BEACON
BIBLE
EXPOSITIONS

BEACON BIBLE EXPOSITIONS

1. Matthew
2. Mark
3. Luke
4. John
*5. Acts
6. Romans
7. Corinthians
8. Galatians, Ephesians
9. Philippians, Colossians, Philemon
10. Thessalonians, Timothy, Titus
11. Hebrews, James, Peter
12. John, Jude, Revelation

BEACON BIBLE EXPOSITIONS

VOLUME 5

ACTS

by

ARNOLD E. AIRHART

Editors
WILLIAM M. GREATHOUSE
WILLARD H. TAYLOR

BEACON HILL PRESS OF KANSAS CITY
Kansas City, Missouri

Library of Congress Catalog Card No. 74-78052

ISBN: 0-8341-0316-8

Printed in the United States of America

Contents

Editors' Preface

No Christian preacher or teacher has been more aware of the creating and sustaining power of the Word of God than the Apostle Paul. As a stratagem in his missionary endeavors, he sought out synagogues in the major cities where he knew Jews would gather to hear the Old Testament. No doubt he calculated that he would be invited to expound the Scriptures, and so he would have a golden opportunity to preach Christ. That peripatetic preacher was confident that valid Christian experience and living could not be enjoyed apart from the Word of God, whether preached or written. To the Thessalonians he wrote: "And we also thank God constantly for this, that when you received the word of God which you heard from us, you accepted it not as the word of men but as what it really is, the word of God, which is at work in you believers" (1 Thess. 2:13, RSV). Strong Christians—and more broadly, strong churches—are born of, and nurtured on, authentic and winsome exposition of the Bible.

Beacon Bible Expositions provide a systematic, devotional Bible study program for laymen and a fresh, homiletical resource for preachers. All the benefits of the best biblical scholarship are found in them, but nontechnical language is used in the composition. A determined effort is made to relate the clarified truth to life today. The writers, Wesleyan in theological perspective, seek to interpret the gospel, pointing to the Living Word, Christ, who is the primary Subject of all scripture, the Mediator of redemption, and the Norm of Christian living.

The publication of this series is a prayerful invitation to both laymen and ministers to set out on a lifelong, systematic study of the Bible. Hopefully these studies will supply the initial impetus.

—William M. Greathouse and
William H. Taylor, *Editors*

Introduction

Luke's two-volume work, commonly referred to as Luke-Acts, spans the ministry of Jesus and the early story of the Church. It has been the focus of a great deal of recent scholarly attention, much of it upon the question of the author's purpose. Was Luke's intention only to faithfully record events in the narrow sense of history, or was it to carefully select events as the basis for a theological statement? The answers that emerge tend to reject the either-or form of the question, and to suggest that Luke was both a first-class historian and a purposeful theologian. I. Howard Marshall, in his recent book *Luke: Historian and Theologian,* prefers to call Luke an evangelist, including both the other terms.

The Purpose of Acts

1. The purpose in Acts is still the purpose stated in the preface to the Gospel: *to present an accurate historical document.* But, as made clear there, the purpose is not history for its own sake, or facts for facts' sake, but rather history that tells a story, a purposeful story. Luke has made use of *history in the service of theology.*

Such a decision is really not optional. Although Christian faith is concerned with "things not seen," it is dependent upon historical facts; it is grounded in historically verifiable occurrences. True enough, mere "raw" facts are without significance until interpreted; but before facts and events can be interpreted, they must have happened. As an evangelist Luke was concerned with history and its theological interpretation.

2. Luke writes *history through the eyes of faith.* The Church's history is seen as divine activity, a more-than-human shaping of her course. The Holy Spirit is protect-

ing, prompting, controlling. This supernaturalistic stance is objectionable only to the historian who works entirely within a naturalistic framework. Because of its perspective Acts might well be called the Gospel of the Holy Spirit. The Spirit's baptism, fullness, and guidance are always in the foreground. It is the story of the continuing acts of Jesus through the Spirit.

3. It is evident that Luke is *highly selective in recording events,* as we would expect in keeping with his purpose. Not the whole story but a simplified account is provided. In effect, one strand of the history, the tale of how the gospel got from Jerusalem to Rome, is told. That accomplished, the story ends, almost abruptly.

4. From the human standpoint, two characters, *Peter and Paul, dominate the action.* Peter's voice and activity are mainly central in cc. 1 through 12. Thereafter, it is Paul. Both personalities are vividly represented. There are interesting, perhaps intentional, parallels. Both exercise a miraculous ministry of healing, both restore the dead, both face sorcerers, both are imprisoned. But Luke makes no attempt to present accounts of the other apostles, and he omits mention of developments outside the range of his purpose. The incidents selected, one feels, are intended to be typical.

5. Within the one strand of the narrative, George Eldon Ladd, in his book *The Young Church,* sees *a twofold purpose.* The first is to establish the connection, theologically, between Israel as the people of God, and the Church, especially the Gentile church, as the new Israel, God's people worldwide. By the consistent appeal to the Old Testament, the Church is presented as the fulfillment of Israel's hope, the working out of God's age-old purpose. The second purpose is more apologetic than theological, and probably is the lesser of the two. This is to present proof that the Christian faith is not a threat to the Roman power; it is, in fact, politically harmless; and is not guilty of improper conduct. This is accomplished in part by recounting the experiences of Paul with Roman officials. Some authors have pursued

the theory that Theophilus was a high-ranking Roman official whom Paul sought to influence; others, that Luke sought to correct a current musunderstanding about Christianity; but these are speculation. It is certain that the theme of the triumph of Christianity against all odds runs through the entire story.

The Historicity of Acts

Luke tells us that he used great care in compiling his information. The natural inference from the passages where he speaks of what "we" did, rather that "they," is that he was, at least at that time, an eyewitness. Much material was doubtless orally transmitted from Paul, Barnabas, Silas, Mark, Titus, Timothy, and such folk as Philip and his daughters, or Mnason (Acts 21:16). Sir William Ramsay, through his extensive studies, made a great contribution toward confirmation of the historicity of Acts. No anachronisms have been found in the book, a remarkable fact in the light of the complex situations described. The accuracy of Luke's knowledge of politics, geography, and Roman law has been sustained.

The Value of the Book

The function of the Book of Acts for us today is manyfold. Other than the Epistles, it is the only historical account of primitive Christians. The Epistles themselves would not be fully intelligible without its light. Although its doctrine is presented in noncreedal form, and with no attempt at a system, it is still very informative, providing us with assurance concerning the *kerygma,* and all the fundamentals of our own faith.

Acts knows nothing of the highly organized and fragmented Church of our times. The oneness of the Church is a main theme, a unity not of organization but of spirit. The essence of the Church consists in the new life imparted by the Spirit and experienced in a shared fellowship. This fellowship is in the Spirit, but is also very tangible. It manifests itself in the gradual transcending of racial and social barriers. The Church's mission is to the whole world, to witness everywhere and to all in the power of the Spirit that God is redemptively at work in the world through Jesus Christ. The Church's purpose is not to "find its own life" but to lose itself in its testimony to Christ. The Church belongs to two worlds; it is in the world but not of it. The Church's mission, its message, and its basic methods are tested and found adequate in the pages of Acts.

Authorship

There is every reason to accept the unbroken tradition that the author of Luke-Acts was "the beloved physician" (Col. 4:14), a Gentile convert, Paul's longtime companion and friend (cf. 2 Tim. 4:11), and a doctor-scholar of ability. Nothing else about him is known.

Date

There is good reason to date the writing of Acts before A.D. 64. That was the year that Nero's persecution of Christians began, and there is no hint of it in Acts. Neither is there any hint of the destruction of Jerusalem in A.D. 70. Likewise there is silence about Paul's death. The favorable attitude reflected by Roman officials, coupled with the general primitve atmosphere of the events throughout the book, points to an early date for the writing, following Paul's arrival and imprisonment at Rome.

Topical Outline of Acts

The Preface

Acts 1:1-5

ACTS 1

The Author's Purpose

Acts 1:1-2

> 1 The former treatise have I made, O Theophilus, of all that Jesus began both to do and teach,
> 2 Until the day in which he was taken up, after that he through the Holy Ghost had given commandments unto the apostles whom he had chosen:

Luke clearly intended this Book of Acts to be the second volume of a two-volume work, the Third Gospel being Volume One.

1. As in the Gospel, the author's Subject is Jesus; Jesus is central; not the Jesus who was, but the One who is alive here and now. Luke begins on an exciting note. Jesus, he implies, is not finished doing and teaching. In one sense He is just beginning *to do and to teach.* This book will record His continuing action.

Of course, Acts is also about the Church, its life and work. But the Christian community is a Jesus-centered fellowship, inspired, not by the mere memory of a life of its teachings, but by the living Presence in the midst. The life of Jesus is expressed in the Church. The Church's work is Jesus' work. There is no break in the continuity between the divine-human, risen, ascended Lord and the Christian community.

Furthermore, this book is open-ended. The action, Jesus' action, is still going on.

2. The work is addressed to Theophilus, as is the Third Gospel. The Greek name means "a friend of God." Was Theophilus a Christian? a pagan? a Roman official? Was he perhaps connected in some way with Paul's trial at Rome? We do not know. Doubtless, Luke writes to enhance his reader's knowledge of the Christian way, perhaps to confirm his faith. The view that *one* of Luke's purposes in writing was to show to Roman officialdom by means of the selected events of his narrative that the Christian faith is the true flowering of the faith of Israel and therefore no threat to Rome politically, has a good deal to commend it.

3. The Ascension was the final event in the earthly life of the Lord. However, it did not occur until He had *given commandment* as to the continuance of His work. The *commandment* is what we commonly call the Great Commission and is expressed most fully in Matt. 28:18-20. It is repeated in another form in Acts 1:8, where it sets the stage for what is to come in the Book of Acts.

4. In his Gospel, Luke had emphasized the work of the Holy Spirit. *Through the Holy Spirit* is, however, a key idea in this second book. All that Jesus did in the days of His flesh He did in the power of the Holy Spirit (cf. Luke 4:1, 14, 18). The title of this book might well be "The Continuing Acts of Jesus in the Person of the Holy Spirit Through the Lives of the Apostles." The reminder in v. 2 prepares for the outpouring of the Holy Spirit promised in c. 1 and recorded in c. 2. It is through the Holy Spirit that both the presence and the power of Christ are made known in the Church. The continuing work of Jesus is by way of the Spirit's action within the lives of the apostles and, indeed, of all Christians.

The Lord's Provision

Acts 1:3-5

3 To whom also he shewed himself alive after his passion by many infallible proofs, being seen of them forty days, and speaking of the things pertaining to the kingdom of God:
4 And, being assembled together with them, commanded them that they should not depart from Jerusalem, but wait for the promise of the Father, which, saith he, ye have heard of me.
5 For John truly baptized with water; but ye shall be baptized with the Holy Ghost not many days hence.

Luke places great stress on the cruciality of the apostles' witness in relation to the whole redemptive enterprise (cf. 1:21-22). The crucial fact and event in the entire case for Christianity is the resurrection of the Lord. The main task of the apostles was to affirm the reality of the Resurrection. Jesus, we remember, did not show himself alive to the public at large, but only to chosen witnesses.

For the apostles, so solemnly charged with responsibility, the risen Saviour did three things. Each was essential to their success. The first was a personal, satisfying assurance with respect to himself: *he showed himself alive after his passion by many . . . proofs.* The second was a necessary instruction in the light of the Cross and the Resurrection about *things pertaining to the kingdom of God.* The third was embodied in a command and a promise: *wait for the promise of the Father . . . ye shall be baptized with the Holy Ghost not many days hence.* It was the indispensable gift and enduement of the Holy Spirit.

1. That the first, the assurance of the resurrection, was fully accomplished, is to be seen in the subsequent fearless witness of the apostles even in the face of death. Although they had to be convinced and were at first skeptical, the evidence of the several appearances was demonstrative, compelling, and incontestable, as the Greek word translated *proofs* suggests.

2. The second thing, the illumination of their understanding, was well begun but was to be progressive and even at best partial, as is indicated by vv. 6-7. The believers had

also to become adjusted to a new kind of relationship with their Lord, and one cannot but see in the 40-day period a gracious provision for this process.

3. It is to the third provision, the baptism with the Holy Spirit, that special attention is given (4-5). The instructions to stay in Jerusalem until the Father's promise was fulfilled were probably given on a special fellowship occasion as Jesus shared a meal with the believers. The Father's promise had been made in the Old Testament, declared by John the Baptist, and confirmed by the Son, especially in the Last Supper Discourse recorded by John. For its fulfillment it now depended on the believers' careful obedience as they waited for the appointed day in the appointed place. Such obedience would demonstrate their faith in *the promise,* their expectation of the gift.

Jesus' words (v. 5) are reminiscent of the prophecy of John the Baptist to whom they refer. (Cf. Matt. 3:11-12.) John's baptism with water was unto repentance. The baptism with the Spirit is Jesus' baptism and is for spiritual purity and power. It became possible because the crucified, ascended, and exalted Lord received in His glorified humanity that gift on behalf of men and bestowed it upon His obedient followers.

The Birth and Growth of the Church at Jerusalem

Acts 1:6—5:42

The Church's Commission

Acts 1:6-8

> 6 When they therefore were come together, they asked of him, saying, Lord, wilt thou at this time restore again the kingdom to Israel?
> 7 And he said unto them, It is not for you to know the times or the seasons, which the Father hath put in his own power.
> 8 But ye shall receive power, after that the Holy Ghost is come upon you: and ye shall be witnesses unto me both in Jerusalem, and in all Judaea, and in Samaria, and unto the uttermost part of the earth.

This last appearance of Jesus with the disciples is apparently later than the one referred to above. Luke here expands the brief account in the Gospel (cf. Luke 24:50-52).

The disciples seem to have shared the Jewish hope of a final king on David's throne in Jerusalem, perhaps with supernatural powers, sovereign over the nations, with Israel at the center. Such was their confidence in their risen Lord's power and wisdom that they saw no barrier to an immediate, visible kingdom of righteousness. It was the question uppermost in their minds. They would see the true nature of the Kingdom more clearly after the coming of the Spirit at Pentecost.

The disciples' question and the Lord's answer contain several ideas in striking contrast.

1. There is the contrast between divine sovereignty and human responsibility. "Lord," they say, "will You . . . ?"

and in effect He replies, "Not without you. You are necessary to the redemptive plan." Their laudable confidence in His sovereign power and in the promises of Scripture needed to be matched by a deep sense of personal responsibility. (Cf. the same truth in the wording of the Great Commission, Matt. 28:18-20.)

2. There is the contrast in the disciples between the absence of full knowledge even amounting to misunderstanding and the presence of a divine and sufficient power. It was not for them (or us) to know, and it is profitless to speculate on either the duration or the time periods in God's plan for the Church. What was to be theirs was the gracious strength to see it through. God's most precious gift is entirely compatible with our necessary human limitations.

3. There is the contrast between the splendor of a material kingdom and the glory of an inward spiritual dynamic. The gift to the disciples was not the "authority" of v. 7 (the Greek word should be translated "authority") but the energy or strength to carry out the Commission, resulting from the new relationship with the Holy Spirit in their lives.

4. There is the contrast between a kingdom based on authority and a kingdom propagated by love. The conquest would not be by overwhelming force but by witnessing—the loving, faithful, certain testimony of those who have been with the Lord.

A witness need not be influential or brilliant or learned. He must tell not what he thinks or what he assumes, but what he knows to be true, and that not from hearsay but from his own experience. And what he tells with his lips must be backed up by his known and observed character lest his witness be discredited.

5. There is the contrast between the narrowness of mere national or racial concepts and the universality of the Lord's plan. Restore the kingdom to Israel? Yes, but not as

they understood it. Waves of Christian witnessing would reach out in ever widening circles, bursting through every barrier until every shore and every nation had been touched. Jerusalem . . . Judea . . . Samaria . . . and then through Asia into Europe and on to Rome! This is the keynote verse (8) of the Book of Acts, giving as it does an outline of the story to follow.

The Church Age: Dawning and Ending

Acts 1:9-11

> 9 And when he had spoken these things, while they beheld, he was taken up; and a cloud received him out of their sight.
> 10 And while they looked stedfastly toward heaven as he went up, behold, two men stood by them in white apparel;
> 11 Which also said, Ye men of Galilee, why stand ye gazing up into heaven? this same Jesus, which is taken up from you into heaven, shall so come in like manner as ye have seen him go into heaven.

1. The 40 days between the Resurrection and the Ascension constituted *a transition period* in the relationship of the disciples with the Lord. Vital lessons were being learned as again and again He appeared and then vanished from their sight. For the disciples, the Ascension marked the end of our Lord's earthly and visible ministry, but it would be another 10 days until at Pentecost the new relationship through the Spirit would be fully inaugurated.

We should remember that for our Lord it was the Resurrection that marked the end of His state of humiliation, and His exaltation to the glory which He had before the world was. The Resurrection and the Ascension are, in fact, parts of one event.

2. There had to be a time when the post-Resurrection appearances ceased, and it was necessary that they cease in *a way denoting finality*. If one considers the concepts of the physical world which the disciples held (concepts quite different from our own), then one can grasp the appropriateness of the way in which Jesus finally vanished, moving upwards and out of their sight into the clouds of the sky. During the 40 days they had already learned that "out of

sight" did not mean out of reach. They would be assured of His nearness.

3. Nevertheless, it was *a loving provision* which in a moment or two sent back two messengers from the unseen world to reassure them. Certainly it eased the pain of parting. In the Gospel, Luke records that they returned to Jerusalem "with great joy." When our children were small and it was necessary for their parents to leave them for a time, my wife sometimes arranged for them something special to take place right after we had gone. It was intended as a lingering token of their parents' love.

4. The angels interrupted the apostles' rapt gazing into the heavens with *the reminder* (the apostles were already familiar with this teaching) *of the return of the Lord.* As the Church age was dawning with His departure, so it would close with His return. To be addressed as *men of Galilee* and to have their Lord described simply as *Jesus* must have filled them with sudden memories of their humble Galilean origin where as plain men they had also known Him as the Man of Galilee. Thus Jesus departed; so Jesus will return.

This is a very precious truth. He who in the miracle of incarnation took unto himself our real humanity did not and never will lay it aside. The One in the heavens at the Father's right hand who intercedes for us is a glorified *man,* one of us forever. The hand He reaches out to us is the hand of Deity to be sure, but it is also a human hand. The Face which will receive us at last is a face like our own.

Not only is it true that *This same Jesus* will come again, but He will come back in the same way that He departed, that is, His return will be visible and in the ordinary world of space and time.

The angels' brief word reminded them, and reminds us, that we who look for Him have work to do: a commission to fulfill, a witness to give in the power of the Spirit. We must not be so preoccupied with the heavenward gaze as to be uninvolved with the needy world, but neither must we cease to live in the light of "that blessed hope."

Preparation Through Prayer

Acts 1:12-14

12 Then returned they unto Jerusalem from the mount called Olivet, which is from Jerusalem a sabbath day's journey.
13 And when they were come in, they went up into an upper room, where abode both Peter, and James, and John, and Andrew, Philip, and Thomas, Bartholomew, and Matthew, James the son of Alphaeus, and Simon Zelotes, and Judas the brother of James.
14 These all continued with one accord in prayer and supplication, with the women, and Mary the mother of Jesus, and with his brethren.

1. From the Mount of Olives (here called Olivet) it was little more than a half mile back to the city where in obedience to the Lord the apostles began to "wait for the promise of the Father." The location of the *upper room* is not known. It was likely in a private house, perhaps that of John Mark's mother (cf. 12:12). Apparently they were making this room their Jerusalem headquarters.

2. Included in *the company* of approximately 120 persons were the 11 apostles; a number of women, of whom only Mary the mother of Jesus is named; and the brothers of Jesus. Others are not classified, but we may suppose that many whose names appear later in Luke's narrative of the Jerusalem church were also present. No doubt some of the women where the wives of the apostles; others would be those women to whom Jesus first showed himself after His resurrection. The Spirit would be poured out upon both "sons and . . . daughters," "servants and . . . handmaidens." Evidently it was not until after the Resurrection that Jesus' brothers (the term probably refers to the children of Joseph and Mary) believed on Him. The company was a group with widely diverse backgrounds and personalities, brought together by a common faith in, and love for, the Lord.

3. Although they attended to their daily tasks, their main business was *prayer*. They were in the Temple for the

regular and appointed prayer times. Praise was uppermost in their praying (cf. Luke 24:53). They prayed with a constancy nourished by expectancy and a settled obedience. And well they might pray! On that tiny company lay the burden of the plan to give Christ to the world. Because they succeeded gloriously, no other Christian ever need lose heart.

4. They were together *with one accord.* The expression denotes a unity of mind or spirit, the absence of discord (cf. 2:46; 4:24; 15:25). It had not always been so, for earlier there had been jealousy and party strife. No doubt the differences had been reconciled, adjustments made. Such oneness of spirit and purpose was essential to their praying. This open and honest relationship with one another was needed preparation for the fullness of the Holy Spirit in their lives.

The Dark Shadow of Judas

Acts 1:15-20

> 15 And in those days Peter stood up in the midst of the disciples, and said, (the number of names together were about an hundred and twenty,)
> 16 Men and brethren, this scripture must needs have been fulfilled, which the Holy Ghost by the mouth of David spake before concerning Judas, which was guide to them that took Jesus.
> 17 For he was numbered with us, and had obtained part of this ministry.
> 18 Now this man purchased a field with the reward of iniquity; and falling headlong, he burst asunder in the midst, and all his bowels gushed out.
> 19 And it was known unto all the dwellers at Jerusalem; insomuch as that field is called in their proper tongue, Aceldama, that is to say, The field of blood.
> 20 For it is written in the book of Psalms, Let his habitation be desolate, and let no man dwell therein: and his bishoprick let another take.

The tragic case of Judas intrudes upon the scene with chilling sadness. Peter had again become the spokesman of the apostles. He too had turned his back on the Lord. But unlike Judas, Peter's defection had been neither wilful nor premeditated, and his repentance for his sin had been prompt, sincere, and deep. He had been fully restored.

1. Just as the apostles had found in the Psalms of David adumbrations of the suffering, death, and resurrection of Jesus, and had been comforted by them, so too they had discovered in the passages where David cried out against his enemies, *a foreshadowing* of the falseness and fate of Judas. It would be quite wrong to think that they saw in this a fatalistic predetermination of Judas' course. The language rather connotes their assurance that God's plan is to be fulfilled in spite of human failure, and that further, they themselves are actively involved in that play.

What motivated Judas to live a double life over a period of time remains a mystery; sin is exceedingly deceitful. It is enough to know from the Gospel records that Jesus had chosen him an apostle, had later seen into his falseness, had continued to love him, and had given him repeated opportunities to make good. Judas had of his own stubborn wilfulness taken the road to ruin.

2. The reconciliation of *the details of this account* of Judas' suicide with those in Matthew's account presents several problems. No doubt both reasons given for naming the burying ground *the field of blood* are equally valid. Even though Matthew records that the chief priest purchased the field, it might logically be said that Judas himself was the purchaser since the money used was actually the 30 pieces of silver he had received as the price of betrayal. And finally it is possible to reconcile the two accounts of Judas' violent death by the use of Augustine's method of combining them into one event. It is assumed that having hanged himself from one of the trees which overhang the steep clifs of the Valley of Hinnom, Judas' body fell upon the sharp rocks beneath and was disembowelled.

3. Judas' story is *a solemn and awful warning.* As verse 25 makes clear, it was the tragedy of deliberate and mistaken choice, contrary to the Lord's choice to apostleship. Judas went to *his own place,* a tactful expression; that is, he went

to the place of his own choosing, rather than to the ministry for which he had been chosen.

The Leadership of the Church

Acts 1:21-26

> 21 Wherefore of these men which have companied with us all the time that the Lord Jesus went in and out among us,
> 22 Beginning from the baptism of John, unto that same day that he was taken up from us, must one be ordained to be a witness with us of his resurrection.
> 23 And they appointed two, Joseph called Barsabas, who was surnamed Justus, and Matthias.
> 24 And they prayed, and said, Thou, Lord, which knowest the hearts of all men, shew whether of these two thou hast chosen,
> 25 That he may take part of this ministry and apostleship, from which Judas by transgression fell, that he might go to his own place.
> 26 And they gave forth their lots; and the lot fell upon Matthias; and he was numbered with the eleven apostles.

1. Taking seriously the scripture in Psalm 109, *his bishoprick let another take,* the apostles felt it imperative to fill the vacancy created by Judas' defection. A fourfold method was used. First, the entire company was consulted (cf. v. 15). Thus they set a precedent which was observed later. Second, two men who were apparently equally qualified were *appointed* or proposed, that is, nominated. Third, earnest prayer was made that the will of God should be done in the selection. They were confident that the Lord had already chosen one of the candidates. The prayer was addressed to Jesus, the Lord, quite naturally, since He had chosen the original apostles. Fourth, they cast lots in order to make the final choice.

2. While *the use of the lot* seems odd to us, it was in keeping with the Old Testament and was the method then used in selecting officers for the Temple. Usually the names were written on stones which were put in a vessel and shaken until one fell out. It was natural to them and they coupled it with prayer. Nevertheless, after Pentecost, and in the age of the Spirit, the method disappeared.

3. It is important to note *the qualifications* which they recognized as necessary *for an apostle.* First, he must be

one who had been in Jesus' company from the beginning of His ministry. Second, he must be a witness of the Resurrection. In fact, the basic function of an apostle was to bear witness to Jesus. Actually, they recognized a third quality which is implicit in their prayer. Men may appear equally qualified on the outside, but God knows their hearts, and the final selection must be determined by what God sees there.

The lot fell upon Matthias, and they at once took him to their hearts as one of the Twelve. Sometimes the argument is advanced that the whole thing was a mistake, that God had really chosen Paul, and that the proof of it is that Matthias was never heard from again in the Scripture. But then, neither were eight of the other apostles mentioned again. The apostleship of Paul was of a special character.

ACTS 2

The Outpouring of the Holy Spirit

Acts 2:1-4

> 1 And when the day of Pentecost was fully come, they were all with one accord in one place.
> 2 And suddenly there came a sound from heaven as of a rushing mighty wind, and it filled all the house where they were sitting.
> 3 And there appeared unto them cloven tongues like as of fire, and it sat upon each of them.
> 4 And they were all filled with the Holy Ghost, and began to speak with other tongues, as the Spirit gave them utterance.

There is a true sense in which all the gracious dealings of God with mankind before this day were leading toward this climactic hour. A new day was dawning in human history. With the outpouring of the Spirit at Pentecost, new privileges, blessings, and opportunities, hitherto only yearned after, were opened wide for all believers to receive. It was not that the Spirit had not been, already and always very much present and at work in the world and in human hearts; it was that on the Day of Pentecost there began a human-divine relationship through the Spirit in which the very truth, power, love, and life of Christ are now imparted to His followers, and this experience has been ever since the personal, collective, and universal birthright of the Church.

It is not possible to conceive of the Church without the Spirit. It is the Spirit who makes the Church truly the Church. The Church is rooted deep in pre-Pentecost history, but Pentecost marks the arrival of the Church as the body of Christ, and as God's instrument of saving mission to the world.

With this in mind, let us look at the significance of the day itself, the phenomena which accompanied the event, and the abiding fact which underlies the external happenings.

1. *The day of Pentecost* was, as we have noted, a day of beginnings. It was also a day of great grace when, as on the days of the incarnation, crucifixion, and resurrection of our Lord, God took yet another long redemptive stride of mercy toward us. But it was especially a day of fulfillment and that is what is mainly implied in the language of verse 1.

a. The Jewish Feast of Pentecost was one of the three great annual religious festivals. It was a one-day celebration. It observed the completion of the harvest and was known as Pentecost because it came on the fiftieth (Greek *pentekostas*) day after the presentation of the harvest's firstfruits. It was also known as the Feast of Weeks because it fell seven weeks (a week of weeks) after Passover. In later times it commemorated the giving of the law at Sinai.

b. Thus, symbolically, the day itself signified three great truths related to the Spirit: the Spirit's coming signals the gathering of the great spiritual harvest which Calvary purchased; it relates the gift of the Spirit to the Cross and the empty tomb; and it suggests the truth that the law of God is now to be written by the Spirit, not externally upon stone, but very personally within our hearts.

c. More literally, the long-awaited day brought fulfillment to the believers' prayers and faith. They had been tarrying in obedience to the Lord's promises and commands (see especially 1:4-8, and the passages on the Comforter in John 14—16). The "promise of the Father" (1:4) was being fulfilled as well as the word of John the Baptist (Matt. 3:11-12), and the numerous prophetic passages on the Spirit in the Old Testament.

2. *To the prepared hearts of the believers the Holy Spirit came.* They had come together in oneness, in faith, and in total obedience. They seemed to have finished praying, for they were *sitting,* apparently in expectant waiting. It may be that they had attended the early-morning Temple worship on that special day and had returned (see Luke 24:53). The advent of the Holy Spirit was accompanied by both audible and visible signs and resulted in immediate, appropriate action.

a. Suddenly, all who were present heard *a roaring sound,* such as that made by a tornadolike wind. The sound (not a literal wind) permeated the whole house. If, as usually is assumed, the house was a private home, the place of "the upper room," the group would be occupying all of its rooms.

The wind is one of the biblical symbols of the Holy Spirit, the life-giving Breath of God. (See Ezek. 37:9-14 and Jesus' words in John 3:8.) Here the symbol denotes supernatural, heaven-sent power. The Spirit was bringing to their human weakness, in fulfillment of Jesus' promise (1:8), the gracious ability and the divine energizing which would make them adequate to be what they ought to be, and to do what they were called to do.

b. The visible sign was like fire, another familiar symbol of the Spirit of God. The language seems to indicate that the phenomenon appeared to them first like a cluster of flamelike tongues, which then divided so that one of the tongues sat upon the head of each person. This spoke of the unity of the Spirit within the diversity and individuality of His work in every believer. The impression must have been indelible. Every one, without exception, was to have the Spirit's fullness and was to be empowered to witness. Still more fundamentally, the fiery display signified purity and cleansing, a work of the Spirit in their personalities. It was the fulfillment of the Baptist's prediction in Matt. 3:11-12 and Luke 3:16-17: "He shall baptize you with the Holy Ghost and with fire. . . . He will throughly purge."

This is expressed in Charles Wesley's lines, "Refining fire, go through my heart." Still another symbolic truth is in another Wesley hymn:

O Thou who camest from above,
The pure celestial fire to impart,
Kindle a flame of sacred love
On the mean altar of my heart!

There let it for Thy glory burn
With inextinguishable blaze,
And trembling to its source return
In humble prayer and fervent praise.

c. The third accompaniment of the outpouring of the Spirit apparently occurred as an immediate result. It is stated in language which designates a solemn and exalted thing: *the Spirit gave them utterance.* Under the Spirit's inspiration they began to witness of the mighty works of God in languages which they had not learned. This is the obvious meaning indicated in vv. 5-11.

If the sound like a mighty wind signified power, and the fiery tongues signified purity, the speaking in tongues was the sign of the universality of the gospel and its complete adequacy for people of all nations and dialects. This third sign was particularly useful in the infancy of the Church, signifying as it did the imperative to break through the boundaries of Jewish provincialism and take the gospel to the whole world.

3. The accompanying signs were important, deeply memorable, and were gloriously used for this epochal occasion. Just as at the giving of the law at Sinai, the signs produced a sense of awe and reverence, appropriate to an inaugural event of such immense importance. They were, however, temporary and, in fact, incidental to the main issue. It would be entirely improper to insist on any one or all of them together as necessary evidences of the Holy Spirit's presence or indwelling.

The abiding and fundamental fact is simply expressed: *they were all filled with the Holy Spirit.* Such a spiritual fact of personal experience can never be defined in merely physical, spatial terms. God, in the person of the Holy Spirit, entered with them into an abiding relationship deeper than words, but described in Scripture as fullness. They belonged to God in completeness: the Spirit possessed and controlled them without hindrance or barrier. They drew upon the life and resources of Christ through the Spirit just as a branch is sustained by the vine.

They were faced with immense responsibilities and great perils as witnesses to Christ's resurrection. As events would prove, they were no less human than before Pentecost. They were not immune to either suffering or loss. Nevertheless the Spirit's deep work in them would produce inspired, Christ-centered lives, and would provide a constant dynamic sufficient for their daily needs and for their victorious witness.

The Outworking of the Spirit

Acts 2:5-13

5 And there were dwelling at Jerusalem Jews, devout men, out of every nation under heaven.
6 Now when this was noised abroad, the multitude came together, and were confounded, because that every man heard them speak in his own language.
7 And they were all amazed and marvelled, saying one to another, Behold, are not all these which speak Galilaeans?
8 And how hear we every man in our own tongue, wherein we were born?

9 Parthians, and Medes, and Elamites, and the dwellers in Mesopotamia, and in Judaea, and Cappadocia, in Pontus, and Asia,
10 Phrygia, and Pamphylia, in Egypt, and in the parts of Libya about Cyrene, and strangers of Rome, Jews and proselytes,
11 Cretes and Arabians, we do hear them speak in our tongues the wonderful works of God.
12 And they were all amazed, and were in doubt, saying one to another, What meaneth this?
13 Others mocking said, These men are full of new wine.

The Holy Spirit is the caring, sharing, ministering Spirit. He is the Church's dynamic for service. The Spirit-filled believers at Pentecost bagan at once a ministry to others. These erstwhile uncertain and fearful disciples were now impelled by love to share their good news with everyone.

1. *The ministry of the Spirit* through these believers demonstrated and *forecast that worldwide concern* which has always characterized a Spirit-filled church. In addition to the many Jews who had moved to Jerusalem from other countries, there were large numbers of both Jews and Gentile proselytes who were there for the Feast of Pentecost. Proselytes were Gentiles who had turned to the Jewish faith and had been received into full fellowship. With foreigners, Pentecost was the most popular of the annual religious festivals because at that season the weather for sailing was safest. Thus the number of visitors in Jerusalem was at its peak. The list of nations represented constituted a kind of geographical survey of the whole ancient world surrounding Jerusalem. The first four countries lay to the east, where literally millions of Jews had dispersed. Judaea seems to be used here as a general term for the whole central area lying between the countries to the east and west. Moving counterclockwise, countries in Asia Minor are next named, then North Africa, where as many as 1 million Jews lived; and finally Rome itself, the home of a thriving Jewish colony. Crete and Arabia seem to have been added as if overlooked in the first list.

Converts to Christ on that first Christian Pentecost would carry the gospel back into each of these nations.

This may well have been the origin of the church at Rome. On the day the Church was born, the great missionary impulse and movement which has swept around the world was already in view.

2. *The ministry of the Spirit,* here as always, *exalted Christ* and pointed men to Him. The multitude which gathered in response to the sound of either the wind or the witnessing or both, recognized in the speech of the disciples, whom they easily identified as Galileans, meaningful words spoken in their own national tongues. The message which was so conveyed, as well as the miracle of the languages, made a profound impression. The people were hearing of *the wonderful works of God.* Under the Spirit's inspiration the believers' great theme would be God's mighty saving acts in history and especially in Jesus Christ, and that would be climaxed in the Lord's resurrection from the dead. It was Christ-exalting evangelism.

The witnessing in many languages at Pentecost pointed men of diverse nations to their oneness in Christ. It was the reversal of the divisiveness of the confused tongues at Babel.

3. *The ministry of the Spirit provoked contrasting responses.* First, attention was arrested; then minds were engaged in earnest inquiry. The multitude was on the threshold of spiritual conviction, ready for the preaching of Peter.

The same spiritual influences which brought about an openness to the truth in many, began also to produce a profane reaction in others. Either as an insensitive joke or as a deliberate spurning of serious inquiry, they charged the believers with drunkenness. Those in the crowd who had supported the crucifixion of Jesus might well wish to close their ears to the word that He was alive again. In one sense their accusation was unwittingly close to the truth: the disciples were, in fact, God-intoxicated men and women, filled with the "new wine" of the Kingdom.

The Spirit's ministry is ever a dividing influence. The

human response produces either spiritual illumination or blindness of heart.

Preaching in the Power of the Spirit

Acts 2:14-21

14 But Peter, standing up with the eleven, lifted up his voice, and said unto them, Ye men of Judaea, and all ye that dwell at Jerusalem, be this known unto you, and hearken to my words:
15 For these are not drunken, as ye suppose, seeing it is but the third hour of the day.
16 But this is that which was spoken by the prophet Joel;
17 And it shall come to pass in the last days, saith God, I will pour out of my Spirit upon all flesh: and your sons and your daughters shall prophesy, and your young men shall see visions, and your old men shall dream dreams:
18 And on my servants and on my handmaidens I will pour out in those days of my Spirit; and they shall prophesy:
19 And I will shew wonders in heaven above, and signs in the earth beneath; blood, and fire, and vapour of smoke:
20 The sun shall be turned into darkness, and the moon into blood, before that great and notable day of the Lord come:
21 And it shall come to pass, that whosoever shall call on the name of the Lord shall be saved.

It is not necessary to think that we have a stenographic, full-length report of Peter's entire sermon. The inspired record is undoubtedly a faithful account of the content of the message, not omitting the big fisherman's characteristic style, which must have lodged unforgettably in the memory of the listeners. The sermon was likely delivered in the commonly understood Aramaic tongue spoken in Judea. Luke reported it in Greek, and we have an English translation. It is the Spirit, not the letter, which gives life.

1. The miracle of speaking in unlearned languages necessarily gave way to *the superior gift of prophesying* or preaching. Preaching, testifying, verbally communicating —these are divinely ordained means for reaching out with the gospel.

2. *The characteristics of apostolic preaching* are illustrated in Peter's opening words and throughout the entire sermon. Always the ready spokesman, Peter was now *courageous* and confident in the Lord. "Stand up and speak

up" is good advice for any preacher. The preaching was *forthright:* With one sentence Peter demolished the charge of drunkenness. It was *authoritative:* It declared with certainty historic facts and momentous contemporary truths. It was *scriptural:* It included both the interpretation and the application of biblical passages. It *focused upon Jesus Christ:* His life, death, and resurrection. It was *personal* in its appeal: The crowd is directly addressed, using personal pronouns. It *called for action* and decision (note v. 37): No sermon is effective which does not create some such response in the listeners, and no sermon is really finished which does not answer the question "What shall we do?" In that sense it was dialogical preaching. *The secret of preaching* and witnessing is disclosed as the Pentecostal enduement of the Spirit.

3. *The explanation of Pentecost* is to be found in God's gracious purpose announced centuries earlier through the prophet Joel. *In the last days* "all the Lord's people" will be anointed to prophesy, as Moses had longed for so long before (Num. 11:29). The prophecy of Joel has been fulfilled, Peter declares, and this is the explanation for the amazing actions of the apostles and of the other Christian believers.

The last days, in which all this will come true, have already commenced with the advent of Christ and will not conclude until He returns in power *with wonders in heaven above, and signs in the earth beneath.*

The baptism with the Holy Spirit is no longer for the select few as in the previous dispensation. The Spirit may be received without distinction as to sex *(sons and . . . daughters),* or as to age *(young . . . old),* or as to station in life *(servants . . . handmaidens).*

The Old Testament prophetic gift was expressed in *visions* and *dreams.* Translated into contemporary terms, the Spirit will endue Christian youth to "expect great things from God, and attempt great things for God." Working through the experience of age. He will inspire spiritual insights into the events and issues of the times.

The great redemptive fulfillment of such a prophetic ministry is expressed in a universal invitation coupled with an unfailing pledge: *Whosoever shall call upon the name of the Lord shall be saved.*

Proclaiming Jesus as Lord

Acts 2:22-40

22 Ye men of Israel, hear these words; Jesus of Nazareth, a man approved of God among you by miracles and wonders and signs, which God did by him in the midst of you, as ye yourselves also know:
23 Him, being delivered by the determinate counsel and foreknowledge of God, ye have taken, and by wicked hands have crucified and slain:
24 Whom God hath raised up, having loosed the pains of death: because it was not possible that he should be holden of it.
25 For David speaketh concerning him, I foresaw the Lord always before my face, for he is on my right hand, that I should not be moved:
26 Therefore did my heart rejoice, and my tongue was glad; moreover also my flesh shall rest in hope:
27 Because thou wilt not leave my soul in hell, neither wilt thou suffer thine Holy One to see corruption.
28 Thou hast made known to me the ways of life; thou shalt make me full of joy with thy countenance.
29 Men and brethren, let me freely speak unto you of the patriarch David, that he is both dead and buried, and his sepulchre is with us unto this day.
30 Therefore being a prophet, and knowing that God had sworn with an oath to him, that of the fruit of his loins, according to the flesh, he would raise up Christ to sit on his throne;
31 He seeing this before spake of the resurrection of Christ, that his soul was not left in hell, neither his flesh did see corruption.
32 This Jesus hath God raised up, whereof we all are witnesses.
33 Therefore being by the right hand of God exalted, and having received of the Father the promise of the Holy Ghost, he hath shed forth this, which ye now see and hear.
34 For David is not ascended into the heavens: but he saith himself, The Lord said unto my Lord, Sit thou on my right hand,
35 Until I make thy foes thy footstool.
36 Therefore let all the house of Israel know assuredly, that God hath made that same Jesus, whom ye have crucified, both Lord and Christ.
37 Now when they heard this, they were pricked in their heart, and said unto Peter and to the rest of the apostles, Men and brethren, what shall we do?
38 Then Peter said unto them, Repent, and be baptized every one of you in the name of Jesus Christ for the remission of sins, and ye shall receive the gift of the Holy Ghost.
39 For the promise is unto you, and to your children, and to all that are afar off, even as many as the Lord our God shall call.
40 And with many other words did he testify and exhort, saying, Save yourselves from this untoward generation.

Having identified the amazing events of the day as resulting from the foretold outpouring of the Holy Spirit, Peter proceeded to elaborate his main theme. The theme: Jesus. The conclusion: Jesus is both Lord and Saviour.

1. *He begins with the Lord's person* and with events which were well known to the great majority of those present. From this vantage point he leads them on by successive steps to saving faith—a wise and winsome procedure. They identified Peter's Lord as *Jesus of Nazareth,* whose mighty miracles had been understood by all but the perverse as evidence that God was at work through Him. Thus far, Peter's hearers would agree.

2. *The Lord's death,* meaning the humiliating and scandalous death by crucifixion and as a common criminal, was the unavoidable stumbling block to faith in Him as the Messiah. Did not the Mosaic law itself place a curse on one who so died? The Cross is still the so-called scandal of Christianity.

Peter faces the problem by forthrightly declaring that the death of Jesus was God's will, something both planned and foreknown by God, and therefore an event full of divine significance and wisdom. The idea of atonement is not expanded upon, but it was logically evident.

At once, this sobering statement places those who had cried "crucify him" in direct and fearful opposition to Jehovah. The sovereign purpose of God does not absolve them of their guilty responsibility for Jesus' death. Nor does the fact that the physical deed was carried out by men outside the laws of Moses, that is, by the Romans. The sermon was beginning to take hold.

3. It is *the Lord's resurrection* from the dead which is the clinching piece of evidence in Peter's case for the Lordship of Jesus. This is the crowning proof, the great fact to which the apostles were to bear witness. For so recent an event (only some seven weeks past) Peter confidently invites full investigation by any who care to do so.

He invokes again the prophetic Scriptures, this time

from David, acknowledged by all as a prophet. The quotation is from Psalm 16. David had rejoiced in God's care of him during his lifetime and had expressed his confidence that he would not be abandoned even in death. (The term here translated "hell" is better understood as "the place of death" or "the realm of the dead.") But the language, says Peter, goes far beyond application solely to David. David died, was buried, saw corruption. His tomb is with us as evidence of that, Peter observes. (The implicit contrasting reference to Jesus' tomb can be felt.) Therefore David's words were really inspired prophecy. They can apply only to Jesus, and so both His death *and* resurrection were in the plan of God.

Furthermore, says Peter, probably with a gesture toward the other apostles, we ourselves are all personal witnesses that Jesus is alive from the dead.

4. Peter now moves swiftly to the climax of his sermon. *The exaltation of Jesus by the right hand of God* is an expression which includes His glorification, His ascension, and His ministry at the Father's right hand. It is the explanation of both His physical absence from the disciples and the outpouring of His Spirit. It was of this that Jesus himself said, "All power is given unto me." The crucified, risen, exalted Man of Nazareth, having accomplished a full atonement for sin, is now our perfect Forerunner, the Pioneer of a new race of men, and in Him is restored all (and more) that was lost to our race because of sin. In His glorified humanity He has received (has had restored on our behalf) the promised Holy Spirit, and now as our Representative He shares the Gift with His brethren, as Pentecost demonstrates. In believers the gift of the Spirit is the pledge or down payment of their full inheritance which awaits the hour when He makes His foes His footstool.

Once again Peter appeals to a well-known Messianic psalm, the 110th. The fulfillment can point only to Jesus. Therefore Jesus is the Messiah. And now the full meaning is inescapable; all the Jesus events coupled with the Scriptures speak with one voice: Jesus is Lord.

5. The preaching of Christ's Lordship produced *pungent conviction.* The word of the preacher was like a stab to the hearers' hearts. They were conscience-smitten. Deeply aware of their sins, they nonetheless sensed that the situation was fraught with hope and enquired, "What are we to do?" The question signified humble confession and obedient submission.

The response indicated that there was indeed something they could and must do.

a. Repentance was necessary—a turning away from sin and a turning to the Lord in faith, a complete renovation of attitude.

b. Water baptism, which they understood, signified public witness in token of a new life and of the forgiveness of sins. The words translated "for the remission" can carry the meaning "because of the remission." Such public confession *in the name of Jesus Christ* would be confession to His Lordship and diety.

c. Thus obedient, they would become proper candidates with all believers to receive also the gift of the Holy Spirit, the gift which is the supreme privilege and the badge of membership in the new Kingdom. Peter reassures them of the all-inclusive scope of the promise (of the Father). It is to all generations. It includes those who are far off in both time and place. It is for all whom God calls, and His call is: "Whosoever will."

The New Life in the Spirit

Acts 2:41-47

41 Then they that gladly received his word were baptized: and the same day there were added unto them about three thousand souls.
42 And they continued stedfastly in the apostles' doctrine and fellowship, and in breaking of bread, and in prayers.
43 And fear came upon every soul: and many wonders and signs were done by the apostles.
44 And all that believed were together, and had all things common;

45 And sold their possessions and goods, and parted them to all men, as every man had need.
46 And they, continuing daily with one accord in the temple, and breaking bread from house to house, did eat their meat with gladness and singleness of heart,
47 Praising God, and having favour with all the people. And the Lord added to the church daily such as should be saved.

On the first day of the Church's life as the "habitation of the Spirit," it grew from 120 to 3,000, a ratio of 1 to 25, It was the harvest in the fields already ripe; the disciples reaped where they had not sown; the reapers had overtaken the plowman. Entrance into the fellowship of the believers was outwardly signified by water baptism.

In brief outline Luke sketches for us the characteristics of that life-pulsating, infant Church.

1. There is a glimpse of the *dynamics of the fellowship* in terms of both spiritual exercises and social expression.

a. The spiritual exercises included instruction, the discipline of the fellowship, the observance of the Lord's Supper, and purposeful prayer.

Following Jesus' example, the apostles, and later others, gave careful instruction to the believers. There was as yet no written Gospel. Doubtless we have the substance of this instruction within our New Testament in its narrative, doctrinal, and ethical forms. The teaching ministry was basic to the successful life of the newborn church. In our own churches this means careful Bible study with application to our own times.

The *fellowship* would be based upon a common faith, common loyalties, a common code of conduct, and common purposes. Such a powerfully supportive bond would be deeply cherished.

The *breaking of bread* (v. 42) indicates the Lord's Supper, perhaps as part of an ordinary meal, but with extraordinary significance as they solemnly remember the Lord's death. Prayer was their "vital breath." The suggestion is of regularly appointed times for this sharing fellowship.

b. We have a lovely sketch of the church in its *social expression, the fellowship of the shared life.* It reflects their loving concern about each other's material needs and their understanding that they also needed each other in the daily common places of life such as work and making meals (vv. 44-46). Something about eating together enhances fellowship.

The community of goods was not enforced but voluntary and spontaneous (see also 4:32-35). Those who had possessions (doubtless some were wealthy and many had some surplus) from time to time, as the need arose, turned them into cash in order to assist the needy or the destitute. There was no other social provision for the poor. It expressed love and unselfishness.

2. *The external impact of such a fellowship* upon their immediate world is noteworthy. The ministry of the apostles, so unitedly supported by the fellowship, was attended by wonderful works as promised by the Lord. A deep reverence, a profound impression of God at work, came upon those who observed the Church (v. 43). Moreover, the happiness and wholesomeness of the lives of the believers produced in the minds of the people of the city genuine respect and goodwill toward them. The later persecution did not come from the common people. Best of all, as a result of all this, the Lord, who alone can do it, was day by day adding to the Church those who were being saved. The winsomeness of the believers' lives together with the witness of their lips produced a winning combination.

ACTS 3

Power to Make Men Whole

Act 3:1-11

1 Now Peter and John went up together into the temple at the hour of prayer, being the ninth hour.
2 And a certain man lame from his mother's womb was carried, whom

they laid daily at the gate of the temple which is called Beautiful, to ask alms of them that entered into the temple;
3 Who seeing Peter and John about to go into the temple asked an alms.
4 And Peter, fastening his eyes upon him with John, said, Look on us.
5 And he gave heed unto them, expecting to receive something of them.
6 Then Peter said, Silver and gold have I none; but such as I have give I thee: In the name of Jesus Christ of Nazareth rise up and walk.
7 And he took him by the right hand, and lifted him up: and immediately his feet and ancle bones received strength.
8 And he leaping up stood, and walked, and entered with them into the temple, walking, and leaping, and praising God.
9 And all the people saw him walking and praising God:
10 And they knew that it was he which sat for alms at the Beautiful gate of the temple: and they were filled with wonder and amazement at that which had happened unto him.
11 And as the lame man which was healed held Peter and John, all the people ran together unto them in the porch that is called Solomon's, greatly wondering.

The "Many wonders and signs . . . done by the apostles" (2:43) served, in that day when the Church was beginning and there were no New Testament Scriptures, as authenticating credentials to establish the apostles' authority. In this passage Luke describes one of these miracles. The account also marks the occasion of the beginning of official opposition to the apostles, a force which would soon fall on the Church with the full fury of persecution. This miracle probably took place not long after Pentecost.

1. *The condition of the crippled beggar* is strikingly symbolic of the moral and spiritual plight of man in his sins. He had been born with his deformity. He was helpless within himself, and insofar as human remedy was concerned, his condition was hopeless. Friends carried him up a flight of steps to the gate called Beautiful, one of nine gates surrounding the Temple, this one probably the entrance from the Court of the Gentiles into the Court of the Women. The gate was a splendid structure of Corinthian bronze, adorned richly with gold and silver. Here the pauper's plight appeared in ugly contrast, seen by the worshippers passing through. It was the best place to beg. The most advantage he could gain however, from the religious

ceremonies which daily surrounded him was a few coins from the more sympathetic worshippers, a slight alleviation of his misery, but no cure.

2. *The response of Peter and John* to the man outside the gate represents well the message and power of the gospel as will as the challenge and opportunity of the Church. Evidently the believers still observed the Temple prayer times, for the apostles were dutifully on their way, at about three in the afternoon, to the Court of Israel to share in the prayer service at the evening oblation. Then the unpredictable ministry of the Holy Spirit through these good men turned a routine meeting into a shining hour.

a. Such as I have give I thee was Peter's response. Good people will always share what they have in the face of need. The great question for us and for the Church is: What is it that we have to share? None can share what he does not possess. There is an old story that Thomas Aquinas once called on Pope Innocent II and found him counting a huge sum of money. "The church can no longer say," said the pope, "'Silver and gold have I none!'" "True," said Thomas, "but neither can she now say, 'Arise and walk.'"

b. The beggar evidently expected little and was no doubt further depressed by Peter's opening remark. But the mood was transformed as Peter first commanded his attention and then, coupled with the encouraging pull of his own strong right hand, thrillingly challenged him to the impossible. The miracle was not gradual but immediate. The twisted feet and ankles were made whole; he who had never in his lifetime stood erect on his own two feet, not only stood but walked, and not only walked but leaped for joy.

3. The key phrase is *in the name of Jesus Christ of Nazareth.* "The name" stands for all that Jesus is in the full measure of His revelation to His own followers. In our prayers it ought to be no mere formula, but the affirmation

of His living presence and power amongst us. "All that Jesus began both to do and teach" (1:1) He is evidently able to continue through the Spirit and through Spirit-filled human instruments.

4. Peter and John were likely moved solely by compassion in taking this action. The Spirit, however, made of the occasion an *opportunity for preaching the gospel.* The gathering crowd was amazed. The miracle could not be denied. The sign was convincing. Had not Isaiah prophesied of the Messianic age, "Then shall the lame man leap as an hart"? (Isa. 35:6).

Nothing exalts Christ more nor gives greater opportunity for further witnessing than does the miracle of a transformed life. The Church's task is to make men whole in the name of Jesus.

Jesus, the Lord of Life

Acts 3:12-16

12 And when Peter saw it, he answered unto the people, Ye men of Israel, why marvel ye at this? or why look ye so earnestly on us, as though by our own power or holiness we had made this man to walk?
13 The God of Abraham, and of Isaac, and of Jacob, the God of our fathers, hath glorified his Son Jesus; whom ye delivered up, and denied him in the presence of Pilate, when he was determined to let him go.
14 But ye denied the Holy One and the Just, and desired a murderer to be granted unto you;
15 And killed the Price of life, whom God hath raised from the dead; whereof we are witnesses.
16 And his name through faith in his name hath made this man strong, whom ye see and know: yea, the faith which is by him hath given him this perfect soundness in the presence of you all.

Men who had once displayed overweening desire for place in the Kingdom now demonstrate a remarkable reluctance to take credit or to hold the spotlight. Peter denies that it is either their ability or their piety which is responsible for the miracle. Actually this inevitable and subtle test was crucial. Failure under pressure to give all the glory to the Lord would have ruined them before they were well started.

With great courage and presence of mind Peter seizes the occasion of the gathered crowd to preach his second sermon of record. It is very reminiscent of the first. Certain features stand out.

1. *Christ is exalted* by ascriptions of honor and by His names. Peter is appealing to Jews.

a. Jesus is God's Servant (v. 13; the better translations have this term) and this is mindful of the "servant passages" of Isaiah 42; 52; and 53. The audience would identify the Servant of Jehovah with suffering.

b. Jesus is the Holy One and the Just or Righteous One. These names also were rooted in Old Testament Messianic passages. The Holy One is God's specially chosen vessel. The Righteous One is He who perfectly fulfills God's requirements, God's will.

c. Jesus is the Prince, or Captain, or Author of life itself. He has life in himself and therefore death cannot hold Him; nevertheless the Source of life was himself killed. This is the mystery of the atonement for sin, expressing in a paradox both the cost and the certainty of our deliverance from death. As the Prince of life He is the Forerunner, leading the way to life, bringing "life and immortality to light."

2. *Sin is uncovered* in several incisive contrasts.

God glorified and exalted Jesus; they (the Jews) disowned and repudiated Him and delivered Him to death.

Even the pagan Roman governor would have loosed Him; they refused.

They preferred a murderer, one who destroys life; they killed Him, the Author of life. God raised again the One whom they killed.

Sin is perverseness. It is utter opposition to God. It chooses what God rejects, and rejects what He chooses. Sin is self-defeating, self-destructive.

3. *Faith is set forth* as the principle on which God makes men whole again. Faith alone is the condition because sal-

vation is a gift, totally undeserved, only to be gratefully received. It is faith in His name and therefore implies acceptance of His revealed Person and thus submission, obedience. Even faith itself is by or through Him (v. 16), which is to say that it is made possible by the gracious work of the Spirit.

Great Blessings—Great Responsibilities

Acts 3:17-26

17 And now, brethren, I wot that through ignorance ye did it, as did also your rulers.
18 But those things, which God before had shewed by the mouth of all his prophets, that Christ should suffer, he hath so fulfilled.
19 Repent ye therefore, and be converted, that your sins may be blotted out, when the times of refreshing shall come from the presence of the Lord;
20 And he shall send Jesus Christ, which before was preached unto you:
21 Whom the heaven must receive until the times of restitution of all things, which God hath spoken by the mouth of all his holy prophets since the world began.
22 For Moses truly said unto the fathers, A prophet shall the Lord your God raise up unto you of your brethren, like unto me; him shall ye hear in all things whatsoever he shall say unto you.
23 And it shall come to pass, that every soul, which will not hear that prophet, shall be destroyed from among the people.
24 Yea, and all the prophets from Samuel and those that follow after, as many as have spoken, have likewise foretold of these days.
25 Ye are the children of the prophets, and of the covenant which God made with our fathers, saying unto Abraham, And in thy seed shall all the kindreds of the earth be blessed.
26 Unto you first God, having raised up his Son Jesus, sent him to bless you, in turning away every one of you from his iniquities.

Having set forth great evangelical truths in the first part of his sermon, Peter now appeals directly to his hearers on the basis of God's great kindness to them—a mercy which now calls for action on their part. The appeal is within the context of the nation of Israel.

1. *Great promises,* great offers of blessing, phrased in Old Testament language are made dependent on the listeners' repentance (vv. 19-21). Not only forgiveness but *the times of refreshing* will come. This is coupled with the promise of the *restitution of all things.* These two expressions in the

minds of Peter's hearers could only mean the promised, longed-for Messianic kingdom. It would be God's kingdom on earth with blessings for all men and all nature. The first term suggested deliverance into an ideal state; the second connoted freedom from captivity with marvellous results.

Whatever might have been had Israel received Jesus when He first came, the fact now is that this final Kingdom awaits Christ's second advent. He has ascended to the Father and has poured out His Spirit upon His people, but He will return. In the meantime the spiritual blessings of the future final consummation have reached back into this age of the Holy Spirit. It is already our privilege to enjoy the "seasons of refreshing" and the making of all things new within our own hearts.

2. The great privileges which the Jews have been given carry with them *commensurate responsibilities.*

a. Prophecies regarding the Messiah have now been fulfilled before their very eyes. They now can see that the *Christ should suffer,* a radically new understanding of the Messianic scriptures. What they did to Jesus was in ignorance in the sense that they did not grasp His identity as Messiah. Now they know, and their sin (cf. Num. 15:27-29) is no longer mitigated by ignorance. God's great generous offer is that if they will turn to Him in repentance and faith, the whole guilty past will be cancelled out.

b. The most revered name in Israel, other than Jehovah, was Moses. Moses' striking prophecy (Deut. 18:15 ff.) concerning a prophet *of your brethren, like unto me,* had a primary reference to the prophets in Israel, but had for a long time been understood as pointing to one great leader to come, a second Moses, a new mediator between God and the people. This Messianic hope, Peter declares, has been fulfilled in Jesus. They must therefore heed Moses' stern warnings concerning disobedience to Him.

c. Furthermore, *all the prophets from Samuel* and on *have likewise foretold of these days.* All that they had said about "the Lord's anointed" (David, for example) found its true fulfillment in Jesus. As *the children of the prophets* all the honors, blessings, and high responsibilities have come now to rest fully on them. They are living in the days of fulfillment. It was a powerful appeal.

d. Finally, Peter reminds them of their rich national heritage as heirs of *the covenant which God made with our fathers,* that is, with Abraham at the first. Jesus, Abraham's promised seed, has been in their very midst, raised up (both in the sense of resurrection and in the sense that God raised up Moses as a deliverer). The covenant blessings are for all men, but for them first as Jews. God has sent Jesus to bless them with new covenant blessings, which Peter defines specificially as salvation from sin, *turning away every one of you from his iniquities.*

ACTS 4

Kept by the Power of God

Acts 4:1-12

1 And as they spake unto the people, the priests, and the captain of the temple, and the Sadducees, came upon them,
2 Being grieved that they taught the people, and preached through Jesus the resurrection from the dead.
3 And they laid hands on them, and put them in hold unto the next day: for it was now eventide.
4 Howbeit many of them which heard the word believed; and the number of the men was about five thousand.
5 And it came to pass on the morrow, that their rulers, and elders, and scribes,
6 And Annas the high priest, and Caiaphas, and John, and Alexander, and as many as were of the kindred of the high priest, were gathered together at Jerusalem.
7 And when they had set them in the midst, they asked, By what power, or by what name, have ye done this?
8 Then Peter, filled with the Holy Ghost, said unto them, Ye rulers of the people, and elders of Israel,
9 If we this day be examined of the good deed done to the impotent man, by what means he is made whole;
10 Be it known unto you all, and to all the people of Israel, that by the name of Jesus Christ of Nazareth, whom ye crucified, whom God

raised from the dead, even by him doth this man stand here before you whole.
11 This is the stone which was set at nought of you builders which is become the head of the corner.
12 Neither is there salvation in any other: for there is none other name under heaven given among men, whereby we must be saved.

This entire passage turns upon verse 8, and the key expression in it is: *filled with the Holy Spirit.* In this testing experience, the apostles must have remembered vividly Jesus' forewarning as well as His promise (Luke 21:12-15). The promise, "For I will give you a mouth and wisdom, which all your adversaries shall not be able to gainsay or resist," was proved utterly trustworthy. Let us examine their triumph under testing.

1. Consider the *pressures under which they were tested.*

a. The onslaught of the test was *sudden.* It came, as it often does, right on the heels of a great spiritual experience and right in the midst of great opportunity. Apparently Peter's sermon was rudely interrupted before he could finish.

b. The faithful and anointed witnessing of the apostles had made the test *unavoidable.* Although the arrest itself was carried out by the chief of the Temple police, acting along with the priests who were on duty that day at the Temple services, it was doubtless the Sadducees who were really behind it. The Sadducees were the most powerful religious-political party in Jewish affairs. They were wealthy, socially prestigious, kept the high priesthood within their group, and cooperated with Rome. Religiously they were rationalists; they denied the existence of angels, spirits, the resurrection, or any life after death. They could not afford to ignore the threat of the new Jesus movement to their whole position. They were distressed, exasperated by the power of the movement, and by the believers' assertion that Jesus was alive again. Now, the startling miracle at the Beautiful Gate suddenly brought the whole irritating problem to a head.

c. The pressures involved in the test were nearly

overwhelming. Peter and John, and probably the healed man too, were seized roughly and thrown into jail overnight. (At least that gave them time to pray and to recall the Lord's promises.) The next morning they were placed before the whole Sanhedrin, the supreme court of the Jewish nation. These humble Galileans would be properly overawed by such an august, powerful assemblage. Ordinarily men cringed or became speechless, surrounded by 70 dignitaries, many of them learned and famous.

The atmosphere was hostile. The apostles were addressed, as the Greek wording indicates, with contempt. Both Caiaphas, the actual ruling high priest, and his father-in-law, Annas, the former high priest and the real power in the council, were there, along with many of their powerful family. Only weeks before, they had condemned Jesus of Nazareth to death. It could be suicidal to bear witness to that name now.

2. In spite of all this, consider *the wide margin of their victory.*

a. Filled with the Spirit, Peter, never in the old days noted for anything like poise under pressure, answers the insinuation that they have used some form of magic or occult power, with poised, clear, courageous statements.

b. Inspired by the Spirit, they make their points forcefully. It was a *good deed* which they had done to the cripple; he had been made whole (this same word is translated "saved" in v. 12); it was for doing good they were being questioned. Further, it was not their own doing at all; it was the work of Jesus, the One the council knew had done such miracles before they had killed Him. This miracle was evidence that Jesus was alive.

c. In the power of the Spirit, Peter sketches again the now familiar sharp horns of the dilemma confronting his accusers: They had killed Jesus; God had raised Him from the dead; they, the self-appointed builders, had rejected Him as unworthy of a place in their building; God had revealed Him as the very Cornerstone of it all. Peter may have consciously used Ps. 118:22 since Jesus had used it of himself in witnessing to these same people (Matt. 21:42-44).

This tremendous statement is climaxed with a superlative declaration of faith. Salvation is in Jesus alone. Israel's salvation, the salvation of the council members, the salvation of the apostles, of anyone, anywhere, is inextricably bound up with the name of Jesus. Reject that Name and no deliverance will come from any other source. Believe in that Name and spiritual wholeness is yours, even if your case seems as hopeless as that of the erstwhile cripple, now standing before them in silent testimony.

d. Dramatically, just as with Jesus before Pilate, the positions of the judges and those being judged is reversed. Jesus' word to them has been vindicated, "Ye shall receive power . . . and ye shall be witnesses unto me."

Nonconformity with the World

Acts 4:13-22

13 Now when they saw the boldness of Peter and John, and perceived that they were unlearned and ignorant men, they marvelled; and they took knowledge of them, that they had been with Jesus.
14 And beholding the man which was healed standing with them, they could say nothing against it.
15 But when they had commanded them to go aside out of the council, they conferred among themselves,
16 Saying, What shall we do to these men? for that indeed a notable miracle hath been done by them is manifest to all them that dwell in Jerusalem; and we cannot deny it.
17 But that it spread no further among the people, let us straitly threaten them, that they speak henceforth to no man in this name.
18 And they called them, and commanded them not to speak at all nor teach in the name of Jesus.
19 But Peter and John answered and said unto them, Whether it be right in the sight of God to hearken unto you more than unto God, judge ye.
20 For we cannot but speak the things which we have seen and heard.
21 So when they had further threatened them, they let them go, finding nothing how they might punish them, because of the people: for all men glorified God for that which was done.
22 For the man was above forty years old, on whom this miracle of healing was shewed.

The dramatic intensity of this vivid event is hardly matched in literature. Life in the Spirit is more exciting than fiction. Notice the elements in the brief unfolding of the drama.

1. There is the headlong *clash of the opposing forces.* The apostles versus the council suggests the picture of the real Church facing its worldly opposition in all times and places. The confrontation is inevitable. They represent two opposing systems, two opposite sets of values, principles, ethical codes. Unbelief challenges faith, conscience confronts expediency, materialism meets the realm of the spirit. "Don't let the world around you squeeze you into its mold" (Rom. 12:2*a,* Phillips) points up the issues at stake.

The learned members of the court of the Sanhedrin, well trained in intellectual subtleties but less cultured in heart, marvelled at the poise of Peter and John. How could these men argue from the Scriptures with such fluency and skill, seeing that they were technically untrained in the rabbinical schools *(unlearned)* as well as being mere private citizens or laymen without official position (the meaning of *ignorant* here)? They finally recognized them as having been the close, personal associates of Jesus. That fact no doubt answered their question, for they were well aware of Jesus' masterful skill with Scripture as well as with vital issues.

This clash, however, is *not* between an educated, cultured world on the one hand, and a naive, unrefined Church on the other. The issue in these terms is rather that of the underlying, implicit principles molding the education or the basic assumptions structuring the culture.

2. There is also in the drama *the unanswerable argument* in favor of the Church. Here is the healed man standing before their eyes! The man is the sign of the living presence of Jesus Christ. He is the stubborn evidence which will not go away. He represents the supreme dilemma confronting the skeptics. This man stands for the miracle of transformed people everywhere the gospel is preached in power and Christ is uplifted. He stands for the healing of broken hearts, broken homes, and twisted lives.

Wherever the Church lacks such an argument, all her entreaties fall on deaf ears; with this evidence her credentials are unassailable.

3. The drama also unfolds *the sinister plot* to destroy the Church. The evidence in favor of the apostles' message is irrefutable. The logic of the opposition is correct: The only way to fight the gospel is to hush it up, to silence the witnesses. If the facts favor the gospel, then use force, threats, intimidation, anything to keep others from finding out the truth. It is of great significance that the Sanhedrin made no attempt at this point to refute the preaching of Jesus' resurrection, the supreme fact on which the whole gospel stands or falls. The reasons are self-evident. What they did do was to use the immense pressure of their supreme authority to order the apostles to seal their lips against ever again uttering the name of Jesus.

This is still the enemy strategy to cripple the Church. Where the conspiracy of silence has succeeded, the Church has miserably failed. But the Spirit-filled Church cannot keep silence!

4. The drama finally reveals *the true character* of the protagonists. Not good times but hard times bring out what is really in people.

Peter and John, gifted by the Spirit with spiritual insight, answer without hesitation. Their reply is both courageous and unanswerable. They appeal their sentence to a higher court, to the Supreme Judge of all men, including the Sanhedrin. They will not conform to outside pressure because the pressure on the inside—the voice of conscience, the obligation to truth, the sense of responsibility, the power of love—is greater still. Conformity with God's will means nonconformity with the world.

Their words (vv. 19 and 20) indicate clearly their great intellectual-moral-ethical foundations. Truth, they are saying to us, is real, not relative but absolute, having God as its Source. Truth has been revealed so that we can understand it. Truth accepted brings assurance in place of insecurity and despair. Men who have refused the truth can be manipulated by the unscrupulous, but for Christians the revelation in Christ is authoritative. Furthermore, men are finally accountable to God for what they do in response to the truth. To suppress the saving truth is unthinkable.

In contrast with the joyous obedience of the apostles is the wilful, blind unbelief of the council. Although they marvel, they refuse to believe. Their blindness is self-induced. They suppress truth while the apostles confess it. The apostles are joyful; they are gloomy. The apostles are open and forthright; they are covert and complicated. The council is frustrated; the apostles are confident. The world has nothing to match the Church, when the Church is really the Church.

The Church moves forward on the faith of those who will not be pressured into mere conformity; men like Moses, Elijah, Daniel; men like the apostles; men like Luther, Knox, and Wesley. The ease of conformity is costly in the long run. Said a Christian leader, "If some of you [Christians] are not careful, you will die in your beds and it will serve you right!"

Prayer in the Church's Life

Acts 4:23-31

> 23 And being let go, they went to their own company, and reported all the chief priests and elders had said unto them.
> 24 And when they heard that, they lifted up their voice to God with one accord, and said, Lord, thou art God, which hast made heaven, and earth, and the sea, and all that in them is:
> 25 Who by the mouth of thy servant David hast said, Why did the heathen rage, and the people imagine vain things?
> 26 The kings of the earth stood up, and the rulers were gathered together against the Lord, and against his Christ.
> 27 For of a truth against thy holy child Jesus, whom thou hast anointed, both Herod, and Pontius Pilate, with the Gentiles, and the people of Israel, were gathered together,
> 28 For to do whatsoever thy hand and thy counsel determined before to be done.
> 29 And now, Lord, behold their threatenings: and grant unto thy servants, that with all boldness they may speak thy word,

30 By stretching forth thine hand to heal; and that signs and wonders may be done by the name of thy holy child Jesus.
31 And when they had prayed, the place was shaken where they were assembled together; and they were all filled with the Holy Ghost, and they spake the word of God with boldness.

Characteristically, the apostles met the first crisis in the Church's career through prayer. The critical situation was this: Their continued preaching and teaching had henceforth to be carried on in violation of the orders of the civil authority, the highest court in their nation. There was no human resource or earthly court to which they might appeal. Providentially, they were thrust entirely upon God.

1. *Prayer and the fellowship of believers* are closely entwined. They sought out *their own company,* probably the other apostles and such others as were known to be gathered in prayer. In that concerned and open-hearted company they shared the burden and the need.

To be sure, they needed the touch of God, but they also needed each other, the warm clasp of hands in mutual faith, the strength each could lend to his brother. They prayed *with one accord.* The prayer fellowship is the "place where spirits blend." It is noteworthy that "Peter and John" become "they," the larger company to which the concern is transferred, and later "they" becomes "the multitude of them that believed."

2. We catch also the significance of *prayer and the affirmation of faith.* Real praying takes us past merely superficial, petty things, back to the great realities in our lives. We are at our best at such times.

a. They quickly pushed through the distressing outward circumstances and planted their feet firmly on the bedrock of the sovereignty of the eternal God who made and sustains all things. The term by which they addressed God is not the ordinary word for *Lord,* but one which indicates absolute, unrestricted power. From the tyranny of men they appealed to the changeless, omnipotent Creator.

b. From another of the Messianic psalms, the second, they affirmed their faith and found assurance in the divine wisdom and foreknowledge. They saw their opposition in its true light, as against Jesus, the Lord's Anointed. The Psalmist had prophesied the opposition of Herod, Pilate, the Gentiles (Roman authorities), and the people (the Jewish authorities) long before. If all was foreknown, then nothing takes God by surprise, and nothing is out of His control. Let the foes of Jesus unite in apparent universal strength; their plans will nevertheless be futile. God is on the throne of the universe. His overruling providences make all human opposition mere vanity.

c. The great faith statement contains important implicit affirmations about Jesus. He is sinless. He is the Messiah. His death is more than tragedy; the Cross is God's great victory over sin and death.

Thus they expressed the great convictions which shaped their faith and conduct in the crisis, and found them not wanting.

3. Listening to them pray, we sense the meaning of *prayer and deliverance from fear.*

It is moving to note what they did *not* pray for. Not for deliverance from suffering, or hardship, or even death. The reference to themselves as *thy servants,* along with their petitions, makes clear that they prayed in a spirit of total humility, dependence, and yieldedness to His will. There was no complaint voiced.

What they asked for was *boldness,* deliverance from fear or any cowardly action. There was no indication of retreat on the one hand, or of recklessness on the other, but there was a sensible, careful, factual assessment of their needs. They were concerned that Jesus should be vindicated and His truth upheld through continued signs done in His name.

4. Finally, we are taught the place of *prayer and the renewal of the Church.*

The physical shaking of the place where they were

praying was a sign assuring them of the nearness of the divine power, similar to the sound of the roaring wind at Pentecost. Perhaps it was God's way of reminding them that all things merely temporal will fail us in the crisis, but true values, the things of the Spirit, are unshakable.

Their prayer for boldness to speak was answered at once: *They were all filled with the Holy Spirit.* For most of those present this was not an initial experience of being filled with the Spirit. The fullness received at Pentecost had been maintained. It was, however, a necessary and fresh anointing of the Spirit. There ought to be many such times of refreshing in the life of Spirit-filled Christians. Renewal within the Church, ability to face the crises, comes not first from innovative programs or strategy-planning sessions, good as they may be, but from prayer and fresh infillings of the Spirit. Then the rest will follow.

From every stormy wind that blows,
From every swelling tide of woes,
There is a calm, a sure retreat;
'Tis found beneath the mercy-seat.

There, there on eagle wings we soar,
And sin and sense molest no more;
And heaven comes down our souls to greet,
And glory crowns the mercy-seat.

The Church at Its Best and Its Worst

Acts 4:32—5:11

32 And the multitude of them that believed were of one heart and of one soul: neither said any of them that ought of the things which he possessed was his own; but they had all things common.
33 And with great power gave the apostles witness of the resurrection of the Lord Jesus: and great grace was upon them all.
34 Neither was there any among them that lacked: for as many as were possessors of lands or houses sold them, and brought the prices of the things that were sold,
35 And laid them down at the apostles' feet: and distribution was made unto every man according as he had need.
36 And Joses, who by the apostles was surnamed Barnabas, (which

is, being interpreted, The son of consolation,) a Levite, and of the country of Cyprus,
37 Having land, sold it, and brought the money, and laid it at the apostles' feet.

1 But a certain man named Ananias, with Sapphira his wife, sold a possession,
2 And kept back part of the price, his wife also being privy to it, and brought a certain part, and laid it at the apostles' feet.
3 But Peter said, Ananias, why hath Satan filled thine heart to lie to the Holy Ghost, and to keep back part of the price of the land?
4 Whiles it remained, was it not thine own? and after it was sold, was it not in thine own power? why hast thou conceived this thing in thine heart? thou hast not lied unto men, but unto God.
5 And Ananias hearing these words fell down, and gave up the ghost: and great fear came on all them that heard these things.
6 And the young men arose, wound him up, and carried him out, and buried him.
7 And it was about the space of three hours after, when his wife, not knowing what was done, came in.
8 And Peter answered unto her, Tell me whether ye sold the land for so much? And she said, Yea, for so much.
9 Then Peter said unto her, How is it that ye have agreed together to tempt the Spirit of the Lord? behold, the feet of them which have buried thy husband are at the door, and shall carry thee out.
10 Then fell she down straightway at his feet, and yielded up the ghost: and the young men came in, and found her dead, and, carrying her forth, buried her by her husband.
11 And great fear came upon all the church, and upon as many as heard these things.

This entire passage is a study in contrasts. We might almost be tempted to feel that the account of the Church as the Spirit-filled community is too ideal a picture, or to wish on the other hand that the dark story of spiritual treason within the same community had not been told. The characters of Barnabas and Ananias are set forth in deliberate contrast. The Bible records human events with realism. Luke wishes his readers to see the real Church, "warts and all." The spiritual lessons taught are profound.

1. *The Spirit-filled community* is described in terms of four attractive characteristics.

a. It was a fellowship without divisions or factions of any kind. The believers had increased first to 3,000, then 5,000, and by this time to many more, and yet they *were of one heart and of one soul.* This *oneness* of faith and purpose, but especially of love, is an identifying mark of the

Christian Church, just as love is the true badge of a Christian.

b. Generosity of the most unselfish kind made them different from the world. We have already noted (see comments, c. 2) the practice of a community of goods which prevailed. This was a world apart from what we know as Communism. It was completely voluntary. It was based on love, not law. It upheld, rather than denied, the right to private property. It was an astonishing display of love in action, of selfless concern for the needs of others. It must be interpreted in the light of its own time and social conditions.

However, it demonstrates a timeless principle: Christians, whose faith in its essence holds to the ascendency of the spiritual over the material values, must prove this faith in everyday life by holding rather loosely to material things. So-called love that does not involve one's money is a mere sentiment and does not really involve the person himself.

c. It is no wonder that such a dynamic fellowship was marked by the *effectiveness* of its witness for Christ. Witnessing backed up by such living is always a powerful, convincing force. If the Church's testimony lacks impact or is easily brushed aside, perhaps attention should be given to the quality of its fellowship.

Luke's choice of words here, "the apostles gave witness," indicates also that they saw the sharing of the Good News as a glad obligation, part of their total stewardship.

d. This united, caring, witnessing community was enjoying the outpoured *blessings* of God. *Great grace was upthem all;* not just upon the leaders, or the spiritually elite, but upon the whole Church.

Unity, generosity, and effective evangelism are sought-after qualities in Church life today. They are never successfully promoted or organized or talked up. Their secret is the secret of Spirit-filled lives, the Spirit-empowered Church. It is the Holy Spirit who makes the Church winsome.

e. No doubt Luke could have brought forward many examples of outstanding generosity and service, but he here introduces Barnabas because of the prominent place which he filled in the subsequent outreach of the Church. The name given him by the apostles characterized him aptly as the helper, the encourager, the friend who stands at the side of one in need. Luke, interpreting the name, uses the same root word as Jesus used in describing the Holy Spirit as the Comforter.

ACTS 5

2. *The sad, dark contrast* to Barnabas and the bright portrait of the Church's life is sketched in bold, honest realism, and with a minimum of detail. This was the Church's first internal crisis. The Church has often been in greater peril from internal betrayal than from external persecution.

a. Much of the admitted strangeness of the story will be removed if we can grasp clearly the real *nature of the sin* of Ananias and Sapphira. The initial temptation to deceitfulness was born in the pure atmosphere of the devotion and generosity of their fellow believers. The issues of the stewardship of money are crucial in a Christian's life. Money becomes either our useful servant or our diabolical master. In this case the love of money and praise was the root of a situation which grew quickly into horrendous proportions. We must be clear, however, that their sin was not in giving only part of their possessions to the Church. As Peter made plain, that would have been proper and right. The sin lay in the planned deception.

Double-mindedness in this couple sponsored a fierce internal struggle. Avarice contested with the impulse to share. The desire for human recognition and praise fought with purer motives. How sad that they did not permit the Spirit's fullness to cleanse them of their double-mindedness!

How deceitful sin is! In a setting in which the Spirit flamed within the Church in living generosity and honest openness of heart, this pair plotted together, deliberately and carefully, to deceive the Church. They would receive praise and be credited for great piety for performing such a generous act. Perhaps later they themselves could draw upon the communal resources, even while enjoying their secret hoard.

They were actually willing to test the mercy of God and the Spirit's probing light within the Church. Their lie was not to men only, but to God. Refusing the Spirit's reproof, they were filled instead with Satan's delusion. Their consciences were seared until they contemplated gross hypocrisy without trembling. Their sin was, in the end, brazen, defiant, and contemptuous of the Spirit himself.

b. Knowing as we do the amazing forbearance of God with sinners, *the punishment* of these brazen hypocrites seems at first strangely severe. But we remember that they sinned wilfully against the most intense spiritual light possible. Spiritual death followed. While physical death appears to have been a divine judgment, the intense shock of discovery was in itself enough to produce heart failure. The Old Testament case of Achan who had stolen the thing devoted to God and had been punished with death, would be very familiar to them.

Peter acted, not as the agent in their deaths, but as God's spokesman in uncovering their deceit. Apparently, as the questioning of Sapphira makes clear, Ananias had presented a sum of money publicly, pretending that it represented the entire sale price. Peter had been given special discernment to detect the lie. Perhaps he was as surprised as anyone at Ananias' death. By the time Sapphira arrived before the apostles, expecting to receive her share of the credit, Peter was able also to discern her fate. The quick burial of the victims outside the city is accounted for by usual burial customs in that climate.

c. Both the deity and personality of *the Holy Spirit* are clearly taught. Comparing vv. 4 and 5, it is evident that only a person can be lied to, and that to lie to the Holy Spirit is to lie to God.

d. There are other *lessons* for the Church. The warnings against hypocrisy and a brazen attitude towards the Spirit's ministry were taken to heart by all who heard of these things. It is evident that the purity of the Church is a very precious thing in the eyes of God. The Church will not be a perfect society. There will be tares amongst the wheat. But defiant sin is to be dealt with in the Church's discipline; purity is to be the Church's standard.

The attack of Satan against the Church is real; the only defense is Spirit-fullness, the cure for double-mindedness. This is the first instance of the use of the word "church" to describe the body of believers. The use may be deliberate. In spite of inward crisis, this group is still the true people of God. Let the Church move on!

From Revival to Outreach

Acts 5:12-16

> 12 And by the hands of the apostles were many signs and wonders wrought among the people; (and they were all with one accord in Solomon's porch.
> 13 And of the rest durst no man join himself to them: but the people magnified them.
> 14 And believers were the more added to the Lord, multitudes both of men and women.)
> 15 Insomuch that they brought forth the sick into the streets, and laid them on beds and couches, that at the least the shadow of Peter passing by might overshadow some of them.
> 16 There came also a multitude out of the cities round about unto Jerusalem, bringing sick folks, and them which were vexed with unclean spirits: and they were healed every one.

Luke seems to place this passage in apposition to the preceding story. There the emphasis is on purity within the Church; here it is upon outreach to the world through works of power and compassion. The Spirit who discerns and judges sin in the Church is also the Spirit of Jesus, the Healer of the sick in soul and body.

1. The great *respect for the leadership* of the apostles was a major aspect of the Church's early success. The apostles were, of course, God's special gift to the Church (see Eph. 4:11) for that special time, in a unique, unrepeatable sense. Their authority to speak for Christ (in the absence of any written New Testament tradition) had to be vindicated, and for that reason God especially empowered them to perform signs and miracles.

The populace generally revered them at this point. So great was the influence of Peter, acknowledged as the leader, that people carried the sick into the streets on couches and pallets so that in passing Peter might bless them, if not verbally, at least by the shadow of his presence. The evidence is that people thought of the apostles as holy and gifted men, through whose ministries the healing touch of Jesus was given. Thus it was that men of no social or civil reputation, sometimes flogged by the authorities, and always under the interdict of the civil law, became the most powerful human influence for truth and good in the whole Christian era.

They were respected and yet in some sense were separate from other men. V. 13*a* means either that unbelievers held them in such awe that they feared to mingle with them or molest their meetings, or else that those within the fellowship did not dare to usurp their authority. The judgment on Ananias had produced a salutory reverence for leadership.

2. The *compassionate ministry* of the Church reached for the first time outside Jerusalem to the surrounding towns.

Luke recognized three distinct ministries of the Church although they are interrelated. The first is given prior place: the ministry of salvation. Multitudes of people (no attempt is now made to number the converts) were coming to faith in Christ and were being *added to the Lord.* True evangelism gets people in touch with the Lord himself, not merely the church. It is significant that women are here given a place of honor in the Church.

The other two ministries were to *sick folk,* the ministry

of physical healing, and to *them which were vexed with unclean spirits.* These two are not confused but are separate ministries. It would be contrary to the biblical evidence to infer because at this time *they were healed every one* that this is God's will regarding the physically sick in all cases. In His sovereign wisdom God was authenticating the apostolic ministry by signs and wonders.

A Lesson on Divine Providence

Acts 5:17-26

17 Then the high priest rose up, and all they that were with him, (which is the sect of the Sadducees,) and were filled with indignation,
18 And laid their hands on the apostles, and put them in the common prison.
19 But the angel of the Lord by night opened the prison doors, and brought them forth, and said,
20 Go, stand and speak in the temple to the people all the words of this life.
21 And when they heard that they entered into the temple early in the morning, and taught. But the high priest came, and they that were with him, and called the council together, and all the senate of the children of Israel, and sent to the prison to have them brought.
22 But when the officers came, and found them not in the prison, they returned, and told,
23 Saying, The prison truly found we shut with all safety, and the keepers standing without before the doors: but when we had opened, we found no man within.
24 Now when the high priest and the captain of the temple and the chief priests heard these things, they doubted of them whereunto this would grow.
25 Then came one and told them, saying, Behold, the men whom ye put in prison are standing in the temple, and teaching the people.
26 Then went the captain with the officers, and brought them without violence: for they feared the people, lest they should have been stoned.

The Christian movement which was being grudgingly tolerated for expedient reasons had so grown that the opposition could tolerate it no longer. The simmering resentment of the Sadducees had reached the boiling point. More intense persecution was to come. All of the apostles were summarily and roughly arrested this time and placed in jail as common criminals under lock and key. By the end of the ordeal they had been beaten and had "suffered shame."

Once more there is presented a study in contrast.

1. *The ways of God with unbelievers* and those who resist His will are partially illustrated here. Again and again God brings evidence to bear upon the issues of faith and unbelief. Those who stubbornly oppose Him find that their efforts to destroy the evidence only produce more startling evidence about Him. Yet, because God never coerces, the evidence is never completely overwhelming; faith is always a choice, an alternative, not a compulsion.

Jealousy of the growing popularity of the believers, fear for their own doctrinal position which denied the supernatural, and sheer political expediency moved the rulers to action. Blinded by self-interest, they could not see the obvious. Although perplexed by the evidence of divine intervention, yet they were so motivated by pride and so controlled by their own naturalistic prejudices that they chose unbelief in spite of all the facts. Unbelief is always more difficult than faith.

2. Doubtless *God's ways with His own children* are harder to fully fathom.

a. Just *how* the apostles were released from the jail is an interesting question. There are five occurrences in Acts of the *angel of the Lord.* (It is intriguing that God sent an angel to take the apostles from the custody of the Sadducees who didn't believe in angels.) Sometimes the reference is to a visible appearance in human form as in Peter's escape from prison (c. 12), and sometimes the supernatural intervention is not apparent to the senses. Angel means "messenger," and many Christians can testify that God has sent special messengers in various guises who either consciously or unwittingly acted as the Lord's personal representatives to supply a need or change a situation. One has little trouble believing in angels after such an experience of divine care.

In this case the angel spoke a direct command and the apostles obeyed to the letter.

Evidently only the apostles were aware of the intervention. The guards must have seen nothing. No one was aware that the prisoners were gone.

b. It is easier to discuss how the apostles were released than to answer *why*. Certainly it was not to save them from facing the Sanhedrin. Further, the God who miraculously delivered them could have kept them from arrest in the first place.

Certain lessons must have come through to the apostles and the Church. The Lord will not crush their opposition so that it ceases altogether; yet there is assurance that He is always able to take care of any situation concerning them. They will not be immune to trials and setbacks; yet He will know where they are and what they are enduring at any time. There will be opposition; but nothing can stop the progress of the gospel. God does not use miracles indiscriminately; but He will not let His own be tried beyond endurance.

The apostles also learned that their message was more important than their comfort. Just as Jesus is the Source of life, so the gospel brings life itself. To suppress the gospel is to deny life.

One can imagine the acute embarrassment of the high priest, who, having summoned the entire council early in the morning, discovers the prisoners missing. Then, as if to add to the humiliation, an eyewitness reports that the prisoners are even then preaching in the Temple area. At that point they must awkwardly wait while the Temple officials go in person to see if they can bring "the prisoners" in. All of this had its effect on at least some of the council, as the outcome of the trial indicates.

The apostles acted as men would act who had been doubly reassured in their faith. Although no force was applied, they went without resistance to face the court, knowing that even a word from them could have produced a violent uprising in their favor.

Blessed Assurance: The Spirit's Gift

Acts 5:27-42

27 And when they had brought them, they set them before the council: and the high priest asked them.
28 Saying, Did not we straitly command you that ye should not teach in this name? and, behold, ye have filled Jerusalem with your doctrine, and intend to bring this man's blood upon us.
29 Then Peter and the other apostles answered and said, We ought to obey God rather than men.
30 The God of our fathers raised up Jesus, whom ye slew and hanged on a tree.
31 Him hath God exalted with his right hand to be a Prince and a Saviour, for to give repentance to Israel, and forgiveness of sins.
32 And we are his witnesses of these things; and so is also the Holy Ghost, whom God hath given to them that obey him.
33 When they heard that, they were cut to the heart, and took counsel to slay them.
34 Then stood there up one in the council, a Pharisee, named Gamaliel, a doctor of the law, had in reputation among all the people, and commanded to put the apostles forth a little space;
35 And said unto them, Ye men of Israel, take heed to yourselves what ye intend to do as touching these men.
36 For before these days rose up Theudas, boasting himself to be somebody; to whom a number of men, about four hundred, joined themselves: who was slain; and all, as many as obeyed him, were scattered, and brought to nought.
37 After this man rose up Judas of Galilee in the days of the taxing, and drew away much people after him: he also perished; and all, even as many as obeyed him, were dispersed.
38 And now I say unto you, Refrain from these men, and let them alone: for if this counsel or this work be of men, it will come to nought:
39 But if it be of God, ye cannot overthrow it; lest haply ye be found even to fight against God.
40 And to him they agreed: and when they had called the apostles, and beaten them, they commanded that they should not speak in the name of Jesus, and let them go.
41 And they departed from the presence of the council, rejoicing that they were counted worthy to suffer shame for his name.
42 And daily in the temple, and in every house, they ceased not to teach and preach Jesus Christ.

The words of the apostles here are similar to the response to the Sanhedrin at the earlier trial of Peter and John (4:19-20). But there is an added dimension: They offer a precise statement on the question of how they know and why they are sure that they are right in the face of the contradiction of Israel's highest court. In complete contrast to the apostles' assurance is the "play if safe" counsel of Gamaliel. The episode ends with a demonstration of the joy of assurance and obedience.

Blessed assurance, Jesus is mine;
O, what a foretaste of glory divine!

1. *The accusations* brought against the apostles were specific. They had not only disobeyed the command of the authorities to never again speak of Jesus, but they were actually filling Jerusalem with His teaching. It was an eloquent tribute to the growth of the Church's influence.

In the second accusation there can be detected the remonstrance of a pained conscience: you *intend to bring this man's blood upon us.* The high priest would not use the name of Jesus, but he remembered His death and also that daring statement to Pilate which had seemed so safe at the time: "His blood be upon us." Fear of reprisal from the populace of Jerusalem also lay behind this rather subjective accusation.

The charges were deadly serious. The apostles were not unaware of the severe consequences if found guilty.

2. In the face of this, the apostles, speaking through Peter, responded with composed *assurance.* Every Christian knows that the "accuser of the brethren" challenges his right to security in Christ. There are three foundation facts in the response of the apostles.

a. Their unswerving and complete obedience to God's will was the key which opened the way to full assurance. We have already, in connection with their witness in c. 4, discussed the meaning of their basic convictions about God and truth. The meaning of their actual words here is better conveyed by "We *must* obey God" than by "we ought." Theirs was a settled, total commitment, an imperative claim upon their lives. They could not be silenced. They would not be compromised. They did not even consider the cost.

Of course, their claim to know God's will so surely could not go unchallenged. After all, the judges they faced claimed to be the interpreters to Israel of the revelation and will of God. Peter's next words set forth the apostles' case.

b. There is first, the witness of the great objective, historic evidence about Jesus Christ. Peter boldly flings out the facts: God sent Jesus as the Messiah; He raised Him from the dead after the council itself rejected and slew Him. Peter even adds the detail about hanging on a tree, the sign of the divine curse upon the one so executed. But God was in it all: He exalted the rejected Jesus to the place of honor and power. We have already noted in Peter's sermons the forceful use of this dilemma. As a Prince, the Author of salvation, He requires them now to turn away from their wicked attitude and turn to Jesus. Then as Saviour, He will grant, even to His murderers, forgiveness, a full pardon. As personal witnesses, the apostles can vouch for all these facts.

c. But there is more than this. To the objective witness of the facts must be also added the internal testimony of the Holy Spirit. Peter links this last unerringly with the condition of obedience: the Holy Spirit is *given to them that obey him*. How do the apostles, how do Christians, come to assurance about their faith? For us who were not eyewitnesses of these sacred events, the witness of *the Bible* and the internal witness of the Spirit must go hand in hand. The first without the second will prove sterile and cold; the second without the first may be mistaken or else stereotyped; those who are fully committed to obedience will have both in full assurance.

The prophetic words of Jesus about the Comforter's witnessing ministry (John 15:26-27) ought to be studied in connection with Peter's great statement here.

3. The passage that follows is in vivid *contrast to the assurance* of the apostles. Peter's inspired words had a profound effect. The record states that the listeners' hearts were cut in two (a literal translation). Since they would not yield to the truth, there could be only one answer. They intended to kill the apostles at once. It is a familiar dilemma: Either obey the truth or kill it in your heart.

The murderous action was headed off by Gamaliel,

the most famous and highly respected teacher of his time. He was a Pharisee, and the Pharisees held a minority position in the great council. They opposed the Sadducees, the instigators of the trial, in both doctrine and politics.

Gamaliel's proposal seems to have been prompted partly by piety and partly by politics. It would not do to allow the Sadducees a victory in a situation where the Sadducee doctrinal position was being threatened, a position which the Pharisees also opposed. But genuine piety on Gamaliel's part would have called for a much higher response.

Gamaliel represents a weak and pecular view of divine providence. "Wait and see," he advises in pragmatic vein. Perhaps God is in this movement, perhaps not. If so, it will flourish and its opposers will be found in opposition to God. If not, it will die of its own accord. Such advice has only half the truth. It is essentially agnostic. It says no one can be really sure. It fails to account on the one hand for the deluding deceitfulness of sin and error, or on the other for the call to decision and action which the truth presents. It is the denial of Jesus' and Peter's doctrine of the Spirit's ministry in leading men to assurance of the truth. Men cannot be fence straddlers when the Spirit convicts their hearts and minds.

How tame is Gamaliel's word when contrasted with the joy and decisiveness of the apostles' Spirit-given assurance. Even so, God can and does use unwitting instruments to work His purpose. The council could not condemn without the Pharisees' consent. The apostles were therefore beaten, commanded again to cease witnessing, and let go.

4. The experience had induced *no trace of doubt or indecision* in the apostles' hearts. They wore their wounds as badges of honor. Not one turned back. The council was troubled, uncertain; the apostles rejoiced, remembering Jesus' words in the Beatitudes. Theirs was a divinely given certainty. The shame of the flogging was transmuted into honor inasmuch as it was for His sake.

Not for a day did they cease a full ministry of both teaching and preaching. They did it publicly as well as systematically, from house to house. Such is the assurance which the Spirit gives.

The Expansion and Outreach of the Church

Acts 6:1—12:25

ACTS 6

Solving a Church Problem in the Spirit

Acts 6:1-7

> 1 And in those days, when the number of the disciples was multiplied, there arose a murmuring of the Grecians against the Hebrews, because their widows were neglected in the daily ministration.
> 2 Then the twelve called the multitude of the disciples unto them, and said, It is not reason that we should leave the word of God, and serve tables.
> 3 Wherefore, brethren, look ye out among you seven men of honest report, full of the Holy Ghost and wisdom, whom we may appoint over this business.
> 4 But we will give ourselves continually to prayer, and to the ministry of the word.
> 5 And the saying pleased the whole multitude: and they chose Stephen, a man full of faith and of the Holy Ghost, and Philip, and Prochorus, and Nicanor, and Timon, and Parmenas, and Nicolas a proselyte of Antioch:
> 6 Whom they set before the apostles: and when they had prayed, they laid their hands on them.
> 7 And the word of God increased; and the number of the disciples multipled in Jerusalem greatly; and a great company of the priests were obedient to the faith.

To this point in Luke's great story, the main thrust of the Church's witnessing has been confined to Jerusalem and to Jews. Not only have the disciples greatly added to their numbers, but now the word used to describe the rapid growth is *multiplied.* The Church has been firmly established in Jerusalem; the authority of the apostles has been clearly defined.

At this point changes are introduced which will alter the Church's life and thrust it out beyond Jerusalem. A new kind of leadership and organization is introduced; the ties with Temple and synagogue worship were severed; Stephen's witnessing points the way to outreach to the Gentiles and precipitates a persecution that scatters the believers.

1. It began with *a problem*. The funds which the apostles received from generous donors were used largely to care for the needy. Daily distribution of food or money was made. This must have become an onerous task. One important and sensitive group, completely dependent on this charity, was the widows.

The Greek-speaking Jewish believers *(the Grecians)* developed a grievance toward their Aramaic-speaking brethren *(the Hebrews)* on the grounds that Greek-speaking widows were not being fairly treated. Whether the grievance was real or imagined, the situation had the ingredients for division and scandal. It was likely aggravated by the mild language and cultural barriers. And anyone who has tried to work out an equitable plan for distributing free goods understands the potential for trouble.

Of course ideally, such jealousies and misunderstandings should not occur where love reigns. But the Church was not, and is not, an ideal society.

2. The apostles responded courteously and adopted a *gracious method* in meeting the situation. Not judgment, as with the problem of hypocrisy, but grace was the keynote. The whole assembly was evidently given a large part in the selection of leaders to care for the handling of the money and the distribution of alms. The assembly selected seven men (by what means we do not know) who were presented to the apostles for approval and appointment. Judging by their Greek names, it would seem that all seven came from the Greek-speaking side in the dispute. Goodwill was restored within the fellowship. When attention is focused on "rights," fellowship is threatened; when grace

motivates men to concern for others, fellowship is restored.

The wise delegation and sharing of responsibility freed the apostles to care for their high priorities: prayer, which would include worship, and the preaching and teaching of the Word.

3. The *qualifications* for office of these new leaders as set forth are instructive. In such a position of trust these men must have the full confidence of all and thus be of sound reputation, *of honest report.* Further, they must be *filled with the Spirit,* men whose commitment was total, whose hearts were pure. No amount of energy or cleverness could compensate for a lack here. Finally, it was necessary that they have gifts for their task as well as grace, and thus they should have demonstrated *wisdom,* practical good sense, in the handling of their own affairs. These standards for the election of church officers are as sound today as then.

There is little ground for seeing in this appointment the creation of a new "order" within the Church. Other than the apostles, a temporary order, we do not have any technical designation for church leaders in the Book of Acts.

The leaders were formally installed in office by the apostles. The "laying on of hands" by the apostles designated their full blessing, transfer of authority, and identification with them in their work.

4. The reaffirmation of unity no doubt contributed to a fresh *evangelistic advance.* Luke's summary in v. 7 characteristically indicates his recognition of a new phase in the Church's progress. The special notation about the conversion of *a great company of the priests* highlights by way of tension the imminent break with the Temple worship.

God's Man of the Hour

Acts 6:8-15

8 And Stephen, full of faith and power, did great wonders and miracles among the people.
9 Then there arose certain of the synagogue, which is called the

Synagogue of the Libertines, and Cyrenians, and Alexandrians, and of them of Cilicia and of Asia, disputing with Stephen.
10 And they were not able to resist the wisdom and the spirit by which he spake.
11 Then they suborned men, which said, We have heard him speak blasphemous words against Moses, and against God.
12 And they stirred up the people, and the elders, and the scribes, and came upon him, and caught him, and brought him to the council,
13 And set up false witnesses, which said, This man ceaseth not to speak blasphemous words against this holy place, and the law:
14 For we have heard him say, that this Jesus of Nazareth shall destroy this place, and shall change the customs which Moses delivered us.
15 And all that sat in the council, looking stedfastly on him, saw his face as it had been the face of an angel.

The Christian career of Stephen was short but brilliant. The significance of a man's life cannot be measured by time or the number of things done. Stephen was indeed the first Christian martyr, but that must not obscure the fact that he was the spiritual catalyst of essential change in the Church. He was also the dynamic link between the ministries of Peter and Paul. He was Paul's inspiration in several ways: by the impact of his life and death (see 8:1), by the insights of his central thesis, and by the example of his methods. The great missionary to the Gentiles was to profit much from both the latter. Stephen was God's man at the crossroads, pointing the Church to its world mission.

1. The *character* of the man accounts in large measure for his importance. We have already noted above the qualifications of the seven. Of the seven, both Stephen and Philip exercised a much wider ministry than that of temporal affairs. We need to beware of confining a public witnessing ministry to a special order of clergy. Stephen seems to have been a learned man, a man of ideas, not afraid to innovate. But above all he was endowed by the Spirit with grace, that is, graciousness and divine favor ("grace" is the preferred reading to "faith," v. 8); with power, that is, a God-given effectiveness; and with wisdom, God's gift of insight and practical good sense.

2. Stephen's *message* is implied by the charges against him and expounded in his own defense. As an educated,

Greek-speaking Jew himself, it was natural that his ministry would be to Hellenists, as well as that the challenge should come from them.

Jewish synagogues were congregations formed for simple worship, for instruction in the law, and for needed community functions. The term applies also to the building used. There were many in Jerusalem and probably thousands among the dispersed Jews throughout the world. Stephen's opposition came from a congregation known as the Libertines, likely because they were freedmen, that is, liberated slaves and their families. Luke mentions several national backgrounds of these people. It is noteworthy that Paul was from Cilicia although there is not proof that he was involved. All were Greek-speaking.

There were implications in Stephen's preaching of Christ which certain of these Jews could not ignore. His principles they could not deny, but his conclusions threatened their way of life. It is evident that Stephen stressed the spiritual character of religion, the relation of the gospel to the whole Gentile world, and therefore the temporary character of the Mosaic ceremonial law and Temple worship. When they could not answer his arguments, they determined, supported no doubt by the chief priests, to bring him to the council on charges that could lead to his death. To obtain witnesses they resorted to bribing men to testify falsely.

Stephen was charged with blasphemy against the Temple, against the law, against Moses, and against God. It was true that Stephen's spiritual message, as we have noted, constituted a threat to their narrow system. The new wine of the Spirit would burst the old wineskins of ceremonial religion. It was this threat to the priority of the Temple, and thus to the whole Jerusalem economy, that finally turned the populace against the believers and made Stephen's seizure and the mob scene at his stoning possible.

3. Even before the accused was allowed to defend himself

against the half-truths of the false witnesses, the ugly scene was transformed by a *manifestation of divine glory*. The shining face, suffused with supernatural light, was a sign of God's presence and approval. Every person present would recall that Moses' face shone as he returned from communing with Jehovah. Every eye was drawn to the manifestation of an other-worldly presence. Stephen himself, sensing the crisis of opportunity and responsibility, and remembering how his Lord had been placed in so similar a trial, must have been filled with an overwhelming exaltation of spirit. To the council, God was graciously offering one more sign to bring conviction of the truth.

ACTS 7

Stephen's Defense: The God of Glory Revealed to Abraham

Acts 7:1-8

1 Then said the high priest, Are these things so?
2 And he said, Men, brethren, and fathers, hearken; The God of glory appeared unto our father Abraham, when he was in Mesopotamia, before he dwelt in Charran,
3 And said unto him, Get thee out of thy country, and from thy kindred, and come into the land which I shall shew thee.
4 Then came he out of the land of the Chaldaeans, and dwelt in Charran: and from thence, when his father was dead, he removed him into this land, wherein ye now dwell.
5 And he gave him none inheritance in it, no, not so much as to set his foot on: yet he promised that he would give it to him for a possession, and to his seed after him, when as yet he had no child.
6 And God spake on this wise, That his seed should sojourn in a strange land; and that they should bring them into bondage, and entreat them evil four hundred years.
7 And the nation to whom they shall be in bondage will I judge, said God: and after that shall they come forth, and serve me in this place.
8 And he gave him the covenant of circumcision: and so Abraham begat Isaac, and circumcised him the eighth day; and Isaac begat Jacob; and Jacob begat the twelve patriarchs.

At first glance the long speech of Stephen before the council (it is the longest recorded speech in the New Testament) seems irrelevant to the issues involved. Actually Stephen defended himself against the charges only indirectly. What he did do was to brilliantly set forth the case for faith in Jesus as the Way to the fulfillment of God's purpose for Israel and for the world. This method of rehearsing the working of God in Israel's history was a favorite one with the rabbis.

Throughout his survey of God's dealings with the nation, Stephen, by careful selection of events and persons, makes point after point in support of a thesis which is not lost on his audience. He reasons that God's dealings with His people are earlier than the law; that God was never confined to one land or to the Temple; and that the nation had a long record of rejection of God's voice through their leaders which culminated in the slaying of Jesus. He shows that the great men have been those willing to adventure out into new ways in obedience to God. He skillfully draws attention to events in the lives of Joseph and Moses, so that the parallels with Jesus will be pointed and obvious. All the while, without once referring to Him, he is preaching Jesus as Messiah, Saviour, Redeemer, and Fulfiller of Israel's hopes.

1. Stephen begins with great courtesy. He identifies himself with the faith of Israel and with Abraham, their common father. The reference to *the God of glory* shows him to be no blasphemer.

2. Abraham had a revelation of God and was called while he dwelt in a foreign land, far from the holy places.

3. Moreover, Abraham is an example of those who are willing to move out into a new way in obedience to God's call. All that Abraham had was a promise that not he but his posterity would possess the land; at no time did he personally own even a place to set his foot. The promise itself came before he had an heir, and then it was coupled with the warning that his descendants would live for centuries in bondage in a strange land before the promise was fulfilled.

4. So the great revelation of God, the holy covenant itself, including the sign of circumcision, along with the response of faith and obedience, all came before there was a holy land, or the law, or a temple. These tangible things are therefore not essential to a redemptive relationship with God. Stephen demonstrates an exalted view of God's mercy and faithfulness.

Stephen's Defense: Joseph, a Foreshadowing of Jesus

Acts 7:9-16

9 Are the patriarchs, moved with envy, sold Joseph into Egypt: but God was with him,
10 And delivered him out of all his afflictions, and gave him favour and wisdom in the sight of Pharaoh king of Egypt; and he made him governor over Egypt and all his house.
11 Now there came a dearth over all the land of Egypt and Chanaan, and great affliction: and our fathers found no sustenance.
12 But when Jacob heard that there was corn in Egypt, he sent out our fathers first.
13 And at the second time Joseph was made known to his brethren; and Joseph's kindred was made known unto Pharaoh.
14 Then sent Joseph, and called his father Jacob to him, and all his kindred, threescore and fifteen souls.
15 So Jacob went down into Egypt, and died, he, and our fathers,
16 And were carried over into Sychem, and laid in the sepulchre that Abraham bought for a sum of money of the sons of Emmor the father of Sychem.

1. The well-phrased parallels between Joseph and Jesus are striking. Like Jesus, Joseph was hated and betrayed by his brethen. Even the motive for the rejection is pointed out. But as with Jesus, *God was with* Joseph and delivered him. If Nicodemus was in the council on that day, he must have been haunted by his own words to Jesus, "No man can do these miracles that thou doest, except God be with him" (John 3:2*b*).

Like Jesus, Joseph was exalted by God after being rejected, and the purpose of his exaltation was that he might become his people's saviour, as well as the saviour of other nations through the supply of food during famine. There may also be a deliberate reference to Jesus' second coming in Stephen's notation that it was at *the second time* of confrontation that Joseph was made known to his brothers.

2. In this recital of events, Stephen is glorifying God for His patient and loving providence across the generations in the fulfilling of His promise to Abraham. A man with such a lofty view of God could not be guilty of blasphemy.

3. God was carrying out His purpose and preserving His people far from the Promised Land, that is, in Egypt. Furthermore, the patriarchs themselves were buried in Shechem, which was in New Testament times in Samaria, a fact that probably rankled in the minds of Stephen's accusers. The point of these references is that God is no respecter of places. The redemptive purpose transcends any one nation or locality.

Stephen's Defense: Jesus, a Prophet like unto Moses

Acts 7:17-40

17 But when the time of the promise drew nigh, which God had sworn
to Abraham, the people grew and multiplied in Egupt.
18 Till another king arose, which knew not Joseph.
19 The same dealt subtilly with our kindred, and evil entreated our
fathers, so that they cast out their young children, to the end they might
not live.
20 In which time Moses was born, and was exceeding fair, and
nourished up in his father's house three months:
21 And when he was cast out, Pharaoh's daughter took him up, and
nourished him for her own son.
22 And Moses was learned in all the wisdom of the Egyptians, and
was mighty in words and in deeds.
23 And when he was full forty years old, it came into his heart to visit
his brethren the children of Israel.
24 And seeing one of them suffer wrong, he defended him, and
avenged him that was oppressed, and smote the Egyptian:
25 For he supposed his brethren would have understood how that
God by his hand would deliver them: but they understood not.
26 And the next day he shewed himself unto them as they strove,
and would have set them at one again, saying, Sirs, ye are brethren;
why do ye wrong one to another?
27 But he that did his neighbour wrong thrust him away, saying, Who
made thee a ruler and a judge over us?
28 Wilt thou kill me, as thou diddest the Egyptian yesterday?
29 Then fled Moses at this saying, and was a stranger in the land of
Madian, where he begat two sons.
30 And when forty years were expired, there appeared to him in the
wilderness of mount Sina an angel of the Lord in a flame of fire in a
bush.
31 When Moses saw it, he wondered at the sight: and as he drew near
to behold it, the voice of the Lord came unto him,
32 Saying, I am the God of thy fathers, the God of Abraham, and the

God of Isaac, and the God of Jacob. Then Moses trembled, and durst not behold.
33 Then said the Lord to him, Put off thy shoes from thy feet: for the place where thou standest is holy ground.
34 I have seen, I have seen the affliction of my people which is in Egypt, and I have heard their groaning, and am come down to deliver them. And now come, I will send thee into Egypt.
35 This Moses whom they refused, saying, Who made thee a ruler and a judge? the same did God send to be a ruler and a deliverer by the hand of the angel which appeared to him in the bush.
36 He brought them out, after that he had shewed wonders and signs in the land of Egypt, and in the Red sea, and in the wilderness forty years.
37 This is that Moses, which said unto the children of Israel, A prophet shall the Lord your God raise up unto you of your brethren, like unto me; him shall ye hear.
38 This is he, that was in the church in the wilderness with the angel which spake to him in the mount Sina, and with our fathers: who received the lively oracles to give unto us:
39 To whom our fathers would not obey, but thrust him from them, and in their hearts turned back again into Egypt,
40 Saying unto Aaron, Make us gods to go before us: for as for this Moses, which brought us out of the land of Egypt, we wot not what is become of him.

1. The parallels between Moses and Jesus are even more deliberate and bold than those between Joseph and Jesus. Stephen deals at much greater length with Moses' career. He is coming to the heart of his message.

a. Moses was born *when the time of the promise drew nigh,* a time of great affliction and bondage. The Pharaohs of the Hyksos dynasty who had a common ancestry with the Hebrews, treated them well in remembrance of Joseph, but a new line of kings in Egypt began to exploit them bitterly. Probably in fear of their increasing numbers, they forced them to expose to death their male children.

Jesus had come "in the fulness of time," as prophesied to a nation under Roman bondage.

b. Moses had been saved from death and providentially cared for in infancy; so had Jesus. But it is uncertain if Stephen knew of Christ's infancy. Moses had received the finest education which his day could afford. The traditions say that he was very learned in the sciences and the arts, including the fine arts.

c. Like Jesus, Moses presented himself to his people in his mature manhood. Stephen here indicates that Moses was already, while in Egypt, conscious of his mission, something not given in the Exodus narrative (cf. Heb. 11:27). Like Jesus, Moses was misunderstood and rejected.

d. Moses' mission as deliverer was initiated by the appearance of *the angel of the Lord,* that is, by Jehovah himself, confirming his call and revealing God's purpose to redeem His people. So had the Father confirmed the work of the Son in the beginning of Jesus' ministry.

e. Although the people at first refused Moses, God sent him to be a deliverer; and deliver them he did, with great wonders and signs. These signs also marked Jesus' ministry.

f. Stephen finally uses very plain words with unquestioned reference to Jesus: Moses himself had foretold that God would raise up a prophet for Israel *of your brethren, like unto me; him shall ye hear.* They claimed to revere Moses but had ignored his words.

g. Moses was the mediator between God and the people, speaking to them God's very words, giving them the law. Clearly, that message was intended to be life-giving. A greater than Moses had come, declaring plainly that His words were from His Father and that to receive His word would bring both light and life.

h. The nation had treated Jesus as it had treated Moses. They *would not obey, but thrust him from them.* As with Moses, so with Jesus, they were saying, *as for this Moses . . . we wot not* (we cannot tell) *what is become of him.*

2. Stephen is already driving home with relentless force the lesson concerning the pattern of rejection of God's servants throughout the history of the nation, a lesson which will quickly come to a climax and will be once more illustrated. The unspoken question now is, Who has really rejected Moses? Stephen, as charged, or the leaders of the nation?

3. The overtones of the passage again make the point that

God is unconfined with respect to place or ceremony when He reveals himself. It was in Midian, in the Arabian desert, where Moses sojourned, that God spoke in a flaming bush that was not consumed. Wherever God is, the place is *holy ground.* It was also in the wilderness, not in Jerusalem, that God dwelt with His called-out people, here called *the church in the wilderness.* (The Church is still a pilgrim society.) There in the wilderness God spoke, and the people understood His will. Stephen is indicating that the Jews have made of the Temple and the city something never intended by the Lord.

Stephen's Defense: The House Left Desolate

Acts 7:41-53

41 And they made a calf in those days, and offered sacrifice unto the idol, and rejoiced in the works of their own hands.
42 Then God turned, and gave them up to worship the host of heaven; as it is written in the book of the prophets, O ye house of Israel, have ye offered to me slain beasts and sacrifices by the space of forty years in the wilderness?
43 Yea, ye took up the tabernacle of Moloch, and the star of your god Remphan, figures which ye made to worship them: and I will carry you away beyond Babylon.
44 Our fathers had the tabernacle of witness in the wilderness, as he had appointed, speaking unto Moses, that he should make it according to the fashion that he had seen.
45 Which also our fathers that came after brought in with Jesus into the possession of the Gentiles, whom God drave out before the face of our fathers, unto the days of David;
46 Who found favour before God, and desired to find a tabernacle for the God of Jacob.
47 But Solomon built him an house.
48 Howbeit the most High dwelleth not in temples made with hands; as saith the prophet,
49 Heaven is my throne, and earth is my footstool: what house will ye build me? saith the Lord: or what is the place of my rest?
50 Hath not my hand made all these things?
51 Ye stiffnecked and uncircumcised in heart and ears, ye do always resist the Holy Ghost: as your fathers did, so do ye.
52 Which of the prophets have not your fathers persecuted? and they have slain them which shewed before of the coming of the Just One; of whom ye have been now the betrayers and murderers:
53 Who have received the law by the disposition of angels, and have not kept it.

Through the lips of Stephen the Jerusalem rulers are hearing the final appeal to heed God's voice through His messengers. And yet Jesus had foreknown the result: "O Jerusalem, Jerusalem, thou that killest the prophets, and stonest them which are sent unto thee, how often would I have gathered thy children together . . . and ye would not! Behold, your house is left unto you desolate" (Matt. 23: 37-38).

1. Stephen has been tracing in history the persistent purpose of God throughout all generations and has shown how this has been matched by the perpetual rebellion of Israel. *Idolatry* had actually begun in the wilderness with the golden calf. He seems to suggest that the people had even diverted their sacrifices to other gods. This was only the beginning of a long history of yearning after other gods.

Stephen makes free use of Amos 5:25-27 (*the book of the prophets* is a reference to the 12 minor prophets) to remind his hearers that this idolatry had culminated in the worship of the heavenly bodies. God *gave them up* to their folly and disobedience. They were taken into successive captivities.

2. Stephen now addresses himself directly to the charge related to *the temple* (v. 44). He does not deny that he is in conflict with the view which made the Temple God's only dwelling place, almost an object of worship itself.

What Israel had in the wilderness (and Stephen notes that it was made to God's specifications) was a portable tent which housed all that was necessary to their worship. Indeed, this served the nation until David's time. Stephen contends that David desired to build for God a finer tabernacle or house, but when the project was left to Solomon, he built instead a great rich edifice of stone, permanent and fixed. Stephen's disapproval is implied.

Stephen cites the prophet Isaiah (c. 66) in support of his thesis that the God of the whole earth cannot be localized nor can His Spirit be contained in a building. Even the term *the most High* seems to identify Jehovah with the God of all the nations, the Creator.

That God does not dwell, that is, does not take up His

residence *in temples made with hands,* contains the incipient doctrine of the body of Christ as the true temple of God through the Spirit. It was Paul who would bring Stephen's seed-concept to fruition.

3. As he concludes (vv. 51-53), Stephen suddenly moves from defense to attack. He is deeply moved by his hearers' hardness of heart. They have not resisted him (that would be pardonable), but they have closed their ears to the voice of the Holy Spirit. To be *uncircumcized in heart* was not only to be classed with the pagans, but, since circumcision signified submission, trust, and separation, the epithet also indicated a rebellious, unbelieving, unclean spirit.

Great privilege brings great responsibility! They had the law by the hand of angels. They had the prophets. The Messiah himself had come to them. They had broken the law, persecuted the prophets, and as the climactic act in the tragedy of their rebellion, had murdered the Just One.

For the last time, Stephen was swinging God's red lantern of warning. But it was too late. The issue had already been decided.

Stephen's Death: Eyes for Invisibles

Acts 7:54—8:1a

54 When they heard these things, they were cut to the heart, and they gnashed on him with their teeth.
55 But he, being full of the Holy Ghost, looked up stedfastly into heaven, and saw the glory of God, and Jesus standing on the right hand of God,
56 And said, Behold, I see the heavens opened, and the Son of man standing on the right hand of God.
57 Then they cried out with a loud voice, and stopped their ears, and ran upon him with one accord,
58 And cast him out of the city, and stoned him: and the witnesses laid down their clothes at a young man's feet, whose name was Saul.
59 And they stoned Stephen, calling upon God, and saying, Lord Jesus, receive my spirit.
60 And he kneeled down, and cried with a loud voice, Lord, lay not this sin to their charge. And when he had said this, he fell asleep.
1*a* And Saul was consenting unto his death.

Unreasoning rage is characteristic of those who are condemned by their own consciences as well as by reason but whose wills remain unmoved. Aware of the fury of his hearers, Stephen was looking away from them toward his only Source of help.

"Full of the Holy Spirit" or "filled with the Holy Spirit" are characteristic expressions of the Book of Acts. The triumph of Stephen before the Sanhedrin and in the hour of his supreme testing can be explained only by the fact of the Holy Spirit totally possessing and controlling his personal faculties and attitudes. As a fully obedient servant, he felt and knew himself to be completely in the hands of God in the supreme crisis of his life. Such is the privilege of Spirit-filled believers.

Stephen's martyrdom is a demonstration of the ultimate fact for Christians: Jesus is Lord.

1. *Jesus is Lord in the unseen glory.* Stephen, now completely absorbed with heavenly things, having loosed himself from all other concerns, was granted eyes for invisibles, and saw Jesus in His ascended authority and glory at the right hand of God. It was a vision granted to few in the New Testament record. Certainly John saw it on Patmos, and doubtless Paul also. "Glory" is a word that speaks of the indescribable brightness and beauty which surrounds the presence of God.

Stephen described the glorified Jesus as *the Son of man.* Outside the Gospels this is the only place in the New Testament where this name is used. Jesus used it of himself. It comes from the Old Testament (Dan. 7:13-14) where the prophet saw the Son of Man "with the clouds of heaven" coming to "the Ancient of days" and being given "dominion, and glory, and a kingdom, that all people, nations, and languages, should serve him. . . . An everlasting dominion, which shall not pass away." For Jewish concepts of the Messiah, the name therefore had a revolutionary aspect; it related to all mankind and suggested a world mission. The vision was in keeping with Stephen's preaching in which he declared that Jesus is for all people.

Only short weeks before, this same council had heard Jesus say before them in answer to their question Art thou the Christ? "Hereafter shall the Son of man sit on the right hand of the power of God" (Luke 22:69). Now Stephen declares the fulfillment of that prediction of exaltation. It was more than they could bear. Stephen's death was sealed.

2. *Jesus is Lord in the crises of our life and in our death.* Stephen's arraignment before the council had some of the earmarks of a proper and orderly trial, but at the last his accusers, stung beyond endurance by the prisoner's vision and serenity of spirit, abandoned all semblance of legality. The trial broke up in a scene of mob violence. Stephen was rushed outside the city and stoned to death. There was no consent or sentence by the Roman governor (probably Pilate). No doubt the illegality of the action was patched up with the procurator later.

How triumphantly like his Lord Stephen was in his death! Like Jesus, Stephen was accused by bribed witnesses of blasphemy against Moses, the Temple, and God. Like Jesus before this same council, Stephen witnessed to the exaltation of the Son of Man at the right had of God. Like Jesus, Stephen committed his spirit in the hour of his death to God. (It is noteworthy that Stephen's prayer in death was addressed to Jesus, to whom he commended his spirit, a remarkable witness to the deity of our Lord.) Like Jesus, Stephen prayed for the forgiveness of his cruel executioners. Like Jesus, all of this was accomplished in the power of the Spirit.

Ordinarily, the Scriptures speak of the Son as *seated* at the right of the Father in the position of power and mediatorship, having finished His atoning work on earth. Stephen saw Him *standing* as if to honor and welcome home His faithful witness.

3. *Jesus is Lord of His ongoing Church.* Mosaic law required that in the case of execution by stoning, the witnesses against the accused must strike the first blows. If death did not quickly result from being hurled down from a high place and crushed under the stones of the witnesses,

then all the spectators must see to it that the business was finished. Luke dramatically introduces Saul of Tarsus at this point by recording that he cared for the outer garments of the witnesses which were taken off to free them for the stoning.

Paul himself describes this moment: "And when the blood of they martyr Stephen was shed, I also was standing by, and consenting unto his death, and kept the raiment of them that slew him" (22:20). The statement that *Saul was consenting* to Stephen's death, if it does not imply that he was a voting member of the Sanhedrin, at least indicates full complicity and responsibility.

Stephen's life and death produced an overwhelming and inexcapable impression on the mind of Saul of Tarsus. Augustine said, "The Church owes Paul to the prayer of Stephen." Saul remembered the emphases of Stephen's defense and his prior preaching. Saul was struck by the angelic glory upon his face before his judges. Saul heard him commit his spirit to Jesus and pray for the forgiveness of his torturers. Saul observed the peace of his countenance as *he fell asleep* in hope of the resurrection.

"The blood of the martyrs is the seed of the Church." God is able to make the wrath of men to praise Him. The seeming untimeliness of Stephen's death, the apparent crushing in the bud of Stephen's great concept of Christ's kingdom, were in fact the planting of the seed from which would spring the great world missionary outreach of the Church. If indeed the Church owes Paul to the prayer of Stephen, then Stephen is the spiritual progenitor of the great Apostle to the Gentiles, and through him of the message of a universal salvation as set forth by Paul the theologian.

ACTS 8

Witnessing in All Judea and in Samaria

Acts 8:1b-8

1*b* And at that time there was a great persecution against the church which was at Jerusalem; and they were all scattered abroad through-

out the regions of Judaea and Samaria, except the apostles.
2 And devout men carried Stephen to his burial, and made great lamentation over him.
3 As for Saul, he made havock of the church, entering into every house, and haling man and women committed them to prison.
4 Therefore they that were scattered abroad went every where preaching the word.
5 Then Philip went down to the city of Samaria, and preached Christ unto them.
6 And the people with one accord gave heed unto those things which Philip spake, hearing and seeing the miracles which he did.
7 For unclean spirits, crying with loud voice, came out of many that were possessed with them: and many taken with palsies, and that were lame, were healed.
8 And there was great joy in that city.

Against the background provided by cc. 6 and 7, Luke now begins to sketch selected incidents in the evangelistic thrust of the Church out and away from Jerusalem, the home base. With a brevity of language two important concepts are noted in this passage.

1. *The evil of persecution was turned into the blessing of evangelism.* The furious attempt to destroy the Church led directly to its rapid propagation. The believers in Jerusalem were *scattered abroad* much in the way a sower would scatter seed. And, like scattered seed, they reproduced the Christian life wherever they went.

a. The attitude of Saul the Pharisee is in curious contrast to some of his number. There were those described here as *devout men,* in all probability Jews of the Pharisaic persuasion, who took up Stephen's battered and blood-stained body and gave it a decent burial, just as some of them had done with the body of Jesus. They doubtless expressed their deep chagrin and regret at the illegal mob action. There is a form of protest in the *great lamentation* over Stephen, something forbidden by the law in the case of a blasphemer. One might have thought that Saul, a "Pharisee of the Pharisees," would find himself alongside men of such pious temperament. Instead he became the leader and chief instigator of the persecution, according to his own later testimony (cf. 22:4, 19; and 26: 10-11). The Pharisee allied himself with the Sadducean high priest's party.

It was the theological insight of Saul coupled with his burning zeal for the traditions of his people which gave him to see that this new movement was no mere harmless sect of Judaism. Unless it was utterly destroyed, it would in the end supplant the religion of the Temple. Thus the persecution which he carefully planned was marked for the first time with a religious passion quite different from the jealousy which motivated the chief priests. Saul ravaged the Church, like a wild animal savaging its prey. In a fury of cruelty, both men and women were seized in their homes and dragged to prison. The rest fled.

b. The results of the persecution were in contradiction to Saul's intentions. The first missionary advance of the Church came about not by apostolic authority or decree and not by a careful plan (as did other later advances), but spontaneously and through suffering. Perhaps it took such a means to keep the Church from clinging to Jerusalem.

The heralds of the good news about the deliverance through Jesus (the word which they preached) were not the apostles but the rank and file of the believers, those whom we would call laymen. Thus, this first sweeping advance came about by the spontaneous witnessing of ordinary Christians.

The apostles remained in Jerusalem at their post of leadership, as men of courage. Perhaps they were spared inasmuch as the persecution seems to have been mainly against the Greek-speaking Jewish Christians, the Hellenistic group in which both Stephen and Philip were prominent leaders (cf. 11:19-20). From this time the Jerusalem church took on a Hebrew rather than Hellenistic flavor.

2. *The original power and success of the Jerusalem church was repeated in Samaria.* This is the point which Luke is making in vv. 5 to 8.

Philip, not the apostle, but one of the seven almoners (see c. 6), is now brought to the center of action briefly. He reappears again only in c. 21, where he is called the evangelist and entertains Paul's party in his home in Caesarea. Philip's preaching to Samaritans is selected as exemplifying the work of the gospel beyond Judea.

The Samaritan city (it is "a" not "the" city) is not named. Perhaps it was Neapolis, the ancient Shechem, the religious center of the country near Mount Gerizim. There the Samaritans had once had a rival temple. Theirs was a mixed race and religion caused by intermingling with the Gentiles who had been settled there at the time of the Assyrian captivity of the northern kingdom. The Jews despised them more than even the pagans and had no dealing with them. Nevertheless the Samaritans revered Moses and hoped for the Messiah. Many had seen and believed on Jesus at Sychar (see John, c. 4). To such a despised people came the gospel and the results were the same as in Jerusalem.

The same signs were done under Philip's ministry as under the apostles in the beginning of the Church. These signs were made more necessary by the character of the Samaritans as indicated in v. 10. The most hopeless cases, the demon-possessed, the paralyzed, and the crippled, were healed by the power of God. Seeing the signs, the Samaritans were convinced, and hearing the gospel they believed on Jesus and were saved. A great city-wide work of grace was done. No wonder there was great joy. Wherever the gospel is received with the resultant spiritual transformation and acconpanying social and physical blessings, there is rejoicing and thanksgiving.

The Outpouring of the Spirit upon the Outcast

Acts 8:9-25

9 But there was a certain man, called Simon, which beforetime in the same city used sorcery, and bewitched the people of Samaria, giving out that himself was some great one:
10 To whom they all gave heed, from the least to the greatest, saying, This man is the great power of God.
11 And to him they had regard, because that of long time he had bewitched them with sorceries.
12 But when they believed Philip preaching the things concerning the

kingdom of God, and the name of Jesus Christ, they were baptized, both men and women.
13 Then Simon himself believed also: and when he was baptized, he continued with Philip, and wondered, beholding the miracles and signs which were done.
14 Now when the apostles which were at Jerusalem heard that Samaria had received the word of God, they sent unto them Peter and John:
15 Who, when they were come down, prayed for them, that they might receive the Holy Ghost:
16 (For as yet he was fallen upon none of them: only they were baptized in the name of the Lord Jesus.)
17 Then laid they their hands on them, and they received the Holy Ghost.
18 And when Simon saw that through laying on of the apostles' hands the Holy Ghost was given, he offered them money,
19 Saying, Give me also this power, that on whomsoever I lay hands, he may receive the Holy Ghost.
20 But Peter said unto him, Thy money perish with thee, because thou hast thought that the gift of God may be purchased with money.
21 Thou hast neither part nor lot in this matter: for thy heart is not right in the sight of God.
22 Repent therefore of this thy wickedness, and pray God, if perhaps the thought of thine heart may be forgiven thee.
23 For I perceive that thou art in the gall of bitterness, and in the bond of iniquity.
24 Then answered Simon, and said, Pray ye to the Lord for me, that none of these things which ye have spoken come upon me.
25 And they, when they had testified and preached the word of the Lord, returned to Jerusalem, and preached the gospel in many villages of the Samaritans.

Luke lists four typical outpourings of the Holy Spirit. The first was, of course, the epochal gift of the Spirit at Pentecost. This is the second, the extension of the Pentecostal baptism to the Samaritan believers, the first such extension beyond the circle of Jewish believers. The Samaritans, although non-Jewish, were kin to the Jews, and formed a natural bridge between the Jewish and Gentile worlds.

This passage is a study in contrast. The genuine work of the Spirit is presented against the backdrop of a spurious substitute.

1. *The Samaritan Pentecost,* so called in the sense indicated above, was an historic breakthrough and a divine confirmation of the missionary outreach of the gospel beyond the Jewish world.

a. A genuine work of grace had been done amongst the

Samaritans. Philip had proclaimed "the word" (v. 4), "Christ" (v. 5), "the kingdom of God," and "the name of Jesus Christ" (v. 12). The two latter expressions indicate an exposition of the rule of God in the hearts of men and the way to realize it, as well as the final revelation of God and of His salvation in the person of Jesus Christ.

Great numbers of people "gave heed" (v. 6), "believed . . . the preaching" (v. 12), and "were baptized, both men and women." The tenses indicate that this blessed work of conversion kept going on from day to day. *Samaria had received the word of God* (v. 14).

The believers were being given water baptism without delay as the outward sign of repentance and saving faith in Jesus.

b. Although the believers had received Christian (water) baptism *in the name of the Lord Jesus,* that is, confessing Jesus as Lord, they had not yet experienced the baptism with the Holy Spirit. The expression *as yet he was fallen upon none of them* refers to the fullness of the Spirit as at Pentecost. As believers, they were not destitute of the Holy Spirit, who regenerates, indwells, and witnesses to all who are in Christ. But they did not know Him in the fullness which Pentecost signified.

The prayer of Peter and John was specific: *that they might receive the Holy Spirit.* The answer was definite: They received Him. It is erroneous to confuse this experience with the mere reception of certain signs authenticating the Spirit's presence. Not the gifts of the Spirit but the Gift, that is, the Spirit himself, the Possessor and Sanctifier to each believer, is the great fact at the heart of this passage.

c. For the Church, this was an historic occasion. Was the ancient wall separating Jews and Samaritans being broken down in Christ? Could these Samaritans, so long considered alienated from the true people of God, receive the gospel and the gift of the Spirit just as Jewish believers had done? These thoughts were doubtless in the minds of the apostles when they delegated Peter and John to visit the great Samaritan revival.

The laying on of the hands of the apostles was not a mystical rite through which the Holy Spirit must be given, although this has been taught by a part of Christendom. The hands would be laid on a few to symbolize the whole. It was rather the sign of fellowship, of acceptance, of solidarity between the leaders of the Church who represented Jerusalem and the new Samaritan believers. It was the sign that the Church is one in Christ and in the Spirit.

The Samaritans needed such a sign to assure their full acceptance by the Jerusalem church. As for the apostles, the Spirit's fullness upon these new believers was sufficient evidence that God himself had received the Samaritan believers.

The joyous sequel to the story is told in v. 25. The two apostles, steeped as they were in Jewish prejudice against Samaritans, returned to Jerusalem, but slowly, stopping in many of the Samaritan villages to proclaim Christ. This was the same John who had once suggested to Jesus that they call down fire on an inhospitable Samaritan village (Luke 9:51-55). The spirit of Jesus had triumphed! This is, incidentally, the last mention of the Apostle John in the Book of Acts.

2. *The challenge of a counterfeit Christianity* in this passage only serves to highlight and accent the attributes of the true.

In the city where the revival took place was a religious imposter, a sinister, conjuring sorcerer by the name of Simon, who for a long time through the practice of his black arts had held the people in the grip of fear and superstition. In their ignorance, they considered his magic feats to be a divine manifestation, and Simon accepted and fostered his false status as *the great power of God.*

This strange person was from a not uncommon class for that day of soothsayers, wizards, astrologers, and pseudo-scientific practitioners of the occult. Many of these were charlatans; some saw themselves as Messiahs (some of the many false Christs); each had his following.

Simon Magus, as Christian tradition and legend has dubbed him, plays quite a prominent part in susequent apocryphal Christian literature. Legend has him becoming the father of a Gnostic sect, the Simonians, who were known as late as the third century, and also has him living at Rome and disturbing the Christians there. But all we know for certain is said here in Acts.

Simon lives on infamously in the dictionary, having lent his name in the word *simony,* the term which describes the buying and selling of spiritual or ecclesiastical influence or position. Simon's counterpart in the Old Testament is Gehazi, the servant of Elisha.

a. Simon illustrates the failure of an inadequate faith. Whether he believed sincerely at the first or was only a pretender, might be debated. In any case his faith appears to have been no more than an intellectual assent rather than a true, trustful commitment of the whole person. Simon believed, but his faith was in the miracles which he saw performed by the hands of Philip. It was an enthusiasm for signs and wonders, a shallow, emotional response, without the deep moral surrender of the self which is the essence of saving faith. The Gospels record that many believed on Jesus, seeing His miracles in the same superficial way. The demons also believe because of the external evidence which they acknowledge, but they do not yield or trust. True faith is dependence, confidence, commitment, appropriation—all in relationship with Jesus Christ.

b. Simon apparently confused God's grace with magic, and he is not the last to have done so. He seems to have considered the miracles of Philip's ministry and the prayers of Peter and John to have been only magic of a higher form than his own. Those who expect spiritual blessings or who pray for spiritual power without any consideration of the deep moral issues involved in a personal relationship with God are really saying that they too believe in a (Christian) magic. Those who expect God's grace to continue to operate in their lives in the absence of a continuing obedient relationship through the Spirit are also trying to practice a form of pious magic. Magic is non-moral or possibly immoral; grace is deeply moral, ethical, and personal in its operations.

This truth is at the core of Peter's biting words to Simon. Simon's intentions were to use spiritual privileges, indeed, to use the Spirit himself, for his own self-seeking, materialistic ends. Peter was properly horror-struck at such crass wickedness. With spiritual insight he saw that Simon was a complete stranger to spiritual reality, a mere intruder into the holy place. Only those who seek after God for His own sake with humble reverence and truthfulness have any part or lot in spiritual things. Only the straight in heart can stand in the holy place, and Simon's heart was crooked. There is no question but that Peter's words imply that candidates for the gifts of the Spirit must be those whose hearts are right (straight) before God. Full obedience and yieldedness are required.

c. Simon had a twisted concept of the Holy Spirit. He seemed to confuse the Spirit with a produced effect, a kind of supernatural energy, an impersonal power or influence, a mere thing. He saw God's gift as *something* to be manipulated, used for one's own ends. *This power* was his own description.

Those whose primary quest is for power, and who can substitute that for a deep hunger for God and righteousness come perilously close to Simon's sin. The gift of God, Peter suggests, is God himself through the Spirit. God comes to us in infinite grace and love, offering a relationship with himself beyond all price, made possible only by Calvary. When we by faith enter into this holy relationship of the fullness of His Spirit, we become His cleansed instruments, for His own use, however and wherever He shall choose.

And yet there was hope for Simon if he would repent and find forgiveness. He seemed terrified by Peter's warning of perdition. The thoughts of his heart had been unveiled. There is little in his response to indicate repentance, however. Mere fear of consequences is by itself an insufficient motive.

The Spirit Reaches Out to One "Afar Off"

Acts 8:26-40

26 And the angel of the Lord spake unto Philip, saying, Arise, and go toward the south unto the way that goeth down from Jerusalem unto Gaza, which is desert.
27 And he arose and went: and, behold, a man of Ethiopia, an eunuch of great authority under Candace queen of the Ethiopians, who had the charge of all her treasure, and had come to Jerusalem for to worship,
28 Was returning, and sitting in his chariot read Esaias the prophet.
29 Then the Spirit said unto Philip, Go near, and join thyself to this chariot.
30 And Philip ran thither to him, and heard him read the prophet Esaias, and said, Understandest thou what thou readest?
31 And he said, How can I, except some man should guide me? And he desired Philip that he would come up and sit with him.
32 The place of the scripture which he read was this, He was led as a sheep to the slaughter; and like a lamb dumb before his shearer, so opened he not his mouth:
33 In his humiliation his judgment was taken away: and who shall declare his generation? for his life is taken from the earth.
34 And the eunuch answered Philip, and said, I pray thee, of whom speaketh the prophet this? of himself, or of some other man?
35 Then Philip opened his mouth, and began at the same scripture, and preached unto him Jesus.
36 And as they went on their way, they came unto a certain water: and the eunuch said, See, here is water; what doth hinder me to be baptized?
37 And Philip said, If thou believest with all thine heart, thou mayest. And he answered and said, I believe that Jesus Christ is the Son of God.
38 And he commanded the chariot to stand still: and they went down both into the water, both Philip and the eunuch; and he baptized him.
39 And when they were come up out of the water, the Spirit of the Lord caught away Philip, that the eunuch saw him no more: and he went on his way rejoicing.
40 But Philip was found at Azotus: and passing through he preached in all the cities, till he came to Caesarea.

Luke has carefully selected another incident from the ministry of Philip the evangelist. It is the conversion of the first Gentile, and other than those present at Pentecost, the first representative of a distant land. Special intervention and guidance from the Lord was involved. Philip's ministry took a quite unexpected direction. This was an event of great significance. Philip and the Ethiopian are the human characters, but it is the Holy Spirit who directs each act.

1. *The Spirit responds to hunger after God.* The object of the divine intervention was a man who contrasted with the people to whom Philip had so recently ministered. He had wealth, position, honor, and high responsibility. He was likely of the black race. He was in charge of the finances of Ethiopia, a developed African nation to the south of Egypt on the upper Nile, traditionally ruled by queens who carried the title of Candace. His conversion would be strategic in the evangelizing of his country.

More significant still was the man's spiritual hunger. He was returning from a worship pilgrimage to the Temple at Jerusalem. Possibly he had attended one of the annual Jewish feasts. As a eunuch, he would likely not be a full-fledged proselyte to the Jewish religion, but rather a "God-fearer" or "a proselyte of the gate" with limited worship privileges. Obviously a man of intelligence, he had obtained a costly scroll of Old Testament Scriptures (the Greek translation) which he read aloud, according to the custom of his time, as he sat in his chariot or wagon on the long journey home.

He was plainly a seeker after God. The ritual of the Temple had not satisfied his heart need. Now he searched in the Scriptures, but in ignorance of their meaning.

Jesus had taught, "Blessed are they which do hunger and thirst after righteousness: for they shall be filled." The Ethiopian's conversion illustrates the proposition that God always responds to the need of those whose hearts reach out after Him.

2. *The Spirit uses obedient human channels.* It must have seemed to Philip a startling or strange directive which came to him to leave abruptly his highly gratifying and successful ministry for a journey to a sparsely populated desert area to the south of Jerusalem. Perhaps that explains why the Spirit used an angel to make the directive explicit. The effective mass evangelist became equally effective in one-to-one evangelism.

It is significant that while the Spirit could use an angel to speak to Philip, He needed a Spirit-filled man, not an angel, to reach a hungry-hearted seeker. But for Philip's willingness to leave the warm fellowship for the lonely road, and to do it promptly in unquestioning obedience, the whole enterprise would have failed. Providential timing brought seeker and evangelist together.

3. *The Spirit illuminates and speaks through the Scriptures.* Still directed by the Spirit, Philip came near the slow-moving vehicle carrying the Ethiopian official, and heard him read aloud from the great Messianic passage in Isaiah 53. Luke uses great brevity, but doubtless Philip's question, manner, and entire approach were so Spirit-directed and thus so winsome that the distance between the two, in station, background, culture, was quickly bridged. People are usually won to some Christian person before they are won to Christ.

The eunuch's response, "How can I find the way without a guide?" is the unspoken appeal of multitudes of people. Needed is an army of Philips, Spirit-filled, with warm hearts and prepared, full minds, who can speak with assurance, even authority, about what they have seen, experienced, and understood of God's grace in Jesus Christ.

Philip had an adequate grasp of the Scriptures. One wishes he might have heard the Spirit-anointed discourse on the great Messianic passage on the suffering Saviour. Philip presented Jesus to the hungry seeker, a message he had not heard in the Jerusalem ritual, a message of grace, atonement for sin, forgiveness, and life in the Spirit.

To neglect in the church the careful, painstaking work of interpreting the Scriptures is to abandon all those who need the one sure light which Scripture affords, and to deprive the Holy Spirit of the most effective use of His own special instrument in lifting up Christ.

4. *The Spirit brings Christian certainty and joy.* Philip's witness was not only *about* Jesus, but was a personal introduction *to* Jesus. It led to decision. The great man opened his heart in humble faith and found the answer to his spiritual hunger. At once he desired to clinch and wit-

ness to his faith by baptism. There were servants present, perhaps a caravan of people. Although v. 37 is not found except in certain of the lesser texts, and is thus omitted in the revised versions, it does no doubt represent the typical confession of faith of a baptismal candidate. This was the great turning point in the eunuch's life, and if tradition may be trusted, the beginning of the Christian Church in his own nation.

How typically the record ends: *He went on his way rejoicing!* Philip was suddenly gone, but the new convert was not dismayed at the loss of his interpreter. He who had before read the Scriptures with unseeing eyes now knew the Author and was indwelt by the Spirit, the great Teacher. He was rejoicing in the assurance and certainty which the Spirit brings.

As for Philip, there was no cessation of his outstanding ministry. Luke makes passing mention of his preaching in several cities, moving north as far as the important city of Caesarea. There the narrative of Philip ends, to be resumed briefly in Acts 21, at a time 20 years later when Paul and Luke were entertained for a time at Caesarea in the home of Philip the evangelist.

ACTS 9

The Miraculous Transformation of Saul of Tarsus

Acts 9:1-19a

1 And Saul, yet breathing out threatenings and slaughter against the disciples of the Lord, went unto the high priest,
2 And desired of him letters to Damascus to the synagogues, that if he found any of this way, whether they were men or women, he might bring them bound unto Jerusalem.
3 And as he journeyed, he came near Damascus: and suddenly there shined round about him a light from heaven:
4 And he fell to the earth, and heard a voice saying unto him, Saul, Saul, why persecutest thou me?
5 And he said, Who art thou, Lord? And the Lord said, I am Jesus whom thou persecutest: it is hard for thee to kick against the pricks.
6 And he trembling and astonished said, Lord, what wilt thou have me to do? And the Lord said unto him, Arise, and go into the city, and it shall be told thee what thou must do.

7 And the men which journeyed with him stood speechless, hearing a voice, but seeing no man.
8 And Saul arose from the earth; and when his eyes were opened, he saw no man: but they led him by the hand, and brought him into Damascus.
9 And he was three days without sight, and neither did eat nor drink.
10 And there was a certain disciple at Damascus, named Ananias; and to him said the Lord in a vision, Ananias. And he said, Behold, I am here, Lord.
11 And the Lord said unto him, Arise, and go into the street which is called Straight, and enquire in the house of Judas for one called Saul of Tarsus: for, behold, he prayeth,
12 And hath seen in a vision a man named Ananias coming in, and putting his hand on him, that he might receive his sight.
13 Then Ananias answered, Lord, I have heard by many of this man, how much evil he hath done to thy saints at Jerusalem:
14 And here he hath authority from the chief priests to bind all that call on thy name.
15 But the Lord said unto him, Go thy way: for he is a chosen vessel unto me, to bear my name before the Gentiles, and kings, and the children of Israel:
16 For I will shew him how great things he must suffer for my name's sake.
17 And Ananias went his way, and entered into the house; and putting his hands on him said, Brother Saul, the Lord, even Jesus, that appeared unto thee in the way as thou camest, hath sent me, that thou mightest receive thy sight, and be filled with the Holy Ghost.
18 And immediately there fell from his eyes as it had been scales: and he received sight forthwith, and arose, and was baptized.
19*a* And when he had received meat, he was strengthened.

In the field of Christian evidences (arguments for the truth of Christianity) the conversion of Saul of Tarsus ranks in importance next to the resurrection of Jesus. The importance of the event to Luke may be surmised from the fact that it is recorded three times in Acts: here, in c. 22, and again in c. 26.

1. Something of the *personality of Saul the persecutor* needs to be seen in order to grasp the magnitude of the miracle in his life.

a. Saul of Tarsus was fiercely proud of his antecedents: he was of the best Jewish stock, "a Hebrew of the Hebrews." Besides, his family held Roman citizenship in Tarsus. His education was superior: he had been trained in Jerusalem in the law at the feet of Gamaliel, the greatest contemporary rabbi; living in the university city of Tarsus, he understood Greek literature, culture, and philosophy, although the Greek learning influenced him little. He was a man of two worlds, the Hebrew and the Greek, a learned and brilliant mind.

Religiously, Saul was a Pharisee and rigorously applied its disciplines. That meant that his faith had a supernatural, spiritual orientation; that he revered the Law as the revelation of God and earnestly sought righteousness by strict obedience; that the Law was to him everything, which explains his burning zeal for his faith and hatred of every threat to its supremacy.

Saul was, evidently at a comparatively young age, a person of some influence in Jerusalem, a voice to be heard, if not indeed a member of the Sanhedrin. To sum up, the Church's arch persecutor was an aristocrat, a scholar, a theologian, and a statesman.

b. Saul's motives for persecution are succinctly stated in his own words, "concerning zeal, persecuting the church" (Phil. 3:6*a*); zeal for the law, and for the purity of the fathers' hope and faith. And yet there was a strange fury in his actions, the kind of thing that drives a man who is losing his inner confidence. He pursued the fleeing disciples even beyond Jewish borders. (The Romans permitted the Jewish rulers to extradite lawbreakers from non-Jewish cities and return them for trial.) By his own testimony, Saul flung the believers into prison, required them to blaspheme the name of Jesus, and in some cases harried them to their deaths.

c. We may be sure that there was a fierce inner struggle in Saul's soul. Although it is clearly impossible to simply equate Saul's transformation with the resolving of a psychological conflict, as some have attempted, nevertheless the inner turmoil must have played its part in the story. He could not forget Stephen's cogent message and triumphant death. Those whom he persecuted had found a peace and a victory which was denied him in his pursuit of a legal righteousness, as he tells us in Romans 7. Yet, the Jesus who hung on the cursed tree could not be the Messiah, according to all Saul understood in the law.

Stephen's doctrine, the disciples' faith, would undermine the whole sacred religious system based on the ancient traditions. That would destroy Judaism. If so, the Nazarenes must themselves be destroyed, root and branch!

2. It is the *revelation of the risen Christ* to Saul which is the key to understanding the change that made of the Church's persecutor its greatest missionary statesman.

Damascus was a great, very ancient Syrian city some 150 miles to the north of Jerusalem and about 70 miles east of the Mediterranean on the edge of the desert. A large community of Jews lived in the Gentile city.

The journey to Damascus would take Saul and his company of Temple police through Samaria and Galilee and then northeast by a caravan route, a journey of at least a week, travelling probably on foot. Finally, on the last day, at noon, with the destination in sight, the event occurred which forever changed Saul's purpose and destiny.

a. We are not left in doubt as to the nature of the blinding flash of light which prostrated the whole company on the ground, Saul himself apparently remaining prostrate and helpless even after the others had risen. Ever after, Paul's consistent account was that he had seen the risen and glorified Christ. He was blinded by "the glory of that light" (22:11), the ineffable glory of *the Divine Presence.* Ananias gave confirmation of the event by his reference to "Jesus that appeared unto thee in the way as thou camest" (v. 17). Later on, Barnabas declared to the apostles that Saul had "seen the Lord in the way" (v. 27).

b. It was no impersonal voice that accompanied the appearance, but the voice of Jesus. In awe and wonder Saul asked the identity of the heavenly visitation. In an instant, he realized that in persecuting the believers he was fighting against Jesus himself. It was a beautiful identification of Jesus the Head, with the members of His body on earth.

The ensuing exchange of words between Jesus and Saul indicate Saul's *unconditional surrender.* The last clause of v. 5 and the first of v. 6, although not in the best texts of this passage, are nevertheless completely in accord with the parallel passages where they do occur. The others in the party evidently heard the sound of a voice to which Saul replied but did not distinguish articulate words, just as they did not see the Lord in the blinding light (cf. 22:9). But for Saul the meaning was clear. Jesus *was* the Messiah. He was risen and alive. The people he had been hounding to death were the people of the Lord. Saul was crushed by the realization of his monumental mistake (cf. 1 Tim. 1:13). The arrestor had himself been arrested. The captor was now Christ's captive. The imprisoner had become "the prisoner of Jesus Christ" (cf. Eph. 3:1 and Phil. 3:12).

c. No doubt a *measure of understanding* of the glorious revelation came to Saul in the three lonely days which he spent without food or water in the house of Judas. The full implications would be thought through and worked out much later. But the outline of his own life's work must have begun to form even then in his mind. The message of Stephen would be recalled. Salvation could not be by the Law, if Jesus were the Messiah, but must be God's gift through Jesus, and therefore it must be a salvation, not for Jews only, but for all men.

The Lord's man in Damascus was Ananias, a godly man who evidently still had ties with the synagogue and was highly regarded by the Jewish colony (see the account in c. 22). How he had become a believer is not indicated, but the word had already spread to Damascus. The Church owes Paul the apostle to Stephen, and to Barnabas, but also in large measure to this otherwise unknown disciple. He performed an inestimable service through humble obedience and in spite of what appeared to him to be deadly peril.

Characteristically, the Spirit was at work simultaneously in Ananias and Saul, preparing the way for the meeting that would begin to reconcile Saul with the Church. Saul could scarcely fully experience forgiveness in his own heart until he had felt the assurance of acceptance by the believers. There is always a confirming clinch given to the faith of a repentant sinner when the clasp of a warm hand receives him into the family of God.

We can understand the misgivings of Ananias. Nevertheless, reassured that Saul was humbly praying, that the way had been prepared for the visit, and expecially concerning the sovereign purpose and plan of God for the future apostle, Ananias went in the Lord's name to the still blinded Saul.

How interesting, in passing, are the names found in this passage for the believers. They are called the people of "this way" (v. 2), "thy saints" (v. 13), and "all that call on thy name" (v. 14). The Christian way is more than belief; it is a total way of life with a clear destination. It is the answer to God's call to a separate and holy life (saints are literally "holy ones"). It is characterized supremely by the principle that Jesus is Lord of all.

The purpose of Ananias' visit to Saul was at least fourfold. First, he was to receive him as a Christian brother and to administer water baptism, the symbol of repentance and new life in Christ. How full of forgiving grace and love are the words with which he first addressed the prostrate erstwhile Pharisee: "Brother Saul"! The miracle of our acceptance in the Beloved is mirrored in the fellowship of the church.

Second, Ananias was to restore Saul's sight. The falling away of the scales, a flaky substance, from Saul's eyes is surely symbolic. His spiritual blindness was removed; the old stubborn unbelief, the ingrained prejudice, the deep-seated religious pride—these too fell away.

Third (although it is not expressly stated, it is clearly implied), Saul was filled with the Holy Spirit. As an obedient believer, he entered into the indispensable sanctifying relationship which would equip him for his life's work.

Fourth, we learn from c. 22 that Saul's commission, already communicated to him in "the heavenly vision" (cf. 26:16-18), was confirmed to him by the words of Ananias. Afterward, Paul always insisted that his commission came not from men but by direct revelation. Ananias was but God's mouthpiece confirming and clinching the divine call to special service. The call and its acceptance were the implementation of the sovereign and wise plan of God for the life of Saul of Tarsus.

A great work awaited Saul, and along with this great suffering. But the suffering is for the sake of the Name. It is represented as a badge of honor, and with the prophecy of suffering there is the implicit pledge of grace and glory. Saul would later come to see "the fellowship of his sufferings" as one of the cherished prizes of his career (cf. Phil. 3:7-14).

Spiritual Preparation for a Great Ministry

Acts 9:19b-30

19*b* Then was Saul certain days with the disciples which were at Damascus.
20 And straightway he preached Christ in the synagogues, that he is the Son of God.
21 But all that heard him were amazed, and said; Is not this he that destroyed them which called on this name in Jerusalem, and came hither for that intent, that he might bring them bound unto the chief priests?
22 But Saul increased the more in strength, and confounded the Jews which dwelt at Damascus, proving that this is very Christ.
23 And after that many days were fulfilled, the Jews took counsel to kill him:
24 But their laying await was known of Saul. And they watched the gates day and night to kill him.
25 Then the disciples took him by night, and let him down by the wall in a basket.
26 And when Saul was come to Jerusalem, he assayed to join himself to the disciples: but they were all afraid of him, and believed not that he was a disciple.
27 But Barnabas took him, and brought him to the apostles, and declared unto them how he had seen the Lord in the way, and that he had spoken to him, and how he had preached boldly at Damascus in the name of Jesus.
28 And he was with them coming in and going out at Jerusalem.
29 And he spake boldly in the name of the Lord Jesus, and disputed against the Grecians: but they went about to slay him.
30 Which when the brethren knew, they brought him down to Caesarea, and sent him forth to Tarsus.

From the conversion of Saul to the start of his ministry in Antioch along with Barnabas as recorded in 11:26 is a period of 10 years. Luke passes over these years in this brief passage. It did not fall within his purpose to expand upon them. A little more information may be gleaned from Paul's own statements.

From Gal. 1:16-17 we learn that Saul departed for Arabia following his conversion and then returned to Damascus. Although there may have been some preaching prior to it (cf. v. 20), his main Damascus ministry followed the period in Arabia.

From Gal. 1:18 we know that three years after his conversion (sometime in the third year, by Jewish reckoning), Saul went back to Jerusalem where he conferred with Peter and James, the Lord's brother. Luke tells us the circumstances of his leaving Damascus at this time. We learn more of this in 2 Cor. 11:32-33, where Paul, in recounting his sufferings, refers to the escape from Damascus in a basket let down the city wall from a window, as a humiliating experience. Apparently Saul had offended not only the Damascus Jews who plotted his murder, but also Aretas, the Nabatean king who ruled Arabia. Although Damascus was outside his kingdom, Aretas seems to have had the privilege of a representative or ethnarch (Paul calls him "governor") in that great city to look after the Nabatean community there. This governor joined forces with the Jews against Saul and posted a guard outside the walls to capture him.

The period in Jerusalem was brief. Paul conferred with the only apostles who were present and also ministered, but within the city itself (cf. Gal. 1:22). Luke tells us that this ministry, like Stephen's, was mainly to the Hellenistic Jews. Another murder plot against him caused "the brethren" to escort him as far as Caesarea. In 22: 17-21, Paul indicates that he went willingly with them since the Lord in a vision had told him to depart from Jerusalem. His commission to the Gentiles was also reaffirmed at this time.

From Caesarea, Saul went on to Tarsus, his home city, and "the regions of Syria and Cilicia" (Gal. 1:21).

We have no record of his activities during the approximately six years until we meet him again at Antioch. We may conjecture that they were fruitful years for the Church.

This passage suggests several facets of Saul's spiritual preparation for his great mission to the Gentile world.

1. *He was learning and testing his gospel.* In later years he would write, "For I am not ashamed of the gospel of Christ" (Rom. 1:16*a*). The complete break with the old life, the old associations, the old way of thinking, must have been a traumatic experience. His whole Pharisaic system of religious thought lay shattered at his feet. Time in the desert solitude was needed to think through the implications of Jesus as Messiah, Saviour, and Lord. Especially he pondered the righteousness of God which is God's gift apart from the law, through faith in Jesus Christ. He did not confer "with flesh and blood." His Teacher was the Holy Spirit. Characteristically he would write, much later, "I received from the Lord that which I passed on to you."

The learned teacher of the law now applied his detailed knowledge of the Scriptures to his new understanding of God, sacred history, and salvation. He became reoriented to the Old Testament, with Jesus as the key to his understanding. He preached Jesus in the power of a personal conviction, as the One who had personally spoken, "I am Jesus." He preached Jesus as the Son of God, a testimony to Deity, and to the absolutely unique revelation of God.

As always such preaching was convincing and irrefutable. Saul displayed a growing ability, an increasing ministry. Those who heard were amazed at the transformation in the man. He evidently succeeded in winning many to the Way in the very city where he came to hunt them down.

2. Saul was also *learning humility and the way of suffering.* The hunter became the hunted. He learned what it

was to be despised by his people, to have his message rejected. He experienced the suspicion of the Jerusalem brethren, who understandably felt he might be "a wolf in sheep's clothing."

He learned also, through Barnabas, his need for his brethren, his dependence upon the kindness of others. The mediation of Barnabas with the apostles on Saul's behalf is a beautiful picture of graciousness. The past was to be forgiven and forgotten if God had forgiven Saul, had received him, and commissioned him to preach Christ.

The way in which Barnabas and Saul complemented each other's strengths and weaknesses is instructive. Barnabas was full of kindness, could be generous to a fault, perhaps sentimental, and too easily influenced, as we note from Gal. 2:12-13 and Acts 15:36-39. Saul was ever the man of principle, perhaps to the point of stubbornness.

In preparation for his future perilous ministry, Saul was learning to face severe opposition, threats to his life, disappointments, and reverses. At Jerusalem and Tarsus he would face his whole past life with a willingness to rectify what he could. All of this was prologue to what was to come.

Growth in the Church through the Spirit

Acts 9:31-43

31 Then had the churches rest throughout all Judaea and Galilee and Samaria, and were edified; and walking in the fear of the Lord, and in the comfort of the Holy Ghost, were multiplied.
32 And it came to pass, as Peter passed throughout all quarters, he came down also to the saints which dwelt at Lydda.
33 And there he found a certain man named Aeneas, which had kept his bed eight years, and was sick of the palsy.
34 And Peter said unto him, Aeneas, Jesus Christ maketh thee whole: arise, and make thy bed. And he arose immediately.
35 And all that dwelt at Lydda and Saron saw him, and turned to the Lord.
36 Now there was at Joppa a certain disciple named Tabitha, which by interpretation is called Dorcas: this woman was full of good works and almsdeeds which she did.
37 And it came to pass in those days, that she was sick, and died: whom when they had washed, they laid her in an upper chamber.
38 And forasmuch as Lydda was nigh to Joppa, and the disciples had heard that Peter was there, they sent unto him two men, desiring him that he would not delay to come to them.

39 Then Peter arose and went with them. When he was come, they brought him into the upper chamber: and all the widows stood by him weeping, and shewing the coats and garments which Dorcas made, while she was with them.
40 But Peter put them all forth, and kneeled down, and prayed; and turning him to the body said, Tabitha, arise. And she opened her eyes: and when she saw Peter, she sat up.
41 And he gave her his hand, and lifted her up, and when he had called the saints and widows, presented her alive.
42 And it was known throughout all Joppa; and many believed in the Lord.
43 And it came to pass that he tarried many days in Joppa with one Simon a tanner.

1. *Church growth and the Spirit's guidance.* With the conversion of Saul, the persecution of the Church died down. In this period of peace, the churches formed by the dispersed disciples had opportunity to build up in strength and numbers. V. 31 is another of Luke's summary statements about Church progress.

a. The earliest manuscripts have "church" rather than "churches." This is significant. There are now numerous congregations of believers not only in Judea, but also in Galilee and Samaria. The extension into Galilee is mentioned here for the first and only time in Acts. Nevertheless, the Church is one, under one Lord.

b. The Church was being *edified* (build up) with regard to its internal life, and was being *multiplied* with regard to its external service. The essence of the Church is the action of its mission in the world. For this purpose it is equipped by the Holy Spirit. The Church at rest from persecution is not a static organization; it is strengthening itself internally and purposefully moving forward in its missionary task.

c. The secret of growth was twofold. *Walking in the fear of the Lord* indicates purposeful obedience to the Lord's commands, complete submission to His lordship. *Walking . . . in the comfort of the Holy Ghost* suggest the strengthening, inspiring, illuminating ministries of the Holy Spirit within the Church's corporate life and within Spirit-filled believers.

2. *Church growth and the Spirit's gifts.* At his point in Luke's story, Peter returns to center stage to remain there until he passes from prominence at the close of c. 12. Apparently Peter was systematically visiting the churches in Judea. We assume that the other apostles were at work elsewhere.

Luke selects two remarkable incidents during this ministry, one at Lydda and one at Joppa, both towns on the seacoast opposite Jerusalem, and about 10 miles apart. It is likely that Philip had preached in these centers.

Some commentators see in these two miracles two signs consciously employed by Luke, the first (the healing of the paralytic Aeneas) to denote the spiritual healing and restoration of the helpless, and the second (the raising of Dorcas) to show the gift of life to those spiritually dead in spite of their works. Some apply these signs to the Gentiles, soon to be visited, and others to Israel, suggesting a future restoration.

Whether or not they are signs, they are along with the ministry of Dorcas, examples of the gifts of the Spirit as manifested in the apostolic era of the Church.

a. The Spirit's gifts differ greatly in a beautiful variety. In Peter we see the conspicuous and spectacular gifts of healing and the miracle of the raising of the dead. In Dorcas is displayed the quiet and lovely gift of helping the needy, in this case the unfortunate widows (cf. Rom. 12:6-8 and 1 Cor. 12:28). Both kinds of gifts are demonstrations of love and compassion. Who is to say which is the greater? Dorcas has her memorial in the Dorcas Societies which have encircled the Christian world with works of mercy. Hers was a life lived simply but for values that outlived her years. To be so remembered makes life meaningful.

The gift of "helping" is largely the power to put good intentions into action. V. 36 indicates that Dorcas was able to order her life so that she was continually giving to others.

b. The Spirit's gifts are sovereignly bestowed. Why

Aeneas was singled out for healing we are not told. The reference to him suggests that he may not even have been a disciple. And the raising of one from the dead was, even in apostolic days, a very rare occurrence. Peter obviously got his directions from the Spirit in these matters. Even the apostles did not exercise spiritual gifts in an independent or wilful manner. In His wisdom God had His reasons just as He does today.

c. The Spirit's gifts are Christlike and Christ-exalting in their operation. Peter claimed no authority of his own; the words to Aeneas were *"Jesus Christ maketh thee whole."* The living, present Christ was the Source of power; the human instrument was but a channel. Prayer was the key in the raising of Dorcas. The results of both the quiet and the spectacular gifts inspired faith in Christ unto salvation.

Peter, through whom the Spirit had worked so powerfully, is described here as making his home with Simon, a tanner, certainly a humble place to live. How remarkably different from those who seek notoriety for their wonder-working! Besides, it suggests that Peter was rising above his Jewish prejudices. A tanner, because of his trade, would be ceremonially unclean. God was preparing Peter for his next adventure of faith.

ACTS 10

God Answers an Honest Seeker

Acts 10:1-8

1 There was a certain man in Caesarea called Cornelius, a centurion of the band called the Italian band,
2 A devout man, and one that feared God with all his house, which gave much alms to the people, and prayed to God alway.
3 He saw in a vision evidently about the ninth hour of the day an angel of God coming in to him, and saying unto him, Cornelius.
4 And when he looked on him, he was afraid, and said, What is it, Lord? And he said unto him, Thy prayers and thine alms are come up for a memorial before God.

5 And now send men to Joppa, and call for one Simon, whose surname is Peter:
6 He lodgeth with one Simon a tanner, whose house is by the sea side: he shall tell thee what thou oughtest to do.
7 And when the angel which spake unto Cornelius was departed, he called two of his household servants, and a devout soldier of them that waited on him continually;
8 And when he had declared all these things unto them, he sent them to Joppa.

As with the conversion of Saul, Luke treats the events of c. 10 in detail and as of great importance. They are rehearsed in c. 11, and they become the test case discussed at the Jerusalem conference, recorded in c. 15. These events are set in motion by special divine providences and visitations. For the first time Gentiles are officially welcomed into the Church. This is a pivotal point in the Church's mission to the world.

The Gentile chosen for the high privilege of this epochal event was a professional soldier, probably from Italy, a centurion in charge of some 100 troops stationed at Caesarea, the Roman capital of Judea.

1. Cornelius *exemplifies those* outside the Church *who walk in all the light* they have, however imperfect. He had left the paganism of his countrymen for the revealed faith, the monotheistic worship, and the high ethical values of Judaism. His description is reminiscent of the centurion whose servant Jesus healed as recorded in Luke 7:2-10. He was not a full proselyte to Judaism, but he is described as a pious or godly man, one who reverenced God, whose regular prayers, even with fasting, ascended to God and were heard. His godly influence extended to his entire household, including at least some of the soldiers under him, who also became God-fearers. He enjoyed the high regard of the Jewish community, no doubt because of his generosity toward the poor and the synagogue. Only of one whose prayers and alms were free of the self-centeredness which seeks the praise of men could it be said: *Thy prayers and thine alms are come up for a memorial before God.* These acts were evidence of faith.

2. Cornelius' experience *illustrates the law of light.* If you walk in all the light you have, you get more light. If you refuse the light you have, you soon walk in darkness. That Cornelius had heard about Jesus is implied in vv. 37 and 38. That he was earnestly seeking more light on the way of salvation is clear from the rehearsal of the story in c. 11 (see v. 14).

In one way or another God answers the heart cry of the honest, obedient seeker. Cornelius was visited by an angel, in broad daylight about three o'clock one afternoon while he prayed. He was assured that God had long been preparing the answer to his prayer and that now the time was ripe; there would be no further delay. His response was immediate obedience, a characteristic of a disciplined soldier. He dispatched two servants under the guard of a devout soldier, to find and bring Peter back with them.

Of course, this incident has greater scope than Cornelius' immediate household, and future implications far beyond the lifetime of those then involved. But is not this always true when God finds people who will obey His voice?

God Corrects the Viewpoint of a Christian Leader

Acts 10:9-23a

9 On the morrow, as they went on their journey, and drew nigh unto the city, Peter went up upon the housetop to pray about the sixth hour:
10 And he became very hungry, and would have eaten: but while they made ready, he fell into a trance,
11 And saw heaven opened, and a certain vessel descending unto him, as it had been a great sheet knit at the four corners, and let down to the earth:
12 Wherein were all manner of fourfooted beasts of the earth, and wild beasts, and creeping things, and fowls of the air.
13 And there came a voice to him, Rise, Peter; kill, and eat.
14 But Peter said, Not so, Lord; for I have never eaten any thing that is common or unclean.
15 And the voice spake unto him again the second time, What God hath cleansed, that call not thou common.
16 This was done thrice: and the vessel was received up again into heaven.
17 Now while Peter doubted in himself what this vision which he had seen should mean, behold, the men which were sent from Cornelius had made enquiry for Simon's house, and stood before the gate,

18 And called, and asked whether Simon, which was surnamed Peter, were lodged there.
19 While Peter thought on the vision, the Spirit said unto him, Behold, three men seek thee.
20 Arise therefore, and get thee down, and go with them, doubting nothing: for I have sent them.
21 Then Peter went down to the men which were sent unto him from Cornelius; and said, Behold, I am he whom ye seek: what is the cause wherefore ye are come?
22 And they said, Cornelius the centurion, a just man, and one that feareth God, and of good report among all the nation of the Jews, was warned from God by an holy angel to send for thee into his house, and to hear words of thee.
23*a* Then called he them in, and lodged them.

The Lord was preparing Peter to meet Cornelius at the same time that He was answering Cornelius' prayer. This was taking place as the delegation from Caesarea travelled the 30 miles to Joppa. And the preparation of Peter was crucial to the whole enterprise.

1. The *presence of both error and prejudice in the minds of Spirit-filled people* is illustrated in Peter. At about noon Peter had climbed to the housetop where he was lodging with Simon, the tanner, to engage in prayer. The flat housetops of homes were customarily used as places of prayer and meditation, or for sleeping. After prayer, Peter was very hungry, but the requested meal was delayed; and as he waited, Peter fell into a trance. This means that he was awake but was mentally lifted out of himself so as not to be conscious of his natural surroundings while his mind and senses became open to intense subjective stimuli. God used this method also to speak to Paul (Acts 22:17).

Peter saw what appeared to be a great sheet (perhaps a sail) held by the four corners and descending from the opened heavens down to the earth. In it were all kinds of beasts, reptiles, and birds, representing, with the exception of fish, the whole animal creation. A voice, which Peter recognized as the Lord's, addressed him personally: *Rise, Peter; kill and eat.* To Peter, a Jew who scrupulously followed his dietary laws regarding clean and unclean foods, the suggestion that he should select and eat food from such a mixture of beasts and birds was instantly revolting. On impulse and by long training he refused vehemently.

Actually, the experience challenged Peter's whole system of values relative to the Mosaic laws concerning ceremonial defilement. Deeper still, it challenged his extreme racial bias relative to Gentiles, a bias which had been instilled from his childhood. As a Christian he had come a considerable distance in correcting his thinking, but still not far enough to be used as God's instrument to bless the Gentiles.

2. The *danger of thwarting God's plan* is expressed in the rebuke to Peter. The warning was stern: "Stop your practice of considering unclean what God has already made clean!" God had already in Christ and His cross abrogated the ceremonial law. He had broken down "the middle wall of partition" between Jews and Gentiles. Those who were "far off" had been "made nigh by the blood of Christ" (Eph. 2:13-14). The warning was "Don't thwart God's plan by persisting in your prejudice!"

It was a shock treatment for Peter, understandable inasmuch as the situation was revolutionary for him. Three times the vision was repeated, an illustration of God's loving patience with the infirmities of our humanness.

3. The sequel to the incident teaches that *the Spirit guides those who will listen.* Returning from his trance, Peter pondered in perplexity the meaning of the vision. About food the meaning was clear, but Peter knew there was more than that.

He had not long to wait for the answer. God's timing was perfect. The three from Cornelius were at that moment inquiring at the gate of the house for Peter. But before Peter was called, the Spirit spoke directly through the inner voice, assuring him that he was to accede to their request and go with them. Going down to greet the men, Peter learned about Cornelius, a Gentile, and heard his request that Peter visit his house and give him God's message.

At once the vision's meaning was clear. The Lord was asking him to accompany Gentiles, to enter a Gentile home, to share the gospel with Gentiles. Then it was true indeed that God had opened the door of mercy to the Gentiles also. Stephen had made the same point. The Samaritan Pentecost had pointed in that direction. Peter's Jewish exclusiveness was melting away. He invited the three visiting Gentiles into the house to share the delayed meal and lodging for the night.

The Spirit Breaks Through Cultural and Racial Barriers

Acts 10:23b-33

> 23*b* And on the morrow Peter went away with them, and certain brethren from Joppa accompanied him.
> 24 And the morrow after they entered into Caesarea. And Cornelius waited for them, and had called together his kinsmen and near friends.
> 25 And as Peter was coming in, Cornelius met him, and fell down at his feet, and worshipped him.
> 26 But Peter took him up, saying, Stand up; I myself also am a man.
> 27 And as he talked with him, he went in, and found many that were come together.
> 28 And he said unto them, Ye know how that it is an unlawful thing for a man that is a Jew to keep company, or come unto one of another nation; but God hath shewed me that I should not call any man common or unclean.
> 29 Therefore came I unto you without gainsaying, as soon as I was sent for: I ask therefore for what intent ye have sent for me?
> 30 And Cornelius said, Four days ago I was fasting until this hour; and at the ninth hour I prayed in my house, and, behold, a man stood before me in bright clothing,
> 31 And said, Cornelius, thy prayer is heard, and thine alms are had in remembrance in the sight of God.
> 32 Send therefore to Joppa, and call hither Simon, whose surname is Peter; he is lodged in the house of one Simon a tanner by the sea side: who, when he cometh, shall speak unto thee.
> 33 Immediately therefore I sent to thee; and thou hast well done that thou art come. Now therefore are we all here present before God, to hear all things that are commanded thee of God.

Since the Lord had been dealing graciously with both the Jewish and Gentile parties, we ought not to be surprised at the beautiful display of mutual respect and understanding existing between such diverse groups at this historic Christian meeting at the house of Cornelius. Some of the disciples from Joppa accompanied Peter—six, as we learn from c. 11—and these became helpful witnesses later at Jerusalem.

1. The Spirit produced *a mutual respect* for one another. Cornelius' act of obeisance at Peter's feet cannot be construed as worship except in the lesser meaning of the word, meaning homage to a great personage. As such it is an oriental custom. Even so, it highly embarrassed Peter. One envisions him helping Cornelius to his feet, protesting that they were all equal in God's sight, and then engaging in animated conversation.

2. The Spirit led both parties to *a mutual understanding.* Peter sets the gathered group at ease by explaining how it is that he, a Jew, is present in this place contrary to Jewish law and custom. It is only because of a revelation from God that he has acted thus. He is proceeding under orders from the Lord. Then he politely calls on Cornelius to give his own statement. Cornelius likewise appeals to the precise and clear directions from the Lord. He too is acting on divine orders. What both are saying is that this is God's doing, and it is marvellous in their eyes!

There's a wideness in God's mercy
Like the wideness of the sea;
There's a kindness in His justice
Which is more than liberty.

For the love of God is broader
Than the measure of man's mind;
And the heart of the eternal
Is most wonderfully kind.

"There is neither Jew nor Greek, there is neither bond or free, there is neither male or female: for ye are all one in Christ Jesus" (Gal. 3:28).

3. The Spirit brought about *a mutual readiness* in both preacher and congregation. How full of faith Cornelius' preparation was! He had arranged to fill his house with his

relatives and friends. What a tribute to his godly example! He expected something wonderful to happen and wanted as many as possible to share it. Courteously he expressed gratitude to Peter for coming at his invitation in spite of the barriers. With growing anticipation he invited Peter to speak. He acknowledged the presence of God in their midst. He announced the readiness of himself and the congregation not only to listen to God's messate but to obey.

What a congregation! What a setting! What an opportunity to preach Christ! Peter too was prepared in heart and mind. Preacher and congregation were one.

The Holy Spirit is given to those who obey Him!

The Good News Is for Everyone

Acts 10:34-43

34 Then Peter opened his mouth, and said, Of a truth I perceive that God is no respecter of persons:
35 But in every nation he that feareth him, and worketh righteousness, is accepted with him.
36 The word which God sent unto the children of Israel, preaching peace by Jesus Christ: (he is Lord of all:)
37 That word, I say, ye know, which was published throughout all Judaea, and began from Galilee, after the baptism which John preached;
38 How God anointed Jesus of Nazareth with the Holy Ghost and with power: who went about doing good, and healing all that were oppressed of the devil; for God was with him.
39 And we are witnesses of all things which he did both in the land of the Jews, and in Jerusalem; whom they slew and hanged on a tree:
40 Him God raised up the third day, and shewed him openly;
41 Not to all the people, but unto witnesses chosen before of God, even to us, who did eat and drink with him after he rose from the dead.
42 And he commanded us to preach unto the people, and to testify that it is he which was ordained of God to be the Judge of quick and dead.
43 To him give all the prophets witness, that through his name whosoever believeth in him shall receive remission of sins.

Peter's sermon is a further example of typical apostolic preaching. Before launching into an exposition of the person of Christ at v. 37, Peter prepares his congregation with introductory thoughts appropriate to the occasion.

1. *The introduction* has to do with God's nature and His revelation of himself especially in Jesus the Christ.

a. God is impartial in His justice and His love. The basis of His acceptance of men (Peter has come to see) has nothing to do with the mere accidents of race, or culture, or station, but upon something deeper and more personal. "Fearing God" and "working righteousness" remind one of Micah 6:8, that God's requirements of man are: to do justly, love mercy, and walk humbly with his God. Mere externals will not suffice: an inner heart relationship is needed. Such righteousness and reverence imply repentance and faith.

b. A revelation of God is needed, God's "word," and this God has given in Jesus the Christ. The good news has been proclaimed to Israel: peace, that is, every good thing, comes from God to men through Jesus.

c. But Jesus if Lord of *all,* not just the Jews. He is also Lord of the Gentiles. This explains the present occasion.

2. *The exposition* of Jesus as Saviour begins with things already known to the congregation, and climaxes with an appeal and invitation to saving faith.

a. Several truths which these Gentiles had already heard about Jesus are now confirmed by the apostles who were eyewitnesses. The stress is on the human Jesus, the prophet of Nazareth. He went about doing good, He healed the demon-possessed. The Holy Spirit rested upon Him in power. (This last concept would be understood by students of Judaism.) Obviously, God was with Him. The apostles certify the truth of all this.

b. Nevertheless, Jesus was killed, and that in the accursed manner which to the Jews denied His Messiahship, that is, by hanging on a tree. But the One whom the people rejected, God vindicated by the Resurrection. These facts too are certified by the witness of the apostles, as witnesses carefully chosen, men who actually ate and drank with the resurrected Jesus. Peter's congregation may have had only garbled or conflicting reports of this. Peter assures them.

c. The resurrected Christ is now exalted to the place of judgment at God's right hand. His is the final power and the final word.

d. All of this is confirmed in the Scriptures by the prophets. Therefore, through the name of Jesus, that is, through the saving work of God as revealed in Jesus, whoever comes in faith may be forgiven his sins. Salvation is for everyone.

The Gentile Pentecost

Acts 10:44-48

44 While Peter yet spake these words, the Holy Ghost fell on all them which heard the word.
45 And they of the circumcision which believed were astonished, as many as came with Peter, because that on the Gentiles also was poured out the gift of the Holy Ghost.
46 For they heard them speak with tongues, and magnify God. Then answered Peter,
47 Can any man forbid water, that these should not be baptized, which have received the Holy Ghost as well as we?
48 And he commanded them to be baptized in the name of the Lord. Then prayed they him to tarry certain days.

The parallels between the outpouring of Holy Spirit at Pentecost (Acts 2) and the outpouring here upon the body of Gentile believers at Caesarea, are such as to justify calling this occasion the Gentile Pentecost. This occasion signals and attests the beginnings of the Church among the Gentiles.

1. The baptism of the Holy Spirit was *given to a prepared and expectant group* of Gentile believers. Evidently Peter's sermon was interrupted as the Holy Spirit *fell on all them which heard the word.* No doubt he had intended to go on to expound scripturally the gift of the Holy Spirit, but that would wait another time. The expectant, obedient attitude of this congregation has already been noted. They were walking in the light and following Peter's message with glad acceptance.

Since Pentecost, no special time period of tarrying or seeking seems necessary for the reception of the Spirit. He does not need to be coaxed or begged to infill prepared hearts. Indeed, quite the opposite is true. He is, like the air which surrounds us, graciously seeking to fill us with His presence, and He does so as soon as and wherever the barriers of disobedience, wilfulness, or unbelief are removed.

2. This ourpouring of the Spirit was at once identified as *the same experience as the original Jewish Pentecost.* This was, in fact, a very important matter. It became the clincing argument for the reception of the Gentiles into the church. Just as at Pentecost, these Spirit-filled people spoke in other languages and magnified God. If there had been a difference, it would have been noted and would have produced a problem. But there was no difference. The Jews present, including Peter, were convinced.

Peter responded by calling for the baptism of the Gentile disciples as the sign of their complete acceptance into the brotherhood of the church. There was no mention of circumcision. Defending his action later, he argued, "Forasmuch then as God gave them the like gift as he did unto us, who believed on the Lord Jesus Christ; what was I, that I should withstand God?" (11:17).

Baptism with water *following* baptism with the Holy Spirit is not the usual order, but it serves to remind us that we cannot confine the Spirit's activity within our formulas.

3. This ourpouring of the Holy Spirit is *described as to its results* by Peter's own definition. What happened here and at Pentecost?

a. Peter identified the experience later as the fiery and purifying baptism of the Holy Spirit proclaimed by John the Baptist as the privilege of the disciples of Jesus and later reaffirmed and promised by Jesus himself (cf. Acts 11:16; Matt. 3:11-12; Acts 1:4-5).

b. At the Jerusalem conference, Peter summed up the comparison of the original Pentecost with the Gentile Pentecost in these words. "And God, which knoweth the hearts, bare them witness [that as Gentiles they were accepted on the grounds of faith in Jesus], giving them the

Holy Ghost, even as he did unto us [that is, the Jews at Pentecost]; and put no difference between us and them, purifying their hearts by faith" (Acts 15:8-9).

The baptism with the Holy Spirit is for believers and is the means of the entire sanctification and purification of their hearts.

ACTS 11

Meeting Dissension in the Church

Acts 11:1-18

1 And the apostles and brethren that were in Judaea heard that the Gentiles had also received the word of God.
2 And when Peter was come up to Jerusalem, they that were of the circumcision contended with him,
3 Saying, Thou wentest in to men uncircumcised, and didst eat with them.
4 But Peter rehearsed the matter from the beginning, and expounded it by order unto them, saying,
5 I was in the city of Joppa praying: and in a trance I saw a vision, A certain vessel descend, as it had been a great sheet, let down from heaven by four corners; and it came even to me:
6 Upon the which when I had fastened mine eyes, I considered, and saw fourfooted beasts of the earth, and wild beasts, and creeping things, and fowls of the air.
7 And I heard a voice saying unto me, Arise, Peter; slay and eat.
8 But I said, Not so, Lord: for nothing common or unclean hath at any time entered into my mouth.
9 But the voice answered me again from heaven, What God hath cleansed, that call not thou common.
10 And this was done three times: and all were drawn up again into heaven.
11 And, behold, immediately there were three men already come unto the house where I was, sent from Caesarea unto me.
12 And the spirit bade me go with them, nothing doubting. Moreoever these six brethren accompanied me, and we entered into the man's house:
13 And he shewed us how he had seen an angel in his house, which stood and said unto him, Send men to Joppa, and call for Simon, whose surname is Peter;
14 Who shall tell thee words, whereby thou and all thy shouse shall be saved.
15 And as I began to speak, the Holy Ghost fell on them, as on us at the beginning.
16 Then remembered I the word of the Lord, how that he said, John indeed baptized with water; but ye shall be baptized with the Holy Ghost.
17 Forasmuch then as God gave them the like gift as he did unto us,

who believed on the Lord Jesus Christ; what was I, that I could withstand God?
18 When they heard these things, they held their peace, and glorified God, saying, Then hath God also to the Gentiles granted repentance unto life.

How long it was before Peter returned to Jerusalem is unknown. It was long enough for the news of the reception of the Gentiles at Caesarea to precede him throughout Judea and to become a contentious issue. The apostles themselves were likely laboring in various places. At Jerusalem it was "they that were of the circumcision," that is, those of the believers who insisted on the keeping of the ceremonial law, who challenged Peter to explain his actions. This is the first record of real dissension in the Church.

1. At its roots, *the dissension grew out of misunderstanding.* The report was that Peter had lodged and eaten with Gentiles, something contrary and repugnant to Jewish practice. Further, he had received Gentiles into the fellowship without requiring circumcision. To many Jewish believers this was surprising, not to say scandalous, conduct. Peter was taken to task. It is an interesting comment on the nature of Peter's position as an apostle.

One key to the situation was that nearly all the really important facts were unknown. This is often the case in misunderstandings. Another key is that these Jewish Christians who were involved believed sincerely that the Mosaic regulations as regards clean and unclean foods, and so forth, were still in force. They considered that a Gentile, in order to be a Christian, must first become a Jew; or, to put it another way, a Gentile must come into the Church by way of the synagogue. It was not a mere quibble, but a deep-rooted problem of conscience and creed. It would trouble the Church for a long time.

2. The dissension was handled by Peter, not by the assertion of his authority as an apostle, but by *an earnest consideration of the facts concerning the work of the Spirit.*

Peter did not argue. He asked to let the facts speak for

themselves. But for these facts he would have agreed with his opposition. His rehearsal of the story is very vivid. One imagines that his audience was spellbound. The unmistakable vision at Joppa, followed by the immediate arrival of the delegation from Caesarea; the testimony to the Spirit's guidance; the confirming guidance given to Cornelius—all these events were God's doings. But the decisive thing was God's act in giving the Holy Spirit to the Gentiles just as at Pentecost. This was God's doing from beginning to end. "What was I, that I could withstand God?" is Peter's conclusion. By implication, although it is graciously unstated, the question is, "Do you question God and His acceptance of these Gentiles by your suggestion that I was wrong in receiving them?"

3. The dissension was resolved by *the willingness of good people to admit a wrong attitude* and to change their minds. When Peter's critics heard the facts of the case, explained with the help of the Holy Spirit, their objections ceased. Evidently there was no carping. They were open to the truth, willing to be corrected. The change of mind was not grudging, but accompanied by praise to God for His mercy to the Gentiles. Love "rejoices in the truth," even when admitting an error.

They rejoiced that God had granted the Gentiles *repentance unto life.* The whole gospel is capsuled in this last phrase. Repentance is turning from sin and turning to Christ in faith. The result is life, the life of the Spirit imparted and continuous.

Foundations of a New Missionary Movement

Acts 11:19-30

19 Now they which were scattered abroad upon the persecution that arose about Stephen travelled as far as Phenice, and Cyprus, and Antioch, preaching the word to none but unto the Jews only.
20 And some of them were men of Cyprus and Cyrene, which, when they were come to Antioch, spake unto the Grecians, preaching the Lord Jesus.
21 And the hand of the Lord was with them: and a great number believed, and turned unto the Lord.
22 Then tidings of these things came unto the ears of the church

which was in Jerusalem: and they sent forth Barnabas, that he should go as far as Antioch.
23 Who, when he came, and had seen the grace of God, was glad, and exhorted them all, that with purpose of heart they would cleave unto the Lord.
24 For he was a good man, and full of the Holy Ghost and of faith: and much people was added unto the Lord.
25 Then departed Barnabas to Tarsus, for to seek Saul:
26 And when he had found him, he brought him unto Antioch. And it came to pass, that a whole year they assembled themselves with the church, and taught much people. And the disciples were called Christians first in Antioch.
27 And in these days came prophets from Jerusalem unto Antioch.
28 And there stood up one of them named Agabus, and signified by the spirit that there should be great dearth throughout all the world: which came to pass in the days of Claudius Caesar.
29 Then the disciples, every man according to his ability, determined to send relief unto the brethren which dwelt in Judaea:
30 Which also they did, and sent it to the elders by the hands of Barnabas and Saul.

Immediately following the account of the Gentile Pentecost, Luke records the establishment of the church at Antioch, destined to be the home base for the missionary thrust to the Gentile world. Indeed, Antioch was to become Jerusalem's successor as the Christian center in the years to come and for a long period of time. There are several important facets of the preparation of the Antioch church, the first truly Gentile congregation, for its important missionary role.

1. The Antioch church was itself *the product of missionary evangelism.* The persecution following Stephen's death, recounted in the eighth chapter, had resulted in disciples witnessing as far to the north as Phenice (the present Lebanon area, the country of ancient Tyre and Sidon), the island of Cyprus, and the Syrian capital of Antioch. Antioch was at that time the third greatest city in the Roman world, ranking after Rome and Alexandria. In this teeming center on the Orontes River at the Crossroads of the ancient world, the church first came to grips with Greek and Roman culture. Although it had a large Jewish community, Antioch was a pagan city, known for its immorality, due in part to its proximity to Daphne, the center for the worship of the Greek goddess Artemis.

Characteristically, the scattered believers from Judea preached to the Jewish community at the first. But some who were natives of Cyprus and of Cyrene in northern Africa, perhaps because of their more cosmopolitan Greek-speaking background, began preaching to the Greeks (the obvious meaning here is Gentiles or pagans) also. They had caught the vision and burden of Stephen for the wider world. They presented Jesus as the Lord and Saviour of all men, and found a response in the sin-weary hearts of these pagans. Of course, Jewish converts were won also. The Antioch church was a mixed congregation.

It is interesting that it was a missionary movement on Antioch by believers from Cyprus and North Africa which prepared the way for the missionary movement from Antioch to the Gentile world.

2. *The strong, growing church at Antioch* provided the firm support needed for a base of missionary operation. Evidently the preaching and witnessing was in the power of the Spirit. Great numbers of people turned to Christ. The word of the great movement in Antioch reached the Jerusalem church, which responded wisely by sending Barnabas, a recognized leader, to give guidance. Barnabas found evidence of a genuine and great work of the Spirit in which he rejoiced. Under his direction the revival continued on and on with great numbers being added unto the Lord.

There can be no sustained missionary thrust without a strong home base. This was provided by the dynamic, growing Antioch congregation.

3. The Antioch church was *blessed with outstanding leadership.* Barnabas, whom we have previously met in Acts on two occasions, was a gifted personality, God's man for the hour in various situations. Several qualities in his character were displayed in this situation. He could rejoice in the successful work of others. No doubt there were deficiencies to be remedied, but his major response was to encourage, to promote purpose and unity in the congregation. He was

indeed a son of consolation or encouragement. Luke gives a threefold characterization: As regards his character, he was *a good man,* genuine, competent, capable; as regards his spiritual life, he was full of the Holy Spirit, completely given over to God, living with singleness of heart; as regards his approach to Christian work, he was full of faith, full of true insights, full of optimism and confidence in the Lord. It is evident also that Barnabas was capable of seeing his limitations and assessing his needs, thus unselfishly seeking out Saul to share the leadership with him.

It was a stroke of genius that brought Saul back to Antioch. In the challenging situation of the great pagan city, Barnabas was led to recall Saul's great gifts and especially his divine commission to preach to the Gentiles. Six or seven years had passed since Saul had returned to Tarsus, not far distant from Antioch. Luke seems to imply that Barnabas had to search before finding him, since he was likely busily engaged in the region. Saul sensed the call of God and returned with Barnabas for what must have been an exciting year of ministry to that thriving church.

Leadership is crucial in church growth. Congregations seldom rise higher than their leaders. Barnabas and Saul were God's gift to the church at Antioch.

4. The church at Antioch enjoyed the advantage of *sound indoctrination and sturdy Christian character.* Apparently Saul gave special attention to a teaching ministry. What a privilege was given the church! No wonder it became a strong Christian center and missionary base. The neglect of a teaching ministry produces ineffective congregations.

Luke's statement that the disciples were called Christians first in Antioch is more than just an interesting concluding sentence about the church. It is given following the fact of the teaching of the believers, and the sequence of thought is hardly without meaning. This name, so honored in succeeding centuries and first used at Antioch, says something about the character and reputation of the believers in that great Gentile city.

Since the Jews would shun such a name which would suggest to them the Messiah, and since the believers used other terms for themselves, the name must have been given by the Greek population as a popular way to describe the new movement making such an impression on their city. It indicates that they thought of believers as an independent religious force to be reckoned with, not merely as a Jewish sect. It indicates also that Christ was by then being recognized by Gentiles a proper name, something that speaks of the power of the Christian witness. Most of all, it says that the believers were truly identified in loyalty and life with the Person, Jesus Christ. In doctrine and conduct, Christians could be recognized without question.

5. The Antioch church was *characterized by generosity, unity, and cooperation.* By the statement about the sending of relief to the Judean church during the period of famine in Palestine, Luke shows the goodwill and solidarity which existed toward the Christian Jews by the predominantly Gentile church at Antioch.

Prophets in the Early Church were primarily preachers. Among the gifts of the Spirit they are ranked next to apostles (1 Cor. 12:28). At times they were enabled by the Spirit to predict the future. Agabus did so on another later occasion as recorded in c. 21. Evidently some of this class who were itinerant preachers reached Antioch and ministered.

The action of the Antioch Christians was voluntary and generous. They acknowledged a spiritual debt to the church at Jerusalem. It appears that the collection of money was systematically planned over a period of time. This was a cause very dear to the Apostle Paul's heart in later years because of its contribution to unity between Jewish and Gentile Christians. He and Barnabas personally took the gift from Antioch to the Judean elders so as to provide food for the needy. Elders are first mentioned here. They would be pastors or congregational leaders in the growing church and would supervise the distribution.

All the Antioch believers apparently took part, none holding back. It must have been a heartwarming as well as stomach-filling experience for the brethren in Judea.

ACTS 12

The Boundaries of Evil

Acts 12:1-4

1 Now about that time Herod the king stretched forth his hands to vex certain of the church.
2 And he killed James the brother of John with the sword.
3 And because he saw it pleased the Jews, he proceeded further to take Peter also. (Then were the days of unleavened bread.)
4 And when he had apprehended him, he put him in prison, and delivered him to four quaternions of soldiers to keep him; intending after Easter to bring him forth to the people.

The twelfth chapter of Acts is transitional in Luke's narrative. After tracing the beginnings of the Gentile church and the establishment of a new Christian center at Antioch in cc. 10 and 11, Luke focuses upon the Jerusalem church and the Apostle Peter for the last time. Henceforth, the center of missionary activity will be Antioch, not Jerusalem; and in accord with Luke's purpose, the spotlight will be upon Paul as the central figure and the leader in the Church's advance, rather than upon Peter, the hero of the earlier chapters.

C. 12 is also a fascinating, contrasting study of good and evil in the Church's experience. In it are the glory and the mystery of divine providence.

1. In the persecution of Herod is the picture of *evil's outstretched hands*. This is the first official or political persecution of the Church. Even so, it really arose from the growing animosity of the populace whom Herod was trying to please. The earlier favor which the apostles seem to have enjoyed with the Jerusalem people was gone, the result perhaps of the Church's movement toward Gentiles.

Herod Agrippa I, although an Edomite, was the last king with Jewish blood in his veins to reign over Judea. The Roman province of Judea during the years from A.D. 7 to 41 had no kings but rather Roman procurators. One of these was Pontius Pilate, from A.D. 26-36. But in the brief period A.D. 41-44, Herod Agrippa I ruled not only Judea, but in fact all of Palestine, under appointment of the Caesar. At Herod's death in 44, Judea came again under the rule of procurators, two of whom we meet in Acts, Felix and Festus.

There are several Herods in the New Testament record. This Herod's grandfather was Herod the Great, who had also ruled all Palestine at the time of Jesus' birth. One of this Herod's uncles was Archelaus, who ruled Judea briefly after Herod the Great's death. Another uncle, Antipas, ruled over Galilee, and it was he who executed John the Baptist, and before whom Jesus appeared before His crucifixion. This Herod's son, Agrippa II, later ruled a small part of northern Palestine, and it was he who heard Paul's defense at Caesarea. Two daughters, Bernice, and Drusilla, Felix's wife, also appear in Luke's story.

Herod Agrippa I was an utterly wicked man. He was descended from the Maccabean Jewish kings through his mother. She had him reared in Rome after his father's murder. After a very checkered career, including bankruptcy and prison, the Emporer Caligula released him in A.D. 37 and placed him over two Palestinian tetrarchies. In A.D. 41, Claudius Caesar added Judea to his domain. In order to curry favor with the Jews, he deferred to their religious scruples and himself observed ceremonial worship and practices. He was an unscrupulous politician.

The murder of the Apostle James was the callous act of a ruler, not out of misguided principle, but for reasons of political expediency. James was to Herod a mere pawn. When James's death seemed to favor Herod's popularity, he quickly decided to do away with Peter also. Herod was evidently visiting Jerusalem to keep Passover. Peter had been seized during the Passover feast days however, and so in order to avoid insulting Jewish scruples regarding the feast, his execution had to be deferred until the annual festival was over. Therefore Peter was held in prison, but under a very secure guard of 16 soldiers, in relays of 4. No doubt there were some who remembered Peter's earlier imprisonment and release.

2. Overshadowing the schemes of evil men is *the Lord's unseen hand.* James, the son of Zebedee, the brother of the Apostle John, one of the three close to Jesus during our Lord's ministry, was the first apostle to be martyred. There is no record in Acts of his ministry. His mother had years before requested of Jesus that her two sons should sit next to Jesus in His kingdom, and Jesus had responded, "Ye shall drink indeed of my cup, and be baptized with the baptism that I am baptized with . . ." (Matt. 20:23*a*). Now like his Lord, he had suffered. He was beheaded, a form of execution reserved by the Jews for those who perverted the faith.

There is unremitting mystery in the providences of God in the lives of His people. Why did James die violently when Peter would be miraculously spared? Surely the same power which delivered Peter could have spared James and Stephen! There are times when the case appears to be one of "truth forever on the scaffold, wrong forever on the throne!" We do not have answers to our questions. What we do have is the assurance that God watches and cares, and that the Unseen Hand is at the controls. The narrative which follows illustrates the principle through which God works with respect to undeserved suffering: "Thus far, and no farther."

The Lord Knows How to Rescue the Godly

Acts 12:5-11

5 Peter therefore was kept in prison: but prayer was made without ceasing of the church unto God for him.
6 And when Herod would have brought him forth, the same night Peter was sleeping between two soldiers, bound with two chains: and the keepers before the door kept the prison.
7 And, behold, the angel of the Lord came upon him, and a light

shined in the prison: and he smote Peter on the side, and raised him up, saying, Arise up quickly. And his chains fell off from his hands.
8 And the angel said unto him, Gird thyself, and bind on thy sandals. And so he did. And he saith unto him, Cast thy garment about thee, and follow me.
9 And he went out, and followed him; and wist not that it was true which was done by the angel; but thought he saw a vision.
10 When they were past the first and the second ward, they came unto the iron gate that leadeth unto the city; which opened to them of his own accord: and they went out, and passed on through one street; and forthwith the angel departed from him.
11 And when Peter was come to himself, he said, Now I know of a surety, that the Lord hath sent his angel, and hath delivered me out of the hand of Herod, and from all the expectation of the people of the Jews.

Perhaps Peter was remembering this experience of escape when he wrote, "The Lord knoweth how to deliver the godly out of temptations, and to reserve the unjust unto the day of judgment to be punished" (2 Pet. 2:9).

1. Peter in prison is an example of *the peace that Jesus gives.* Peter would have known that the night in question was intended by Herod to be his last, inasmuch as it ended the days of the Passover. And yet he was asleep, chained to two soldiers, one by each hand. How well he slept may be indicated by the fact that the angel struck him to waken him. His was the peace, not after the storms, but in it.

Peter was well aware of James's grisly fate, and he had no earthly reason to expect a better one for himself. If the Lord had permitted one apostle to be martyred, why not he also? A clear conscience and a complete and final commitment to the will of God produce the security of which the Psalmist wrote: "Yea, though I walk through the valley of the shadow of death, I will fear no evil: for thou art with me; thy rod and thy staff they comfort me." A hundred martyrs of our own generation testify that men of faith can be serene as they face death.

2. Peter's deliverance illustrates the principle that *miracles are only for impossibilities.* It was an angel that delivered Peter; and, while "angels" may at times be God's special human messengers, there seems no doubt that this

was a case of intervention clearly beyond natural explanation. To people of faith who walk closely with the Lord, all of this will have no strange ring but will be familiar ground.

The greater miracle, of course, is the one of which Charles Wesley sang:

Long my imprisoned spirit lay,
Fast bound in sin and nature's night.
Thine eyes diffused a quick'ning ray.
I woke; the dungeon flamed with light.
My chains fell off; my heart was free.
I rose, went forth, and followed Thee.

There was supernatural light in the darkness, there was power which snapped the chains which bound him to his guards, there was the "automatic" opening of the great iron gate, there was an omnipotent escort through the prison corridors to the quiet, fresh, night air on the outside. All of this was "impossible." None of it should have happened by ordinary reckoning. But it did. And Peter himself thought he was in a trance or a walking dream.

Nevertheless, nothing was done for Peter that he could do for himself. He got up himself, he dressed himself, he was not carried, but walked by himself, on the outside he was left to himself and to his own common sense resources. When he came to the house where the church was praying, he was forced to stand outside the locked gate and repeatedly knock before it was opened by his friends on the inside.

3. Peter's experience illustrates the truth that *God's true providences are best understood in retrospect*. It was not in the event itself but only when it was over and he had opportunity to consider thoughtfully what he had passed through that Peter was able to discern in the experience the hand of God. It was after quiet retrospection that he was able to say, "Now I know."

Few of us can discern God's working clearly when the crisis is on. It is good that we really do not need to. He treats us better than we expect to be treated or than we deserve. We are supremely safe when we repose, by "the rest of faith," within the will of God.

Herod had his plans, and "the people of the Jews" their expectations, but it was the plan of God which was fulfilled.

Prayer and the Providence of God

Acts 12:12-17

12 And when he had considered the thing, he came to the house of Mary the mother of John, whose surname was Mark; where many were gathered together praying.
13 And as Peter knocked at the door of the gate, a damsel came to hearken, named Rhoda.
14 And when she knew Peter's voice, she opened not the gate for gladness, but ran in, and told how Peter stood before the gate.
15 And they said unto her, Thou art mad. But she constantly affirmed that it was even so. Then said they, It is his angel.
16 But Peter continued knocking: and when they had opened the door, and saw him, they were astonished.
17 But he, beckoning unto them with the hand to hold their peace, declared unto them how the Lord had brought him out of the prison. And he said, Go shew these things unto James, and to the brethren. And he departed, and went into another place.

Part of the forcefulness of this passage derives from the fact that it is obviously an eyewitness account. Small details made an indelible impression on someone present who supplied them to Luke. Perhaps the eyewitness on that memorable night was John Mark, since the prayer meeting was in his mother's home. There was a close relationship between Peter and Mark, who was apparently Peter's son in the faith (cf. 1 Pet. 5:13). Mark wrote the Second Gospel, which contains many evidences of Peter's style and personality.

1. The church in fervent and continuing prayer (v. 5) was expressing *the confidence of faith* in a power greater than Herod's.

There were probably several prayer gatherings such as the one described here going on in the city simultaneously. What did they pray for? Doubtless after the loss of James, they felt they could ill spare Peter also. But in the light of their reluctance to accept the news of the deliverance, and their amazement at seeing Peter, it is unlikely that the group at this meeting were really asking for Peter's release, at least not in the middle of the night. Perhaps they were resigned to losing him as they had lost James, and were praying for his comfort and faithfulness and for the protection of the church.

It is too easy for us to judge them as lacking in faith. Whatever the case, it is comforting to note that God answered their prayers beyond their expectations and earlier than their anticipation. While they were still praying, the thing was done. "We know not what we should pray for as we ought: but the Spirit . . . maketh intercession for us . . . according to the will of God" (Rom. 8:26-27). In areas where God's will is not revealed, faith is confidence that God will do what is best; it is not dictation of the result. God is our Refuge. We are safe when we pray for His will to be done.

2. Having observed the above, there is something delightful neverthe less in *the childlike simplicity of faith* in the servant-girl, Rhoda, who accepted the miracle without question. In the darkness, and from the inside of the heavy, locked gate opening onto the street, she recognized only the familiar voice of the knocker, but it was enough. In her joy and excitement she forgot to open the gate but ran inside to blurt out ecstatically, "Peter is here!" Immediately there were voices suggesting that she was hysterical or hallucinating. When she could convince them she was not, others suggested that Peter's angel had appeared, reflecting a popular notion that one's guardian angel might assume one's physical form. Finally, it was the persistent knocking of Peter, still on the street, that summoned them all back to the gate. Facts, not speculation, settled the matter.

3. One imagines the hubbub which ensued. One who was an eyewitness remembered how Peter had waved his hand to get silence so he could speak. When he did, we observe

faith linked with common sense. First, he answered their questions. Then in thoughtfulness, he asked that word be sent to James, the Lord's brother, the head of the Jerusalem church, as well as to the other concerned brethren. And then, Peter departed, secretly, to escape the fury of Herod before he was discovered. It would have been not courageous but presumptuous to tempt the providence of God by falling again into the hands of the murderous kings. Miracles are for impossibilities, not for foolhardiness.

The Sternness and the Kindness of God

Acts 12:18-25

18 Now as soon as it was day, there was no small stir among the soldiers, what was become of Peter.
19 And when Herod had sought for him, and found him not, he examined the keepers, and commanded that they should be put to death. And he went down from Judaea to Caesarea, and there abode.
20 And Herod was highly displeased with them of Tyre and Sidon: but they came with one accord to him, and, having made Blastus the king's chamberlain their friend, desired peace; because their country was nourished by the king's country.
21 And upon a set day Herod, arrayed in royal apparel, sat upon his throne, and made an oration unto them.
22 And the people gave a shout, saying, It is the voice of a god, and not of a man.
23 And immediately the angel of the Lord smote him, because he gave not God the glory: and he was eaten of worms, and gave up the ghost.
24 But the word of God grew and multiplied.
25 And Barnabas and Saul returned from Jerusalem, when they had fulfilled their ministry, and took with them John, whose surname was Mark.

In the entire chapter Luke is contrasting the characters of Herod and Peter, but even more the forces of evil and good, falsehood and truth. Two things are clear.

1. *Evil is only for a while.* The end of Herod is not only an illustration of the righteous judgment of God, but typifies the certain fate of all who exalt themselves in defiance of His will. Herod is really pictured as a little antichrist strutting for his brief moment like a self-made deity.

Chagrined by Peter's escape, Herod cruelly punished the hapless prison guards and returned to Caesarea, the

Roman capital of Judea and his ordinary residence. The account of his death is also recorded by Josephus, with more detail.

For some reason, the authorities of the cities of Tyre and Sidon, to the north, had deeply offended Herod, and he had taken out his cruel spite on them by arranging to withhold from them the normal export of produce from his northern domain of Galilee. Since they depended on these food imports, they were forced to sue for his favor but could apparently only gain access to him by currying the favor of one of his close officials named Blastus.

According to Josephus, the "set day" on which Herod made his oration to them was a public occasion, a great planned celebration in honor of the emperor. Herod dressed himself in a robe made entirely of silver particles. The effect, in the morning sunlight, was dazzling. The people, Josephus relates, cried out that henceforth they would regard him not as a man but as a god. In his boundless vanity he accepted their adulation without protest.

Josephus adds the detail that at the same moment, he observed an owl perched above him, which he superstitiously took to be an evil omen. He was seized with dread and a sudden abdominal pain, which grew worse until he died within a few days. Luke indicated that the loathsome disease was the result of God's immediate judgment. The hollowness and fickleness of the crowd's adulation is evident in Josephus' statement that upon Herod's death there was great rejoicing in the streets.

2. *The word of the Lord endures forever.* By contrast, Luke again summarizes the swift growth and spiritual prosperity of the Church. Neither the martyrdom of James nor the departure of Peter could hinder the life-giving word. God blessed that word, and it brought forth a rich harvest.

In the concluding verse, Luke picks up again the thread of purposeful narrative which was dropped at the end of c. 11. Most scholars agree that the visit of Barnabas and Saul to Jerusalem to present famine relief took place after Herod's death, and that they remained only a short time before returning to Antioch. They took with them John Mark, the cousin of Barnbas. He is mentioned here because he was to accompany them a little later on their first missionary tour.

The Establishment of the Church in Asia Minor and Europe

Acts 13:1—20:38

ACTS 13

The First Christian Missionaries

Acts 13:1-3

1 Now there were in the church that was at Antioch certain prophets and teachers; as Barnabas, and Simeon that was called Niger, and Lucius of Cyrene, and Manaen, which had been brought up with Herod the tetrarch, and Saul.
2 As they ministered to the Lord, and fasted, the Holy Ghost said, Separate me Barnabas and Saul for the work whereunto I have called them.
3 And when they had fasted and prayed, and laid their hands on them, they sent them away.

From the beginning, the Church had been characterized by a missionary impulse and activity, but we are justified in saying that this is the first instance of a deliberate, planned movement to select and send out missionaries to the Gentile world. This passage indicates three things about the movement.

1. There was *a strong, prepared base of operations.* It is not accidental that Antioch rather than Jerusalem became the base. The thriving Antioch church was free from the provincial, racial prejudices that beset Jerusalem. Even the description of the five leaders indicates a unity within the diversity of national and social backgrounds.

Barnabas we know, listed first as befits the earliest

leader at Antioch. Saul we know too, at this point listed last, likely because of the five he came last to Antioch. Simeon that was called Niger (meaning black) could well have been of the black race. Lucius of Cyrene was from North Africa. The description of Manaen indicates that he had been at least reared at the court of Herod Antipas and may have been a foster brother of the man who had John the Baptist beheaded.

These men, of such diverse origins, labored together in the Spirit as prophets and teachers, that is, in a preaching and teaching ministry, as they led the great Antioch congregation. The emphasis was on the Word of God, expounded and taught.

2. There was *the divine call to the missionaries.* Just how the Holy Spirit made His will known is not stated. It may have been through one of the prophets. They were open and attentive to His guidance. The expression "ministered to the Lord" indicates the service of public worship. It was in the atmosphere of prayer, praise, and worship that the Spirit spoke. The prophet Isaiah had received his call in a similar setting (cf. Isaiah 6). The church leaders were also engaged in the special spiritual exercise of fasting, commonly practised in the Early Church.

More than 10 years had passed since Saul of Tarsus had received his personal commission to take Christ to the Gentiles. But the Lord's timing is accurate.

3. There was *the cooperation of the sending church.* While v. 3 states that the church sent them, v. 4 says they were *sent forth by the Holy Ghost.* This is a striking picture of the presidency of the Spirit within the church. The church was to *separate,* to set apart, those whom the Spirit had already chosen. This was the necessary act of recognizing the call and commissioning the missionaries. This they did, at once, by the laying on of their hands. It included the assurance of prayerful support.

Doubtless Barnabas and Saul were the most qualified

and outstanding leaders in the church. The missionary enterprise required the best. They would seem the most needed in Antioch. Obediently the church released them, let them go, the literal meaning of the word translated "sent away."

Overcoming Obstacles in the Spirit's Power

Acts 13:4-13

4 So they, being sent forth by the Holy Ghost, departed unto Seleucia; and from thence they sailed to Cyprus.
5 And when they were at Salamis, they preached the word of God in the synagogues of the Jews: and they had also John to their minister.
6 And when they had gone through the isle unto Paphos, they found a certain sorcerer, a false prophet, a Jew, whose name was Bar-jesus:
7 Which was with the deputy of the country, Sergius Paulus, a prudent man; who called for Barnabas and Saul, and desired to hear the word of God.
8 But Elymas the sorcerer (for so is his name by interpretation) withstood them, seeking to turn away the deputy from the faith.
9 Then Saul, (who also is called Paul,) filled with the Holy Ghost, set his eyes on him,
10 And said, O full of all subtilty and all mischief, thou child of the devil, thou enemy of all righteousness, wilt thou not cease to pervert the right ways of the Lord?
11 And now, behold, the hand of the Lord is upon thee, and thou shalt be blind, not seeing the sun for a season. And immediately there fell on him a mist and a darkness; and he went about seeking some to lead him by the hand.
12 Then the deputy, when he saw what was done, believed, being astonished at the doctrine of the Lord.
13 Now when Paul and his company loosed from Paphos, they came to Perga in Pamphylia: and John departing from them returned to Jerusalem.

The first missionary tour began, quite naturally, on the island of Cyprus, home country for Barnabas, and not far from Antioch. Rome had ruled Cyprus from 57 B.C., and after 22 B.C. as a senatorial province under a governor called a proconsul. The missionary party proceeded from the commercial seaport of Salamis, at the northeast, across the entire island to the capital city of Paphos, a center noted for its immoral cult of the goddess Aphrodite or Venus. Leaving Cyprus, they sailed to the south coast of Asia Minor to the coastal area of Pamphylia and the city of Perga.

We infer that they evangelized as they went. Their

method was to go initially to the local synagogues, to "the Jew first." This method had also the advantage of gaining a hearing among the God-fearing Gentiles who attended the synagogues, and through them of finding openings to preach to the Gentiles.

Luke selects only one main incident on Cyprus, along with passing reference to other significant developments. Several rather typical kinds of obstacles to missionary success are found in the passage.

1. There was *the satanic opposition* of Elymas the sorcerer. This incident is reminiscent of the one in Samaria involving Simon Magus. This is opposition of a new kind, to be faced again and again amongst the pagan Gentiles, different from the Jewish opposition of religious prejudice and unbelief. This opposition is from the occult and the false supernaturalism. It stemmed from motives of greed, or gain, or power-seeking.

This renegade Jew, Bar-Jesus (meaning son of Jesus or Joshua), was obviously intent upon saving his position as a court advisor to the governor. If Sergius Paulus, as intelligent, truth-seeking man, became a Christian, he would have no further use for the sorcerer and his superstitious rites. Elymas deliberately attempted to distort the truth, mislead the governor, and prevent him from becoming a Christian. A great deal was at stake, including the soul of the Roman proconsul.

The work of the Holy Spirit through the Spirit-filled and specially anointed Saul is displayed here in the sense of boldness, an incisive insight into truth and falsehood, vindication of truth, and sudden judgment upon extreme wickedness. It is a terrible thing to become a deliberate stumbling block to the salvation of another person. The sternest denunciations that fell from Jesus' lips were against the "blind leaders of the blind." Saul's words echo those of Jesus. This sorcerer, who claimed to have revelations from God, was in reality ready to barter the governor's soul for personal advantage. He was a "son of the devil," a Hebraism meaning that his affinity was with Satan rather than God, with falsehood and wickedness rather than truth and righteousness.

Some scholars think that Luke saw in Bar-Jesus a picture of unbelieving Judaism, opposing the spread of the gospel to the Gentiles, and smitten, as Paul taught, with spiritual blindness "for a season." However that may be, the act of judgment on the opposer was also an act of mercy. Saul must have remembered how his own physical blindness at his conversion had served to enlighten his spiritual understanding.

The effect of the miracle on the governor was salutary. Luke conveys the impression that he became a Christian.

2. There was the potential obstacle of *a leadership crisis*. As inferred in v. 13 and noted in the remainder of Acts, the mantle of leadership within the group passed from Barnabas to Saul, or Paul as he was called from this point on. (Paul was Saul's Roman name, and perhaps it seemed proper to so designate him because of his ministry within the Roman or Gentile world.) Seniority belonged to Barnabas, and to this point it had been recognized (cf. 11:30; 12:25; 13:2), but the superior gifts of leadership were Paul's. To the everlasting honor of Barnabas, the transition was made without a struggle. Barnabas was one of that special breed who are willing to "play second fiddle" if only the work of God prospers and moves on. Much earlier he had graciously recognized the genius of Saul, and doubtless he had properly and humbly assessed his own supporting role in the missionary enterprise.

3. There was the *personal problem of desertion.* John Mark, Barnabas' cousin, began the tour as their attendant, assistant, or helper (v. 5). No doubt he had special qualifications because of his background in the church at Jerusalem. Gatherings were held in his mother's home there. He likely was personally acquainted with many of the events surrounding Jesus' death and resurrection. He had been close to Peter. But before the party started on the

rugged and dangerous mountain road that led up into the Roman province of Galatia, Mark left the party and returned to Jerusalem.

Mark's reasons are never stated. Perhaps he was homesick. Perhaps he had clashed with Paul over the terms of the gospel to the Gentiles. It is useless to speculate. Paul regarded his action as desertion and later refused to have Mark rejoin them. Barnabas saw it in a different light, and this led in the end to their separation (15:36-40). It is to Paul's credit that much later he tacitly acknowledged the worth of Mark (2 Tim. 4:11) and requested his assistance at Rome. It should be encouraging to all that a man who at first seemed to fail, redeemed himself and his career and became the writer of the Gospel bearing his name.

4. There was *the problem of sickness,* if we can connect Paul's statement to the Galatians (Gal. 4:13), as seems proper, with this point in his travels. Paul wrote: "As you know, it was because of an illness that I first preached the gospel to you" (NIV). It seems evident from the following verse (Gal. 4:14) that Paul persevered in his ministry in Galatia in spite of illness.

Each of the above obstacles are experienced today in missionary endeavor. These missionaries won out over their problems by the power of the Spirit.

The Preaching of Paul

Acts 13:14-41

14 But when they departed from Perga, they came to Antioch in Pisidia, and went into the synagogue on the sabbath day, and sat down.
15 And after the reading of the law and the prophets the rulers of the synagogue sent unto them, saying, Ye men and brethren, if ye have any word of exhortation for the people, say on.
16 Then Paul stood up, and beckoning with his hand said, Men of Israel, and ye that fear God, give audience.
17 The God of this people of Israel chose our fathers, and exalted the people when they dwelt as strangers in the land of Egypt, and with an high arm brought he them out of it.
18 And about the time of forty years suffered he their manners in the wilderness.

19 And when he had destroyed seven nations in the land of Chanaan,
he divided their land to them by lot.
20 And after that he gave unto them judges about the space of four
hundred and fifty years, until Samuel the prophet.
21 And afterward they desired a king: and God gave unto them Saul
the son of Cis, a man of the tribe of Benjamin, by the space of forty
years.
22 And when he had removed him, he raised up unto them David to
be their king; to whom also he gave testimony, and said, I have found
David the son of Jesse, a man after mine own heart, which shall fulfil
all my will.
23 Of this man's seed hath God according to his promise raised unto
Israel a Saviour, Jesus:
24 When John had first preached before his coming the baptism of
repentance to all the people of Israel.
25 And as John fulfilled his course, he said, Whom think ye that I am?
I am not he. But, behold, there cometh one after me, whose shoes of
his feet I am not worthy to loose.
26 Men and brethren, children of the stock of Abraham, and whoso-
ever among you feareth God, to you is the word of this salvation sent.
27 For they that dwell at Jerusalem, and their rulers, because they
knew him not, nor yet the voices of the prophets which are read every
sabbath day, they have fulfilled them in condemning him.
28 And though they found no cause of death in him, yet desired they
Pilate that he should be slain.
29 And when they had fulfilled all that was written of him, they took
him down from the tree, and laid him in a sepulchre.
30 But God raised him from the dead:
31 And he was seen many days of them which came up with him from
Galilee to Jerusalem, who are his witnesses unto the people.
32 And we declare unto you glad tidings, how that the promise which
was made unto the fathers,
33 God hath fulfilled the same unto us their children, in that he hath
raised up Jesus again; as it is also written in the second psalm, Thou
art my Son, this day have I begotten thee.
34 And as concerning that he raised him up from the dead, now no
more to return to corruption, he said on this wise, I will give you the
sure mercies of David.
35 Wherefore he saith also in another psalm, Thou shalt not suffer
thine Holy One to see corruption.
36 For David, after he had served his own generation by the will of
God, fell on sleep, and was laid unto his fathers, and saw corruption:
37 But he, whom God raised again, saw no corruption.
38 Be it known unto you therefore, men and brethren, that through
this man is preached unto you the forgiveness of sins:
39 And by him all that believe are justified from all things, from which
ye could not be justified by the law of Moses.
40 Beware therefore, lest that come upon you, which is spoken of in
the prophets;
41 Behold, ye despisers, and wonder, and perish: for I work a work in
your days, a work which ye shall in no wise believe, though a man de-
clare it unto you.

Antioch in Pisidia (a better rendering is Pisidian Antioch, meaning that the city was near the border of

Pisidia, one of the regions of the province of Galatia) was both a civil and military Roman center.

According to their custom Paul and Barnabas attended the sabbath synagogue service. The elders or rulers were in charge of the public worship. This consisted of the recital of the *Shema* (Deut. 6:4-9), prayers, the reading of an assigned portion from the Law (the Pentateuch), another assigned portion from the Prophets, and, if someone was qualified to do so, an exhortation or sermon to the congregation. It was customary to invite learned visitors to speak. It would be a special occasion to have present two distinguished rabbis from Jerusalem. Paul and Barnabas, sitting in the congregation, were politely invited to address them.

The congregation evidently contained both Jews ("men of Israel," although this term may include proselytes as well) and Gentiles who worshipped God ("ye that fear God"). Paul was eager to respond to their invitation. Quieting the crowd with a gesture, he began at once with an arresting statement and launched into a masterful sermon.

The sermon has three basic sections, each introduced by a form of personal address to the audience, at vv. 16, 26, and 38. The first section is very reminiscent of Stephen's sermon (c. 7), although Paul's stress is on God's grace rather than Israel's failure. The second section reminds one of Peter's sermons contrasting God's vindication of Jesus with the people's rejection. But the last section is distinctly Pauline, declaring the great doctrine of justification by faith in Jesus.

1. Paul declares that *the grace of God traced in all of Israel's history has culminated in the coming of Jesus* (17-25).

a. Paul lists the gracious and mighty redeeming acts of God in Israel's history. All this is God's doing, His initiative, His choice. The history is *His story.* It is not Israel's own doing.

He chose the fathers, He exalted and brought them out of slavery, He cared for them as a father in the wilderness (the alternate reading for v. 18), He drove out the seven nations listed in Deut. 7:1, He gave them Canaan. "All this took about 450 years" (NIV). The time-span mentioned in v. 20 seems to be a reference to the period including the Egyptian bondage to the settlement of Canaan, rather than a later period as suggested by the King James translation.

God gave them judges and later, at their request, kings. When Saul failed, God gave them David. God's testimony to David in v. 22 is Paul's joining together of three separate scriptures (Ps. 89:20; 1 Sam. 13:14; and Isa. 44:28).

b. Paul introduces Jesus (v. 23) in the most solemn language. He is the Fulfillment of God's covenant with David and the nation. These Jews would be very familiar with the fact that Israel's hope, the Messiah, would come from David's lineage.

The culminating announcement came from John the Baptist, who, like a king's herald, proclaimed the coming of this royal Person. The great dignity of Jesus' person and office is highlighted in John's statement (v. 25). Paul's language with respect to Jesus could hardly have suggested to his congregation less than Deity.

2. *The promises of God regarding a Saviour have been fulfilled in the death and resurrection of Jesus* (26-37). It was to Abraham that the covenant of blessing for all nations was first given, and Paul now addresses his audience as children of Abraham.

The Jerusalem rulers and people had actually unwittingly fulfilled the Scriptures when they condemned Jesus. The irony was that they read these Scriptures every week but did not understand. The execution of Jesus was done in the complete absence of legal cause or justification. Like Peter, Paul stresses "the tree," the sign of one accursed in death, according to the law.

But in complete and perfect contrast, God has vindicated and exalted Jesus by the Resurrection which has now been validated by many witnesses. Because of the resurrection of Jesus, God's promises are fulfilled, and the missionaries are able to bring "glad tidings."

Paul concludes his evidence regarding Jesus by reference to two of the psalms. In the first (v. 33) the reference seems to be to the manifestation of Jesus as the Messiah, a fulfillment of Psalm 2. In the second (vv. 34-37), Paul uses Psalm 16 in the same manner as Peter had used it on the Day of Pentecost. Jesus' resurrection is the only possible fulfillment of David's statement that God's Holy One should not see corruption, inasmuch as it was not fulfilled in David himself, whose body at death was decomposed.

We have in the preaching of Peter and Paul an outline of the basic content of the apostolic message, the *kerygma.*

3. *The mercy of God through Jesus provides now for forgiveness and justification* (38-41). God's plan, Paul says, is perfect in both its execution and provision. Jesus alone is the Mediator and the Means of salvation. God is now, through the missionaries, announcing the remission of sins because of Jesus.

Furthermore, although those who appear before God's bar of justice with only the works of the law as their hope are doomed to condemnation, those who believe in Jesus may be acquitted or justified freely. God cannot justify men on the basis of law-keeping; He does justify and save them on the basis of faith in Jesus. This is Paul's great theme. It must have fallen upon the hearts of his hearers at Pisidian Antioch under the anointing of the Spirit with indescribable sweetness. This is the gospel, the glad word the Church is to proclaim.

The sermon closes with a word of warning. God's great offer may be disbelieved, refused, despised. If it is, there is no other hope. Making use of Hab. 1:5, Paul solemnly pleads with his audience not to let the prophet's pronouncement be true of them.

Two Responses to the Gospel

Acts 13:42-52

42 And when the Jews were gone out of the synagogue, the Gentiles besought that these words might be preached to them the next sabbath.
43 Now when the congregation was broken up, many of the Jews and religious proselytes followed Paul and Barnabas: who, speaking to them, persuaded them to continue in the grace of God.
44 And the next sabbath day came almost the whole city together to hear the word of God.
45 But when the Jews saw the multitudes, they were filled with envy, and spake against those things which were spoken by Paul, contradicting and blaspheming.
46 Then Paul and Barnabas waxed bold, and said, It was necessary that the word of God should first have been spoken to you: but seeing ye put it from you, and judge yourselves unworthy of everlasting life, lo, we turn to the Gentiles.
47 For so hath the Lord commanded us, saying, I have set thee to be a light of the Gentiles, that thou shouldest be for salvation unto the ends of the earth.
48 And when the Gentiles heard this, they were glad, and glorified the word of the Lord: and as many as were ordained to eternal life believed.
49 And the word of the Lord was published throughout all the region.
50 But the Jews stirred up the devout and honourable women, and the chief men of the city, and raised persecution against Paul and Barnabas, and expelled them out of their coasts.
51 But they shook off the dust of their feet against them, and came unto Iconium.
52 And the disciples were filled with joy, and with the Holy Ghost.

Paul's preaching made a powerful impression upon the listeners. At the end of the service, there was a popular demand that there be more gospel preaching on the next sabbath. Many, both Jews and Gentiles, apparently followed Paul and Barnabas outside the synagogue where the apostles continued to instruct and exhort them. The gist of this was that they should continue in spite of opposition in this new way of faith in Christ.

Doubtless the apostles were active during the days between the sabbaths. By the time of the next sabbath meeting at the synagogue, the word had spread throughout the whole city so that a huge crowd of people was on hand to hear the Word of God. These would be mostly Gentiles. So far as the record is concerned, this was accomplished without the occurrence of miracles of healing or the like.

It bespoke the presence of a vast field white unto harvest.

As always when the gospel is preached there were two contrasting responses.

1. *Jealousy and self-interest were in contrast with honest and open inquiry.* It was envy of the apostles' success and fear of loss of position and influence that moved the synagogue Jews initially to oppose the gospel. They saw that the gospel offer of salvation to the Gentiles without first becoming Jews would undercut the influence of the synagogue. At once they began to try to refute the gospel message. This doubtless led them to make slanderous statements about Jesus. Very quickly they found themselves, because of selfish motives, in diametric opposition to the gospel.

When they saw that the opposition was closed in heart to any appeal, Paul and Barnabas boldly announced that their mission would be directly to Gentiles without regard for the synagogue. It was not that the door of salvation for the Jews was shut. It meant that the Jews of the synagogue had forfeited the privilege of being the vehicle or medium of God's work of salvation in their city. They would be bypassed but the work would go on. For the Jews who regarded themselves as the exclusive depository of divine revelation, such a thing was unthinkable. Paul and Barnabas appealed to the words of Isaiah (c. 49:6). God himself had appointed His servant (fulfilled in the Messiah) to be *a light to the Gentiles,* and the way of *salvation unto the ends of the earth.*

2. *Faith and unbelief are contrasted.* Two statements in the passage need to be seen the one over against the other. Here is unbelief (v. 46): *ye put it* (the word of God) *from you, and judge yourselves unworthy of everlasting life.* Here is faith (v. 48): *there were glad, and glorified the word of the Lord: and as many as were ordained to eternal life believed.* The latter expression does not indicate the unconditional predestination of individuals to salvation. God *has* predestinated all who believe on Jesus to eternal life.

But the word here is "ordained" and it means literally "to set in order." It was used of the marshalling or stationing of troops.

So we see the contrast. The unbelieving Jews had set themselves in opposition to the Word. In doing this they had judged themselves, they had denied themselves eternal life. The decision and the judgment were really on their own. But the believing Gentiles marshalled or stationed themselves on the side of the gospel, on the side of life. One group was disposed against life, the other disposed toward life.

3. *Condemnation is contrasted with joy in the Holy Spirit.* The Jews were able to turn the magistrates (the chief men) of the city against Paul and Barnabas. Luke seems to suggest that this was done in part through leading women, perhaps magistrates' wives, who were attached to the synagogue as worshippers. The sufferings of the missionaries are not stated by they likely were severe. In the end they were expelled from the area as troublemakers. Luke here, as throughtout Acts, is careful to show that official opposition to Christian believers in the Gentile world came at the instigation of the Jews.

Shaking the dust from one's feet (cf. Luke 9:5) was the sign that the persecutors would bear the condemnation and the responsibility for their actions. In contrast to this burden of condemnation is the great joy of the disciples in spite of persecution. Their secret was that they were filled with the Holy Spirit, evidence that the apostles' ministry had been complete.

ACTS 14

Taking Christ to the Pagan World

Acts 14:1-20

1 And it came to pass in Iconium, that they went both together into the synagogue of the Jews, and so spake, that a great multitude both of the Jews and also of the Greeks believed.

2 But the unbelieving Jews stirred up the Gentiles, and made their minds evil affected against the brethren.
3 Long time therefore abode they speaking boldly in the Lord, which gave testimony unto the word of his grace, and granted signs and wonders to be done by their hands.
4 But the multitude of the city was divided: and part held with the Jews, and part with the apostles.
5 And when there was an assault made both of the Gentiles, and also of the Jews with their rulers, to use them despitefully, and to stone them,
6 They were ware of it, and fled unto Lystra and Derbe, cities of Lycaonia, and unto the region that lieth round about:
7 And there they preached the gospel.
8 And there sat a certain man at Lystra, impotent in his feet, being a cripple from his mother's womb, who never had walked:
9 The same heard Paul speak: who stedfastly beholding him, and perceiving that he had faith to be healed,
10 Said with a loud voice, Stand upright on thy feet. And he leaped and walked.
11 And when the people saw what Paul had done, they lifted up their voices, saying in the speech of Lycaonia, The gods are come down to us in the likeness of men.
12 And they called Barnabas, Jupiter; and Paul, Mercurius, because he was the chief speaker.
13 Then the priest of Jupiter, which was before their city, brought oxen and garlands unto the gates, and would have done sacrifice with the people.
14 Which when the apostles, Barnabas and Paul, heard of, they rent their clothes, and ran in among the people, crying out,
15 And saying, Sirs, why do ye these things? We also are men of like passions with you, and preach unto you that ye should turn from these vanities unto the living God, which made heaven, and earth, and the sea, and all things that are therein:
16 Who in times past suffered all nations to walk in their own ways.
17 Nevertheless he left not himself without witness, in that he did good, and gave us rain from heaven, and fruitful seasons, filling our hearts with food and gladness.
18 And with these sayings scarce restrained they the people, that they had not done sacrifice unto them.
19 And there came thither certain Jews from Antioch and Iconium, who persuaded the people, and, having stoned Paul, drew him out of the city, supposing he had been dead.
20 Howbeit, as the disciples stood round about him, he rose up, and came into the city: and the next day he departed with Barnabas to Derbe.

Driven from Pisidian Antioch, Paul and Barnabas came to Iconium, a city about 80 miles to the southeast of Antioch. Here they stayed for some time until again forced to leave. This time they went to the city of Lystra, about 23 miles southwest of Iconium in the region of Lycaonia. Not only the cities but the surrounding villages were evangelized.

It is interesting to note that Luke's careful description of Lystra and Derbe as cities of Lycaonia, and his implication that Iconium was not, was the point at which Sir William Ramsay in his early critical examination became first impressed with Luke's accuracy as an historian. The inference on Iconium was long in dispute but Ramsay found Luke correct.

Lystra is also noteworthy as the home of Timothy. Although not mentioned here, he was likely converted, along with his mother, on this visit.

Luke's summary of work in these cities is very brief. The divine providences involved and the missionaries' preaching invite consideration, however.

1. *The purposeful preaching* of Paul and Barnabas produced a consistent pattern of results.

a. In the synagogue at Iconium they *so spake* that a multitude believed (v. 1). They spoke *boldly in the Lord,* and their message was *the word of his grace* (v. 2). They preached with the Spirit's power, with the courage and clarity which came from His anointing, not from their own resources. They preached "the word," not their own ideas. The "word of his grace" indicates the gospel, the good news about Jesus—His life, death, and resurrection; the promise of His Spirit. It was a gracious word, full of love and mercy.

b. They preached with persistence. It is noteworthy that Luke states that they *therefore abode* a long time preaching at Iconium, because of the opposition to their message (vv. 2-3). Preachers frequently take opposition as the signal to leave. These missionaries found in it a reason to stay and win a victory for the gospel.

c. Their preaching made mere neutrality toward the gospel impossible. In the end the whole city was divided for and against (v. 4). Jesus himself declared that He came not to bring peace, but a sword (Matt. 10:34), meaning that God's Word separates and defines and thus produces division. But it is the division of light from darkness, of truth from falsehood, of life from death. It is only a spurious gospel which does not so discriminate or disturb. The apostles reached the whole city of Iconium, aided paradoxically by those who came to oppose.

d. Their preaching was sometimes with accompanying signs, sometimes without. In Iconium there were miracles performed which vindicated the truth of the message. At Lystra the healing of a cripple gained the attention of the whole city. There is no mention of miracles at Pisidian Antioch earlier, nor Derbe later. The signs were never the thing of major importance; preaching was. The gifts of the Spirit are at the sovereign disposal of the Lord. The gospel is committed to men.

e. Their preaching was intelligent and versatile. They began with people as they found them, varying the style and approach of the message to suit the congregation's needs. In the synagogue they began with the revelation of God in the Old Testament and preached Christ. But preaching in the open air to the pagans at Lystra who knew nothing of the Scriptures, they began with what they did know (vv. 15-17). They seized the opportunity to preach *the living God,* the God who has life in himself and who gives life to all things, in contrast to the *vanities,* the uselessness, of their poor idols.

The message here is at some points similar to Paul's sermon at Athens later (c. 17). God has permitted the Gentile nations to wander in their own ways. They lost the true way because they preferred their own. (With these words the door is being opened to declare God's way of salvation revealed to His people and realized in Jesus Christ.) Even so, God has not left the pagan nations entirely in darkness. There was always the light of nature, the miracle of the earth's rich abundance, the reliability of the seasons, pointing as they do to a purposeful and beneficent Creator. The light of natural theology is dim, but it is light, and followed, it leads to knowledge of God's power and deity (cf. Rom. 1:18-21). But only the revelation in Scripture and the gospel tells us of God's love and saving grace. We may be sure that the gospel was preached to the pagan population of Lystra.

2. *The providential protection* of Paul and Barnabas through a variety of perils characterizes the new missionary thrust. Writing to Timothy at the close of his career, Paul said, "Thou hast fully known my . . . persecutions, afflictions, which came unto me at Antioch, at Iconium, at Lystra; what persecutions I endured: but out of them all the Lord delivered me" (2 Tim. 3:10-11).

a. There is a persistent pattern in persecution. It is stirred up by the unbelieving Jews, who, rejecting the gospel themselves, are determined to also poison the minds of the Gentiles against it (cf. 1 Thess. 2:14-16). Those from Antioch and Iconium even pursued the missionaries to Lystra on their nefarious mission. In each case they were finally able by misrepresentation to turn the Gentile magistrates against Paul and Barnabas. The temptation to discouragement must have been great.

b. The missionaries faced a variety of tests. There was the opposition of hatred, the misunderstanding resulting from lies and poisoned minds, the use of physical violence, the threat of lynching which caused them to flee to the next place.

The attempt of the populace at Lystra to worship the apostles was a test of another kind. The occasion was precipitated by the healing of the crippled man. His story is much like the man's at the Beautiful Gate of the Temple, who was healed through Peter and John (c. 3). He had been listening and evidently responding to Paul's preaching. No doubt Paul felt specially directed by the Spirit to challenge his faith and commitment. The miracle of healing created intense excitement and commotion.

It seems that Paul and Barnabas were at first not aware of what was going on because the excited crowd was calling out in their native Lycaonian tongue. Paul's preaching would have been in Greek, which nearly all would understand. These people had a legend that the gods Jupiter and Mercury (Roman names for the Greek gods Zeus and Hermes) had once come down among men in this same region. They had a temple to Jupiter outside the city. In Greek mythology Zeus or Jupiter was the chief of the gods, and Hermes or Mercury was the gods' messenger, the inventor of speech, and an eloquent speaker. For this reason the crowd identified Paul, the main speaker of the two, as Mercury. Barnabas had to be Jupiter, but besides, he likely was a more imposing figure than Paul. There is a second-century apocryphal *Acts of Paul* which purports to describe Paul as he looked at Iconium: "A man small in size, with meeting eyebrows, with a rather large nose, baldheaded, bow-legged, strongly built, full of grace, for at times he looked like a man, and at times he had the face of an angel."

When the priests of Jupiter had prepared the garlanded bulls before the temple gates and were getting ready to offer their animal sacrifices in honor of the gods, Paul and Barnabas became aware of what was happening. Horror-struck at such a thing, they tore their tunics at the neck, the Jewish sign of sacrilege or grief, and ran among the people to dissuade them. One imagines them crying, "Stop! Stop! We are just humans like yourselves, who feel in the same way you do!" The gods, of course, were considered to be above ordinary human sufferings.

The subtle temptation to accept the adulation of the crowd was instantly rebuffed. How different was the case of Herod Agrippa (c. 12) in a similar situation. This test is a familiar tactic of Satan. Our Lord faced it also in the wilderness temptation. In lesser forms it has proved the ruin of some of God's ministers.

The utter fickleness of these pagans is demonstrated by the fact that later these same people, who would have worshipped him, took part in stoning Paul.

c. Once again we note the mystery of God's providence in His care of His people. At Iconium the missionaries were made aware of the plot to stone them and escaped. At Lystra Paul did not escape. He recalls this in

2 Cor. 11:25, "Once was I stoned." This was evidently the only time. Writing back to these Galatians, he declared, "I bear in my body the marks of the Lord Jesus" (Gal. 6:17), a remarkable reference to the scars of physical violence.

In God's providence the agonizing experience was not avoided, but when Paul's inert body had been dragged outside the city and left for dead, God intervened. One can imagine the tears of the disciples and the grief of Barnabas as they stood around the battered body. Perhaps Timothy was there also. They intended an appropriate burial. Suddenly Paul just stood up. Tears turned to rejoicing. He went with them back into the city and the next day left for Derbe. Had Paul really been dead and raised again to life? Perhaps. Whatever the case, it was a miracle of God's overshadowing care. But in this case it was deliverance, not from suffering, but in and through suffering.

Priorities in the Missionary Enterprise

Acts 14:21-28

21 And when they had preached the gospel to that city, and had taught many, they returned again to Lystra, and to Iconium, and Antioch,
22 Confirming the souls of the disciples, and exhorting them to continue in the faith, and that we must through much tribulation enter into the kingdom of God.
23 And when they had ordained them elders in every church, and had prayed with fasting, they commended them to the Lord, on whom they believed.
24 And after they had passed throughout Pisidia, they came to Pamphylia.
25 And when they had preached the word in Perga, they went down into Attalia:
26 And thence sailed to Antioch, from whence they had been recommended to the grace of God for the work which they fulfilled.
27 And when they were come, and had gathered the church together, they rehearsed all that God had done with them, and how he had opened the door of faith unto the Gentiles.
28 And there they abode long time with the disciples.

1. *The needs of the church came before personal safety.* Derbe was some 50 miles southeast of Lystra. There the missionaries had great success, apparently without per-

secution. From Derbe there was a main road to Tarsus which was not far distant. That would have been the easy way home. It was a courageous act which took them back to the cities where they had suffered so recently, and over many extra miles of dangerous travel.

2. *The results of their evangelism needed to be conserved.* At Lystra, Iconium, and Pisidian Antioch they spent time with the believers, preparing the new converts to carry on in their absence. It was a bold policy to place such responsibility on people so recently won to Christ in a hostile environment. We are not surprised that they commended them to the Lord in earnest prayer combined with fasting. It was an expression of confidence in the keeping power of the Holy Spirit in the midst of the church.

Their ministry of conservation included encouragement, instruction, and organization. The believers needed encouraging because they faced severe opposition. We see from Paul's Galatian letter how vital the teaching ministry was. A good beginning is not enough. They needed to be fortified with scripture and doctrine. Leaders (elders or presbyters) were needed who could oversee the worship and the shepherding of each congregation. These elders were appointed by Paul and Barnabas, but the term used suggests that the people had some voice in selection as well.

3. *It had to be understood that suffering for Christ's sake cannot be avoided in a godless society* (cf. 1 Thess. 3:3). The converts needed to be intellectually as well as spiritually prepared for the persecution and opposition which would come. To become a Christian meant for Gentiles especially a break with idolatrous customs and the acceptance of new personal and social standards of morality in a very immoral society. Family life was often disturbed. New Christians at times seemed in general conflict with the old society. Their new lives were a rebuke to unbelievers around them. The thorny path of hatred, scorn, and ostracism was frequently unavoidable. There might be physical

violence. Jesus had forewarned His disciples of all this.

The persistent teaching that the signs of God's favor are health, good times, and prosperity is really satanic. The rewards of the Kingdom are not given in the poor coin of this world. Christians are not to be shocked nor disillusioned when trouble comes.

This fact underscores the need for the creation and maintenance of warm, loving, reinforcing communities of Christians for fellowship and mutual discipline.

4. *All the glory for success in Christian work was given to God.* The missionaries returned the way they had come, except that they stopped this time to preach in Perga, and then sailed directly back to Antioch in Syria. What a homecoming time they must have had! They had probably been gone for almost a year. Little if any news of them would have been received in that time.

It was to God's grace that they had been committed as they went. Doubtless they had been objects of daily prayer by the sending church. Now at last, it was to God that glory was given for their safety and their exploits in the gospel. They rehearsed not what they had done, but rather *all that God had done with them.* In this concept and attitude there is a secret for success in Christian work.

5. *The door which God had opened challenged the Church to still greater effort.* God had flung open to the Gentiles the door to salvation, and the door itself was faith in Christ. The simplicity of this statement was epochal and far-reaching. The door did not include the ceremonial law. It did not involve becoming a Jew first and then a Christian, nor did it mean adding legalism to faith in order to find favor with God. It was more than a theory. The apostles testified to the transformed and Spirit-filled lives of their Gentile converts. The worldwide implications of all this were breathtaking.

Nevertheless this truth was to be severely challenged shortly. Perhaps it was to meet the challenge that Paul and Barnabas remained at Antioch for a number of months.

ACTS 15

A Crisis Regarding Doctrine and Practice

Acts 15:1-12

1 And certain men which came down from Judaea taught the brethren, and said, Except ye be circumcised after the manner of Moses, ye cannot be saved.
2 When therefore Paul and Barnabas had no small dissension and disputation with them, they determined that Paul and Barnabas, and certain other of them, should go up to Jerusalem unto the apostles and elders about this question.
3 And being brought on their way by the church, they passed through Phenice and Samaria, declaring the conversion of the Gentiles: and they caused great joy unto all the brethren.
4 And when they were come to Jerusalem, they were received of the church, and of the apostles and elders, and they declared all things that God had done with them.
5 But there rose up certain of the sect of the Pharisees which believed, saying, That it was needful to circumcise them, and to command them to keep the law of Moses.
6 And the apostles and elders came together for to consider of this matter.
7 And when there had been much disputing, Peter rose up, and said unto them, Men and brethren, ye know how that a good while ago God made choice among us, that the Gentiles by my mouth should hear the word of the gospel, and believe.
8 And God, which knoweth the hearts, bare them witness, giving them the Holy Ghost, even as he did unto us;
9 And put no difference between us and them, purifying their hearts by faith.
10 Now therefore why tempt ye God, to put a yoke upon the neck of the disciples, which neither our fathers nor we were able to bear?
11 But we believe that through the grace of the Lord Jesus Christ we shall be saved, even as they.
12 Then all the multitude kept silence, and gave audience to Barnabas and Paul, declaring what miracles and wonders God had wrought among the Gentiles by them.

The most serious problem to face the Early Church, possibly the most critical problem in the Church's entire history, is recorded briefly by Luke in this chapter. The meeting which was held to deal with the problem is often called the Jerusalem Council. Actually, it was a gathering of several leaders from Antioch for discussions with the Jerusalem leaders, the apostles and elders (vv. 2-6). The entire Jerusalem church was interested and became involved (vv. 4, 12).

For Paul, the Apostle to the Gentiles, the matters involved were life-and-death issues. They were the occasion for his letter to the Galatians where they are discussed with passionate earnestness. They are likewise dealt with in other of his letters.

The more traditional view is that Paul discusses this Jerusalem conference in Gal. 2:1-10. It is true that in that passage he does not mention the so-called decree which the conference approved and later sent out in letters to the affected churches. But Paul in Galatians was discussing the authority of his gospel as a revelation from God. It would not have fitted his mood or argument to appeal to the decision of a conference. In the Galatian passage, likely for the same reason, Paul records only his meetings with the Jerusalem leaders. Luke's record seems also to suggest that there were private meetings of this sort as well as the public gathering (cf. vv. 4 and 6). But Luke makes no mention of the presence of Titus, an important feature in Galatians.

There is another view, adopted by equally competent scholars, that in the Galatians passage Paul refers not to this Jerusalem visit but to the one recorded in Acts 11:30 and 12:25, the occasion of the taking to Judea the offering for the poor. On this theory, the letter to the Galatians was written not long *before* the Jerusalem conference of Acts 15; also Paul's clash with Peter at Antioch (Gal. 2:11-14) would have been prior to the conference.

If we accept the more traditional view, it seems reasonable to think that Luke writes of the Jerusalem conference from its more public and ecclesiastical aspects, much as a reporter would. Paul in Galatians writes about the same event from the viewpoint of its more private discussions, and as a theologian in defense of his gospel.

1. *The problem which was faced.*

a. The *immediate problem* was that *certain men,* claiming that they were sent by the Jerusalem church, had gone to Antioch and were teaching that the Gentile Christians not only ought to be circumcised and observe the customs of the Mosaic law, but that they could not be saved unless they did. Such was *not* the teaching at Antioch. In that church both Jewish and Gentile believers lived and fellowshipped together without the ceremonial barriers of the Mosaic laws regulating food and other such matters. Paul and Barnabas viewed this intrusion with great alarm and set out to refute it. The struggle grew in size and seriousness. The church decided to send a delegation to Jerusalem in an attempt to end the controversy.

It is clear, especially from his own account, that to Paul the question was never in doubt. God had already spoken decisively. His own mind was crystal clear on the matter. His appeal to Jerusalem was for the sake of peace, to avoid a ruinous schism, not to decide a point of doctrine (cf. Gal. 2:2).

b. The problem had been *developing over a period of years.* The Church began at Jerusalem among Jews and Jewish proselytes, cradled in the ancient faith of Israel. The Church is the fulfillment of God's covenant with His ancient people through the law and through the prophets. Because of that covenant Israel was separate from the rest of the nations. The laws of uncleanness were great, almost impassable barriers between Jews and Gentiles.

Most Jews had become mistakenly exclusive in their religious ideals, although certain of the Hellenists tended to have a wider vision. But to the average Jew who became a Christian, it was simply unthinkable that even in Christ, God could fully accept Gentiles without the separation which Mosaic regulations provided and which circumcision signified. Witness the struggle of Peter at this point. Apparently law-keeping was not an issue in the Jerusalem church itself simply because it was the regular practice.

The preaching of Stephen had pointed in a different direction. The came the conversion and acceptance of the Samaritans, then of the Gentiles at the house of Cornelius. Then, for the first time, there was a great Gentile church at Antioch. Circumcision was not required. Still later, word came of the great work of Paul and Barnabas in Asia Minor. Gentiles would soon form the majority in the Church. To the Jerusalem zealots for the law, the whole structure of their form of faith seemed threatened. Many of them were not willing to concede without a struggle.

c. The threat of schism in the Church was real. Would there be two churches, one Jewish, one Gentile? Would Antioch be severed from Jerusalem? Would there develop two kinds of Christians, two doors to salvation, two forms of Christian faith, in which Jews and Gentiles would live and work in harmony? It is evident that none of the apostles ever shared the views of the extremists. It is incorrect to think of Peter or James at odds with Paul on this issue, although it is obvious that they moved more slowly at times than Paul would have wished. Paul's account in Galatians is evidence of their fellowship.

d. There are no glib and easy answers to *the deeper problems* which this crisis posed. On one extreme the simple answer was: All Gentile Christians must first become Jews, be circumcised, keep the law. Had it prevailed, the Church would have become a sect or adjunct of Judaism rather than the people of the new covenant, the new Israel of God. It would have withered into a minor religious cult. Paul saw that if the works of the law are necessary to salvation, then Christ died in vain; the Cross becomes of no effect.

On the other extreme is lawlessness, antinomianism. Actually, the fears of the Jews that the moral purity of the Church would be compromised by Gentile Christians living without the strictures of the law, were not idle concerns. People saved out of gross paganism surely needed moral guidelines. The Pauline letters demonstrate how the baffling ethical problems were wrestled with through the decades ahead. Paul and the other apostles would lead believers to a better solution than mere legalism. Christians *are* under perpetual obligation to live holy lives, but the way to victory is by subjection to the law of Christ, surrender to the dominance of the Spirit, rather than by slavery to the mere letter, the word contained in ordinances.

These issues are still very much with us in the Church. It is the extreme answers that we need to fear. Led by the Spirit, the Early Church pointed the way.

2. *The way they faced the problem.* The most significant factor in the settlement was not argument but a testimony, the appeal to what God had done before their eyes. The Antioch delegation was sent warmly on its way by the whole church. Along the way, in Phoenicia and Samaria, they preached and witnessed to the churches and were in turn given hospitality. The Gentile story was received with joy.

At Jerusalem they were hospitably welcomed by the church. It appears that, wisely, they first consulted with and witnessed to the apostles and elders in private and only later before the whole church. The key words are: *thy declared all things that God had done with them . . . and what God had wrought among the Gentiles by them* (vv. 4, 12). In this they were on solid ground.

The vocal opposition came from certain believers *of the sect of the Pharisees.* Paul too had been a Pharisee, but these men seem to have remained legalists at heart, whereas Paul was transformed by his faith. In Galatians Paul refers to them as "false brethren," seeking to bring the Gentile Christians into bondage to law. Nevertheless they were patiently heard out.

Once again, as at an earlier meeting (c. 11), they appealed not to authority but to understanding. They sought, not the will of a majority, but a consensus with the help of the Holy Spirit.

3. *The way they sensed where God was leading.* After "exhaustive inquiry" (Phillips), it was Peter who testified decisively about God's work among the Gentiles. Some 10 years earlier, he reminded them, God had led him to the house of Cornelius where he had preached the gospel to Gentiles and fellowshipped with them. All this he had reported to the Jerusalem church (see the discussion on 11: 1-18). This was God's doing, not his own.

The clinching evidence for Peter was that God gave the Gentile believers the Holy Spirit in the same way and with the same results as at the Spirit's coming to the Jewish believers at Pentecost. When the Spirit is outpoured on believers, He sanctifies and purifies their hearts. He was and is given in response to faith. The Gentiles who received the Spirit were not circumcised law-keepers, but simply openhearted Christian believers.

Peter's implicit challenge to the Pharisaic argument was, How can you call Gentile believers unclean, even though they are uncircumcised, if God himself has cleansed them inwardly? He was hearing again the voice from heaven which had said to him, "What God has cleansed, call not thou common [or unclean]." Jesus himself had taught His disciples that it was not outward ceremonial cleansing which mattered, but the cleansing of the heart (Luke 11:39-40).

Peter further reminded his audience that the works of the law had not brought them to peace with God, neither they nor their fathers. A Gentile proselyte, when he became a Jew, was said to "take up the yoke." Many rabbis taught at this time that if a person failed to keep even one of the long list of regulations, he was guilty of them all. Jesus had recognized the intolerable burden of uncertainty and guilt which this produced (cf. His teaching, Matt. 11: 28-30).

If after God has made His will plain, Peter argues, we seek to add something more to it, we "tempt" Him, that is, we invite His judgment. If the Gentiles have been accepted by God *through the grace of the Lord Jesus Christ,* then all, Jews included, are saved without reference to the works of the law. Peter is one with Paul in this ringing declaration of justification by grace through faith (cf. Eph. 2: 8-9).

A period of discussion likely followed Peter's speech. Then, once again, all fell silent and listened as Barnabas (named first here due to his seniority in the Jerusalem church) and Paul again recounted God's wonderful dealings with the Gentiles at Antioch and in Asia Minor. Theirs was more recent evidence which only added to the powerful witness of Peter.

Decisiveness and Unity Within the Church

Acts 15:13-21

13 And after they had held their peace, James answered, saying, Men and brethren, hearken unto me:
14 Simeon hath declared how God at the first did visit the Gentiles, to take out of them a people for his name.
15 And to this agree the words of the prophets; as it is written,
16 After this I will return, and will build again the tabernacle of David, which is fallen down; and I will build again the ruins thereof, and I will set it up:
17 That the residue of men might seek after the Lord, and all the Gentiles, upon whom my name is called, saith the Lord, who doeth all these things.
18 Known unto God are all his works from the beginning of the world.
19 Wherefore my sentence is, that we trouble not them, which from among the Gentiles are turned to God:
20 But that we write unto them, that they abstain from pollutions of idols, and from fornication, and from things strangled, and from blood.
21 For Moses of old time hath in every city them that preach him, being read in the synagogues every sabbath day.

James, the brother of Jesus, had come to be the spiritual leader of the Jerusalem church. He apparently held a position which we would call chairman of the group of elders who administered church affairs. The apostles had long since ceased to reside in Jerusalem. James's ascetic life and continual prayers at the Temple made him respected by the populace. Tradition says that after his death by stoning in A.D. 61, at the instigation of the high priest, many of the people attributed the city's calamities to the loss of his intercessory prayers.

James's summary of the feelings and the findings of the conference was twofold.

1. *The Church is the new people of God,* and it is composed of both Jews and Gentiles in complete equality. Taking his cue from the witness of Peter, whom he calls by his Jewish name, Simeon, James begins his remarks with this remarkable interpretation. The term "people of God," as used in the Old Testament, always placed God's people in total contrast with the Gentiles. Now, James says—and the idea is revolutionary for the Jews—God's people include Gentiles. God is doing a new thing. They must let go of old ideas. Then he provides scriptural support to the arguments presented. He quotes from Amos 9:11-12, evidently from the Septuagint, the Greek text. The wording differs a little from the Hebrew text on which our version is based.

James places the passage from Amos in a Messianic setting. The tabernacle of David stands for the Old Testament "church" or people of God. It had come to ruin, but God purposed to build it up again, a new people, under the Headship of David's greater son, Jesus, who is now exalted and glorified. Amos had prophesied that all the heathen of the nations round about would be possessed by or would share in the restored kingdom. This could only be fulfilled in a spiritual sense. Those from every nation in the world, the residue of men, who are called by Christ's name, would become part of God's rebuilding of His people. Further more (v. 18) James declares that God has intended this, purposed it, from eternity (cf. Ephesians 1).

2. *Fellowship between Jews and Gentiles in the Church must be built upon mutual respect.* The Jewish believers are to cease pressuring or annoying Gentile believers with demands that they keep the ceremonial law. On the other hand the Gentiles are to exercise charity toward Jews by offering no offense by their way of life.

If the Pharisaic party expected support from the ascetic James (the writer of the New Testament book bearing his name), they were disappointed. He stood firmly with Peter and Paul. His wisdom (cf. his own word about that in Jas. 3:17) was shown in both charity and firmness. Several things need to be noted about this decision.

a. The word "sentence" in the KJV is too strong a term to indicated the meaning. Other versions use words like "judgment" or "opinion." James was not handing down an edict but expressing his strong personal conviction in the form of a resolution to be approved by the whole body.

b. The proposal (which was overwhelmingly approved) must not be thought of as a compromise with the Pharisaic party, that is, as a kind of watering down of the law requirements for Gentile Christians to a bare minimum, or, as a kind of summarizing of the whole law. This was not law but guidance or counsel, and its purpose was not to meet a legal requirement but to provide a basis for fellowship within the Church, a society which would usually have Jews and Gentiles working side by side. The areas dealt with (relationship to idols, sexual morality, and food) were the chief problem areas in Jewish-Gentile relationships, as well as areas about which Gentiles recently converted from paganism would be most ignorant. (This is why it is impossible to interpret abstinence from blood as referring to violence or murder. Even Gentile Christians would know enough not to murder! Such a view still suggest a mere legalistic compromise. Paul, for one, would never have accepted it.)

Gentiles were counselled to respect the consciences and scruples of the Jews in areas where they might carelessly offend. Meat offered to idols, indeed other innocent association with idols, would be greatly troubling to some but meaningless to others. Gentiles often were culturally conditioned by very lax or perverted customs related to sex and marriage. This is still true on many mission fields. They would be asked to abstain from every marriage relationship or form of sexual activity contrary to Jewish practice. Particularly offensive to Jews was the Gentile practice of using meat from which the blood had not been drained, or even mixing blood with food or drink as a delicacy. The best commentary on these issues is Paul's discussion in Rom. 14, and 1 Cor. 6 to 8, as well as other counsels in matters of conscience.

The entire decision supports the great New Testament concept that freedom in Christ is freedom by the Spirit to do what is good and right, and that what is right is never automatically known to a Christian but comes by instruction and counsel.

c. It was implied in this decision (possibly also in v. 21), that Jewish Christians were to have on their part freedom to live according to the ceremonial laws if they chose to do so. Jewish Christians might indeed also attend the synagogues where the law was taught. At the least it was important not to unnecessarily offend devout Jews who worshipped according to their ancient customs throughout the whole Gentile world.

The Holy Spirit Is the Church's Guide

Acts 15:22-34

22 Then pleased it the apostles and elders, with the whole church, to send chosen men of their own company to Antioch with Paul and Barnabas; namely, Judas surnamed Barsabas, and Silas, chief men among the brethren:
23 And they wrote letters by them after this manner; The apostles and elders and brethren send greeting unto the brethren which are of the Gentiles in Antioch and Syria and Cilicia.
24 Forasmuch as we have heard, that certain which went out from us have troubled you with words, subverting your souls, saying, Ye must be circumcised, and keep the law: to whom we gave no such commandment:
25 It seemed good unto us, being assembled with one accord, to send chosen men unto you with our beloved Barnabas and Paul,
26 Men that have hazarded their lives for the name of our Lord Jesus Christ.
27 We have sent therefore Judas and Silas, who shall also tell you the same things by mouth.
28 For it seemed good to the Holy Ghost, and to us, to lay upon you no greater burden than these necessary things;
29 That ye abstain from meats offered to idols, and from blood, and from things strangled, and from fornication: from which if ye keep yourselves, ye shall do well. Fare ye well.

30 So when they were dismissed, they came to Antioch: and when they had gathered the multitude together, they delivered the epistle:
31 Which when they had read, they rejoiced for the consolation.
32 And Judas and Silas, being prophets also themselves, exhorted the brethren with many words, and confirmed them.
33 And after they had tarried there a space, they were let go in peace from the brethren unto the apostles.
34 Notwithstanding it pleased Silas to abide there still.

The key expression of this passage is "it seemed good to the Holy Spirit, and to us" (v. 28*a*). Although desire for the Spirit's guidance and seeking after it are not mentioned as part of the proceedings of the conference, it is evident that those present had a deep sense of divine leadership. We do not read into this something dramatic or profoundly mystical. Men who are consciously living under the Spirit's control are not usually unduly exercised to obtain a dramatic or special revelation. There had been thoughtful discussion, earnest debate, a meeting of minds, all with the prayerful desire to find God's will. They had used their best judgment with clear motives. They had arrived at a united consensus and had a sense of divine approval. The Spirit had guided them.

The elements in their response to the Spirit's guidance are of interest.

1. Apparently the decision was reached by *a vote of the entire body* on the resolution offered by James. The expression translated "it pleased" (v. 22) carried (according to the grammarians) almost technical connotation of voting on or passing on a resolution by a group. Approval came from the apostles, the elders, and the whole church. It was a shared decision.

2. Careful *judgment and tactfulness* were employed in the implementation. Two men were chosen with care to convey a written communication as well as a verbal message. Judas Barsabas was obviously a Hebrew, perhaps a brother of the Joseph Barsabas put forward for the apostolate in c. 1. Silas seems to have been a Hellenistic Jew and was a Roman citizen as we learn from 16:37. Thus this pair were somewhat representative of the issues.

3. *Christian courtesy* characterized the entire plan. The letter was *from* "brethren" *to* "brethren."

4. They took pains to ensure the utmost *clarity* in the message itself. The issue was stated in uncompromising language (v. 24). There was a flat denial that the Judaizers at Antioch had any authority or commission whatsoever from the Jerusalem church. They were unauthorized teachers. Their doctrine "subverted," unsettled, tore down the good work at Antioch. This plain language must have completely silenced the false teachers.

5. They made plain that they acted in *unity,* "with one accord" (v. 25). There had been no dissenting voice when the vote was finally taken. We know that later, and over a considerable time, legalistic opposition reappeared in the Church. Its form, however, seems to have shifted to personal attack on the Apostle Paul.

6. The reference to Barnabas and Paul was a deliberate expression of *confidence and love.* Paul records that the Jerusalem leaders gave to him and Barnabas "the right hands of fellowship" (Gal. 2:9). The Antioch leaders were acknowledged affectionately as men who had "hazarded" (better still, devoted, or given up) their lives for the sake of Christ.

7. There is a disarming *forthrightness* about the request to the Gentiles (vv. 28-29). The letter plainly suggests that the requested guidance is being held to the bare minimum of need. They will honor the freedom of the Gentile brethren. Nothing is asked which is not incumbent upon or normal for Christians anywhere acting in love.

We assume that the implications of the word "necessary" were to be verbally clarified by the messengers. These matters were necessary to harmony and fellowship within the Church. They were not legal requirements in order to be saved.

8. The entire matter was carried out with *dispatch* (v. 30).

A great deal might have been lost by dalliance once the Spirit had indicated His leading.

9. *Peace and good fellowship* within the Church were the immediate results (vv. 31-33). The Gentile believers were "consoled," strengthened, encouraged. The men from Jerusalem enjoyed a profitable and appreciated ministry in the church. The church, freed from controversy, resumed its agressive pattern of growth.

(V. 34 is omitted in the recent versions for the reason that it is not found in the most reliable Greek manuscripts. It may have been inserted at a later time by some scribe who thought the addition would explain v. 40. A more likely explanation, however, is that Silas was summoned by Paul to Antioch after a time in Jerusalem.)

When Good Men Disagree

Acts 15:35-41

35 Paul also and Barnabas continued in Antioch, teaching and preaching the word of the Lord, with many others also.
36 And some days after Paul said unto Barnabas, Let us go again and visit our brethren in every city where we have preached the word of the Lord, and see how they do.
37 And Barnabas determined to take with them John, whose surname was Mark.
38 But Paul thought not good to take him with them, who departed from them from Pamphylia, and went not with them to the work.
39 And the contention was so sharp between them, that they departed asunder one from the other: and so Barnabas took Mark, and sailed unto Cyprus;
40 And Paul chose Silas, and departed, being recommended by the brethren unto the grace of God.
41 And he went through Syria and Cilicia, confirming the churches.

The time which Paul and Barnabas spent in Antioch after their return would be nearly a year at the least, and less than two at the most. Luke now recounts the origin of Paul's second missionary tour.

The candor with which Luke describes the apostles' disagreement points up his objectivity with regard to recorded events.

1. *The human limitations of even the best of men* are

painfully illustrated in this scene. Luke makes no attempt to gloss over the facts. Agreeing to make a second tour together, Barnabas had a mind to take John Mark along. Paul would not consent. No amount of argument produced agreement. So, they parted and went separate ways.

It was a question of honest judgment, not mere prejudice. Paul felt clearly that Mark had disqualified himself by his previous desertion under pressure. He had put other considerations ahead of "the work." It would be unwise to risk another failure in such a critical enterprise. Paul's great concern was the welfare of the churches.

Barnabas, Mark's cousin, saw in him great qualities not yet developed. To refuse Mark might discourage him unduly. He was concerned with Mark's future. They represented two differing but equally cogent points of view.

Someone has observed that the clash of keen minds and strong personalities is at least preferable to the acquiescence of thoughtless weaklings. Perhaps the question is Why could not the same Spirit who produced unity at the Jerusalem conference not bring a harmony of view between these two leaders? For one thing, this issue was not concerned with a fundamental, but only an incidental issue. "In essentials, unity; in nonessentials, liberty; in all things, charity." There is no evidence that charity was lacking here. There was no expression of ill will between the two.

But also, the whole issue may have been aggravated by an emotional coloring. How frequently emotional bias distorts thinking and thus decision! Barnabas had a natural attachment to Mark. It has been suggested that Paul may have been unconsciously influenced by the memory of events described in Gal. 2:11-14, where Paul records that "Barnabas also was carried away with their dissimulation," referring to the refusal of Peter and certain Jews at Antioch to eat with Gentiles. After all, was Barnabas not too easily moved? Could his judgment not be faulty again?

There is real sadness in the parting of these men. Each owed much to the other. Doubtless they greatly loved and respected one another in the light of past associations. Such human failure and infirmity as they displayed is not sin, although it needs and receives the covering of the atoning blood.

2. *The overruling providence of God* is the encouraging sequel to the incident. Paul's intention was to revisit the churches which they had started on their first tour. He was motivated by love and concern for the brethren and for the conservation of the Church. In God's providence an even larger purpose, the extension of the Church into Europe, was accomplished.

Not one but two missionary tours resulted. Silas found his opportunity to move into an unforgettable experience and a work of historic significance. John Mark, who probably needed both the severity of Paul and the compassion of Barnabas, made himself indispensable by his faithful labors (cf. Paul's statement in 2 Tim. 4:11). The confidence of Barnabas was vindicated by the man who wrote a part of our New Testament, likely under Peter's tutelage. Barnabas and Paul remained in hearty fellowship (cf. 1 Cor. 9:6).

God has "a thousand ways" to accomplish His purposes when He has people who are fully devoted to His will. It is a false concept of providence which holds that our honest but human blunders confine our lives henceforth to some second-best and inferior path. No one need lose heart so long as his will is in tune with his Lord's.

Luke's narrative is from this point concerned with the expansion of the Church under Paul's efforts. Barnabas and Mark return to Cyprus and drop from view in the Book of Acts, but not from great and useful service.

ACTS 16

Opening a New Field of Service

Acts 16:1-15

1 Then came he to Derbe and Lystra: and, behold, a certain disciple was there, named Timotheus, the son of a certain woman, which was a Jewess, and believed; but his father was a Greek:
2 Which was well reported of by the brethren that were at Lystra and Iconium.
3 Him would Paul have to go forth with him; and took and circumcised him because of the Jews which were in those quarters: for they knew all that his father was a Greek.
4 And as they went through the cities, they delivered them the decrees for to keep, that were ordained of the apostles and elders which were at Jerusalem.
5 And so were the churches established in the faith, and increased in number daily.
6 Now when they had gone throughout Phrygia and the region of Galatia, and were forbidden of the Holy Ghost to preach the word in Asia,
7 After they were come to Mysia, they assayed to go into Bithynia: but the Spirit suffered them not.
8 And they passing by Mysia came down to Troas.
9 And a vision appeared to Paul in the night; there stood a man of Macedonia, and prayed him, saying, Come over into Macedonia, and help us.
10 And after he had seen the vision, immediately we endeavoured to go into Macedonia, assuredly gathering that the Lord had called us for to preach the gospel unto them.
11 Therefore loosing from Troas, we came with a straight course to Samothracia, and the next day to Neapolis;
12 And from thence to Philippi, which is the chief city of that part of Macedonia, and a colony: and we were in that city abiding certain days.
13 And on the sabbath we went out of the city by a river side, where prayer was wont to be made; and we sat down, and spake unto the women which resorted thither.
14 And a certain woman named Lydia, a seller of purple, of the city of Thyatira, which worshipped God, heard us: whose heart the Lord opened, that she attended unto the things which were spoken of Paul.
15 And when she was baptized, and her household, she besought us, saying, If ye have judged me to be faithful to the Lord, come into my house, and abide there. And she constrained us.

It is at this point that we move with Luke into the crowning and most productive period of Paul's great career. The second and third missionary journeys are really in Luke's narrative one undivided campaign. In one sense all that came before them was preparation, and what followed was sequel. Antioch really ceased to be Paul's base of operations. Other cities became temporary and successive centers for his work. The Roman provinces ringing the Aegean Sea (Macedonia, Achaia, and Asia) with their capitals (Thessolonica, Corinth, and Ephesus)—vital, teeming centers of Greek civilization and culture—were the new arena for Christian missionary action. In this period of activity Paul wrote 1 and 2 Thessalonians, Galatians, 1 and 2 Corinthians, and Romans, and to the churches of this area he later sent Philippians, Philemon, Colossians, and Ephesians.

This is the period of the gospel's penetration of the Roman Western world which was thought of as including the great Roman province of Asia, the western end of Asia Minor, rather than ending at the edge of what is modern Europe. Luke would only end his story when Rome itself had been reached.

1. *Faithful helpers* were soon added to the missionary party. Travelling this time by land, Paul and Silas would pass through northern Syria into the province of Cilicia and the city of Tarsus, Paul's native city. From there they would go through the famed Cilician Gates, the mountain pass to the north of Tarsus, then westward to Derbe, and on to Lystra not far to the northwest. At this point Paul was revisiting the churches founded on the first journey a few years earlier.

a. Timothy was a convert from the earlier visit, along with his mother Eunice and grandmother Lois. Luke seems to indicate that his father, a Greek, was dead. Timothy had been brought up as a Jew by his Jewess mother and was well trained in the Scriptures as a child (2 Tim. 3:14-15). Now he enjoyed an excellent reputation among the believers at Lystra and the neighboring church at Iconium, a very important qualification for his new work. Likely because of his mixed parentage, he had not been circumcised. Paul greatly desired to take the young and promising Timothy with them as a skilled helper. No doubt he also saw in him, his "son in the faith," a successor in some aspects of his own work. In order to clarify Timothy's status and thus enhance his acceptance, especially by the Jews, Paul had him circumcised.

b. In the light of Paul's fight against the Judaizers who insisted that Christians must observe Jewish law, some have found this action with Timothy hard to understand. But *Paul's decision* was based not on necessity but expediency. If Timothy had been a Gentile, the problem would have not existed in this form. As a Jew (the Jewish law declared the child of a Jewish mother to be a Jew), his case would be offensive to other Jews. So far as Paul was concerned, circumcision did not make any moral or spiritual difference; what did matter was that the gospel should not be hindered by a needless offense to anyone (see Gal. 5:6). Paul was not acting inconsistently, nor compromising his previous stance, but in accord with a principle which he himself enuciated, expendiency as an expression of Christian love (see 1 Corinthians 8). It is unfortunate that so many Christians find this principle so hard to grasp.

It may be that at this time the prophetic words concerning Timothy's ministry were uttered, and the laying on of hands which set him apart for his life's work took place (cf. 1 Tim. 1:18; 4:14; 2 Tim. 1:6). At any rate, Timothy began a fruitful ministry under Paul's tutelage.

c. The most likely conclusion from the change in pronouns in v. 10 is that *Luke* himself joined the missionary group at Troas. This is the first occurrence in Acts of the so-called "we" sections, where Luke, in referring to the missionaries, changes from the use of "they" to "we." The common-sense inference is that in these portions of the story, Luke was himself present. If this is the case, then Luke probably remained behind at Philippi, perhaps to further establish the church. The greater detail in the description of the city of Philippi, and the space in the account given to the church, lend some weight to this view. More to the point is the fact that the "we" sections, which end with the story of Philippi, resume at Acts 20:5-6, which records Paul's next visit to Philippi. It seems safe to assume that Luke remained at Philippi for some six years before rejoining Paul again.

How Luke came to join the party at Troas can be only conjecture. He omits any word concerning himself. Perhaps Paul was sick again and Luke was called to treat him. Paul does affectionately describe him as "the beloved physician" (Col. 4:14).

2. This is a remarkable record of *special guidance to their field of labor.* Leaving Lystra, the party, which now included Timothy, must have visited the churches at Iconium, and then Pisidian Antioch, in the Phrygian area of Galatia. In these places they faithfully delivered copies of the letter from the Jerusalem conference containing counsel for Gentile Christians.

At Pisidian Antioch they would be at the point of their farthest penetration to the west and north. They had then to decide where next to pioneer new territory. It is just at this point that Luke inserts (v. 5) one of his typical summarizing statements about the Church and its growth. These summaries in Luke's story are points of departure and indicate that the advance of the Church is moving into a new phase.

From Pisidian Antioch on the southern edge of the region known as Phygia, a road went west across the Roman province of Asia to the great city of Ephesus. It would have seemed the natural thing to take this important route leading to the very heart of Aegean civilization and with ready access to Athens and Corinth just across the water from Ephesus. In the Asian province lay cities like Colossae, Laodicea, Philadelphia, and Miletus, and many others up and down the coast. But what seemed plausible was not God's plan. In some way not explained, perhaps through one of the prophets, they were forbidden to preach at all in the province of Asia. So they travelled northward, assuming no doubt that they ought to evangelize the cities of the highly developed province of Bithynia on the shores of the Black Sea. But by the time they had reached the northern area of Asia in the region of Mysia, they were once again forbidden to cross into Bithynia.

The best manuscripts have in v. 7, "the Spirit of Jesus" would not permit them. The Holy Spirit is identified as the Spirit of Jesus. It is Luke's way of saying that Jesus was present, directing the steps of His messengers in their outreach to the world.

The party had really only one viable alternative. They turned west, and after passing through Mysia without stopping to preach, they came to the port of Troas on the sea. It had been a trip of some 400 miles. They had been hedged about in uncertainty with only negative directions. Thus it is that God sometimes leads us by the successive closing of doors which seem to us to be opportunities, so that by elimination we come to the open door of His choosing. The key factor in finding their way and in the proper timing of their arrival at Troas was their sensitivity and obedience to the voice of the Spirit.

At Troas the open door was revealed. Paul must have discussed his vision and the Macedonian call for help with the others. At once the baffling experience of the closed doors fell into place in the overall plan. Without hesitation they made plans to cross over to Macedonia and so take the gospel into Europe. It was a momentous hour.

Now, Luke recalls, nothing hindered the voyage. Favoring winds brought the ship in two days to Neapolis, with an overnight stop at the rugged island of Samothracia. This 150-mile journey required five days on their return some years later (20:6).

Just a few miles inland on the great east-west Roman road to the Adriatic, the Via Egnatia, was the Macedonian city of Philippi. Here in 42 B.C., in civil war, Antony and Octavian had defeated the forces of Brutus and Cassius. To celebrate the victory, the city was made a Roman colony. This meant that it had special privileges, including self-government modeled on that of the city of Rome, full citizenship rights, and freedom from imperial taxation. To this important city the missionary party were confidently led.

3. *The firstfruits of the future harvest* were soon tasted. The new missionary venture had a humble enough beginning. It is surprising that there was no synagogue in Philippi, since only 10 Jewish men were required to begin one. In the absence of a synagogue those of Jewish faith would establish a place of prayer, usually near a stream. Outside the city beside the Gangites River, the missionaries found the place. The worshippers were women. The four visitors were evidently welcome and began at once to teach. No Christian worker need despise "the day of small things."

Paul had seen in his vision at Troas a Macedonian man, but his first convert was a women. Lydia was a Gentile, a God-fearer, who, like many pagan women of the time, had been attracted to Judiasm. She was a businesswoman, a merchant of the purple cloth for which her native city, Thyatira, was famous. The expensive dye was produced there from a shellfish. Thyatira exported fine purple goods of all kinds. Such a business as Lydia's required a good deal of capital; she probably was wealthy. She must have been a very capable person.

The Lord "opened" Lydia's heart to the gospel so that she listened to Paul's words, not just with natural mental grasp, but with an inward spiritual illumination. This is always true when the gospel is declared and the Scripture expounded, unless it is resisted. More than clear explanation or forceful logic is involved in preaching the Word, useful as these are. The inward work is the Spirit's. Only He can do it. Thus it is that the credit never belongs to the human instrument but to God.

The entire household of Lydia, her servants, and children if any, became Christians along with her. Possibly she was a widow, the head of her home. The strong influence of the heads of households in those days is seen here. Her love for Christ produced also a gracious and generous hospitality. Her words of invitation may mean, Let me express my gratitude for the gospel practically by providing you a place to lodge. We know from Paul's letters that he was careful not to be burdensome to anyone, and apparently it was only after persuasion that he and this three companions consented.

The Challenge of Selfish Materialism

Acts 16:16-24

16 And it came to pass, as we went to prayer, a certain damsel possessed with a spirit of divination met us, which brought her masters much gain by soothsaying:
17 The same followed Paul and us, and cried, saying, These men are the servants of the most high God, which shew unto us the way of salvation.
18 And this did she many days. But Paul, being grieved, turned and said to the spirit, I command thee in the name of Jesus Christ to come out of her. And he came out the same hour.
19 And when her masters saw that the hope of their gains was gone, they caught Paul and Silas, and drew them into the marketplace unto the rulers,
20 And brought them to the magistrates, saying, These men, being Jews, do exceedingly trouble our city,
21 And teach customs, which are not lawful for us to receive, neither to observe, being Romans.
22 And the multitude rose up together against them: and the magistrates rent off their clothes, and commanded to beat them.
23 And when they had laid many stripes upon them, they cast them into prison, charging the jailor to keep them safely:
24 Who, having received such a charge, thrust them into the inner prison, and made their feet fast in the stocks.

In its practical outworkings, the gospel is the implacable foe of the greedy exploitation of the weak for the sake of profit. In the Gentile world Paul faced this challenge more than once.

1. *The satanic strategy of alliance* with any force to undermine truth and righteousness is illustrated in the story. With the demon-possessed slave girl the gospel was at work at the other end of the social scale from that of Lydia.

a. Satan's alliance with superstition, greed, and vice is clear in the case of the girl. *A spirit of divination* is literally "a spirit, a Python." In Greek mythology Apollo slew the Python, the dragon at Delphi, and was therefore called the Pythian god. Those who claimed fortune-telling powers were thought to be inspired by Apollo. Apparently the girl's utterances were beyond her control and to the superstitious were the voice of the god. Actually, as Paul recognized, she was controlled by a wicked spirit. Then, as now, spirit mediums, fortune-telling, astrology, palmistry, and all kinds of practices associated with witchcraft and the occult were big business. In August, 1975, a worldwide convocation of practitioners in magic, Satanism, and the occult took place in Bogota, Colombia. We have witnessed a great resurgence of this anti-Christ challenge since World War II.

b. The strategy of the alliance of evil forces with the church itself is suggested in the way in which the girl followed Paul and Silas and kept crying out Satan's testimonial to their ministry. Evil forces welcome alliance with religion so long as truth can be compromised or self-interest is not interfered with. While the girl's cries about the *most high God* and *salvation* may have expressed the faith of the demons who recognize Jesus and tremble, they would have been understood by the pagans of Philippi as one more claim by travelling cultists. Pagan religions had their ideas of salvation and their belief in one god above the other gods.

, Paul was deeply troubled by this distressing satanic advertising. Doubtless it was the subject of prayer at the daily gatherings with the believers. The exorcism of the evil spirit in the name of Jesus after "many days" of suffering this indignity, was no doubt in obedience to the Spirit's guidance. The wretched girl was immediately delivered, although evidence that she became a Christian is lacking.

Jesus! the name high over all,
In hell, or earth, or sky:
Angels and men before it fall,
And devils fear and fly.

c. The unsuccessful attempt at alliance with Paul and

Silas was at once followed by a temporary alliance of Satan with the forces of civil law. The poor girl was now in her right mind and therefore useless as a fortune-teller. Her masters (she had several), who could not be touched by her pitiful plight, were now wounded in their only point of sensitivity, their greed for gold. Of course, they covered up their true motives with a great protestation of concern for the welfare of their city, its venerable customs, and its laws. This has a familiar ring. How quick the gambling interests, the liquor and drug traffickers, the vice combines are to invoke where possible the protection of the very laws which they do not hesitate to flout at other times.

Paul and Silas (apparently Timothy and Luke were unharmed) were rudely hustled to the public square of the city, the *agora,* the place where the magistrates held court. In this Roman city-colony the supreme magisterial powers were vested in two magistrates usually called *duumvirs,* here called *praetors.* Paul and Silas were charged before them as agitators, creating disorder in the city, promoting customs unlawful for Romans, and illegally proselyting Roman citizens to a strange faith. The contemptuous referral to them as "Jews" was an appeal to racism and the anti-Semitism always present in the ancient world.

2. *The Christian strategy of victory through suffering* for Jesus' sake is in sharp contrast with the work of Satan. The mob that gathered was easily stirred to excitement by the clever appeals to patriotism and race prejudice. The suggestion of treason against Rome may have caused the magistrates to panic. They weakly yielded to the threat of mob uprising. There was no reasonable inquiry into the charges, no due process of law. The command was given to the lictors, the police-attendants who stood by, to strip the prisoners and beat them with their rods. If Paul and Silas protested that they too were Roman citizens who could not legally be scourged or beaten, their words were lost in the yelling mob.

The shameful and horrible beating continued until the

blood flowed from their bared backs. Jewish law restricted judicial beatings to 39 stripes. With the Romans it depended on the magistrates. Sometimes the prisoner died. Here it was "many stripes." Paul records that he was three times beaten with rods (2 Cor. 11:25). This is the one time which Luke records. To the Thessalonians Paul wrote that they had greatly suffered and been shamefully treated at Philippi (1 Thess. 2:2).

The sting of the injustice was as hard to bear as the physical pain. Without any attention to their wounds, Paul and Silas were finally dragged to prison and placed in the dank inner dungeon, the maximum security. To make doubly sure of them, the jailor ordered their feet to be locked into the stocks, a heavy wooden beam with leg holes which were so placed that the feet were spread apart in a painful, cramped position.

Nevertheless, as always, Satan overreached himself. Paul was learning that God's strength "is made perfect in weakness" (2 Cor. 12:9) and that "the weakness of God is stronger than men" (1 Cor. 1:25).

Amazing Grace

Acts 16:25-40

25 And at midnight Paul and Silas prayed, and sang praises unto God: and the prisoners heard them.
26 And suddenly there was a great earthquake, so that the foundations of the prison were shaken: and immediately all the doors were opened, and every one's bands were loosed.
27 And the keeper of the prison awaking out of his sleep, and seeing the prison doors open, he drew out his sword, and would have killed himself, supposing that the prisoners had been fled.
28 But Paul cried with a loud voice, saying, Do thyself no harm: for we are all here.
29 Then he called for a light, and sprang in, and came trembling, and fell down before Paul and Silas,
30 And brought them out, and said, Sirs, what must I do to be saved?
31 And they said, Believe on the Lord Jesus Christ, and thou shalt be saved, and thy house.
32 And they spake unto him the word of the Lord, and to all that were in his house.
33 And he took them the same hour of the night, and washed their stripes; and was baptized, he and all his, straightway.
34 And when he had brought them into his house, he set meat before them, and rejoiced, believing in God with all his house.

35 And when it was day, the magistrates sent the serjeants, saying,
Let those men go.
36 And the keeper of the prison told this saying to Paul, The magis-
trates have sent to let you go: now therefore depart, and go in peace.
37 But Paul said unto them, They have beaten us openly uncon-
demned, being Romans, and have cast us into prison; and now do they
thrust us out privily? nay verily; but let them come themselves and
fetch us out.
38 And the serjeants told these words unto the magistrates: and they
feared, when they heard that they were Romans.
39 And they came and besought them, and brought them out, and de-
sired them to depart out of the city.
40 And they went out of the prison, and entered into the house of
Lydia: and when they had seen the brethren, the comforted them, and
departed.

1. Grace that gives songs in the night makes the Christian way attractive and triumphant. The time, the place, the physical pain, the dark prospect, the human disappointment—all these were against the song, and yet paradoxically it was then that God gave them a song. Paul and Silas were mingling prayer and praise. Their prayers were songs (likely they chanted appropriate psalms) and their songs were prayers. It was impossible to sleep in such a physical state. The singing and the praying eased the pain of their wounds and their cramped limbs, and comforted their hearts.

The rest of the prisoners were listening in amazement, perhaps awe. Cursing and groans they could have understood, but what kind of men were these? Only men of firm faith, good conscience, and unshakeable commitment could sing in such an hour.

Our best songs are born in the night of pain and disappointment. George Matheson, going blind, and saying good-bye to his betrothed, sang "O Love that wilt not let me go, I rest my weary soul in Thee." H. G. Spafford, on the occasion of the tragic loss of his loved ones at sea, sang, "It is well with my soul." Charles P. Jones, having suffered the loss of his property, sang, "There's nothing so precious as Jesus to me." Some of the parts for the Lord's "new song" can be learned only in the darkness.

And many a rapturous minstrel among those sons of
light,
Will say of his sweetest music, "I learned it in the
night."
And many a rolling anthem that fills the Father's
home,
Sobbed out its first rehearsal in the shade of a
darkened room.

2. *Grace that transforms the most unlikely persons* is the unanswerable proof of the power of the gospel. If the earthquake was a mere coincidence, it came at a most fortuitous moment. Men and women of faith will see the hand of God is such "coincidences" in their lives. The bars which held the doors were sprung loose, the bolts and staples which fastened the chains to the walls and the hasps on the stocks were shook free, and the prisoners could have escaped. That they did not we must attribute to the influence of Paul and Silas.

When the earthquake brought to the scene the chief prison keeper, who probably lived adjacent to the prison, he could see only enough in the darkness to know that the prison doors were open. If the prisoners had escaped, as he assumed, his own life would be forfeited in the morning when he would be unable to produce his charges. From inside the dark prison, Paul could see that the keeper had drawn his sword, and, in the Roman tradition of the soldier, was about to take his own life rather than await a dishonorable execution. Paul's shout that the prisoners were all present narrowly averted the suicide. The jailor illustrates the pagan world's philosophy: When everything is lost, end it all as quickly as possible.

Luke's account is condensed and dramatic. The prison keeper was overwhelmed with a welter of emotions: fear, relief, amazement, perplexity. The guards brought lights and verified that the prisoners were still there. Shaking from his traumatic experience, but recognizing in Paul and Silas a quality that he could not comprehend, he fell at their feet, indicating his new assumption that they possessed magical or supernatural powers.

Luke tells us that the jailor next removed the two missionaries from the prison, probably to his own house. Fear is a wholesome thing if it awakens a hardened heart from its calloused indifference to spiritual need, but fear of itself is never a sufficient motive. It provides the sobering, jarring opening through which the Spirit is able to do a moral work if He is permitted. And so, likely, as they talked together, the question came from a heart deeply convicted of sin, "What must I do to be saved?" Paul did not suggest that he wait until his nerves were calmer or his emotions had subsided. The good news is: *Believe on the Lord Jesus Christ, and thou shalt be saved.* It is not faith plus reformation, or faith plus education, or faith plus anything. It is "Just as I am, without on plea . . . O Lamb of God, I come." *They spake unto him the word of the Lord, and to all that were in his house.* Faith took hold of the word. Not only the jailor but his entire household believed. Because there was no guarantee of another time, they were all baptized as new believers that same night. What rejoicing! Paul and Silas rejoiced in the fruits of their unmerited sufferings. The new believers rejoiced in the forgiveness of sins and in the peace and love which filled their hearts.

What a change the events of the night had witnessed! This hard-hearted, brutalized prison keeper, so calloused in soul that he could sleep after committing his bleeding, untended prisoners to the dungeon, is now making the wrong right, so far as he can, washing and binding their wounds, and setting his own table for them. What a transformation of values and attitudes Jesus brings!

'Twas grace that taught my heart to fear,
And grace my fears relieved.
How precious did that grace appear
The hour I first believed!

3. *Grace that suffers wrongfully without bitterness* leaves

behind a convincing testimony. With morning came the word from the lictors sent by the magistrates, that Paul and Silas were to be released. It is not necessary to think that the earthquake or time to reflect had produced a change of heart. More likely they were anxious to have "the troublemakers" out of town, Perhaps they suspected that the charges were untrue. They were quite unprepared for the word which the lictors (here called sergeants) brought back. If Paul and Silas were to leave the city, they would leave with the courtesies and dignity due to citizens of Rome. The magistrates would have to come and escort them in person.

To mistreat and beat a Roman citizen as they had done to Paul and Silas could cost the magistrates their positions, not to say something worse. Suddenly the tables were turned. It was now the magistrates who were the lawbreakers. They recognized the truth of Paul's charge: no due process of law, illegal beating and imprisonment of Roman citizens. They could not now expel them from the city, but for them to remain would expose the terrible mistake of the magistrates. There was no recourse for the crestfallen praetors but to swallow their pride, apologize in person, and humbly beg the two "Jews" to leave the city. How dramatically Luke sets up the contrast: thrown into prison like criminals and slaves; entreated courteously to come out!

Vengeance, if Paul and Silas had been so minded, would have been possible. They might have scored a turnabout victory over these magistrates and had them publicly disgraced, while they themselves were vindicated. Of course, in the end it would have been self-defeating for the gospel, and it was never in their hearts. Yet, it would have been wrong to merely acquiesce in this injustice as if it had not occurred. They ought not to condone law violation nor fail to rebuke evil. They were true to their own consciences and faithful to the magistrates, too. Besides, this action likely proved helpful in forestalling further persecution of the believers. One imagines that when the magistrates came to entreat them, that being a captive audience, they too heard the gospel.

Deliberately, without haste, after returning to Lydia's house and spending some time strengthening the believers, they took their leave of Philippi. The church was on a good foundation, and, all things considered, it was time to go on. Luke, as we have noted, was left behind.

ACTS 17

Turning the World Upside Down

Acts 17:1-14

1 Now when they had passed through Amphipolis and Apollonia, they came to Thessalonica, where was a synagogue of the Jews:
2 And Paul, as his manner was, went in unto them, and three sabbath days reasoned with them out of the scriptures,
3 Opening and alleging, that Christ must needs have suffered, and risen again from the dead; and that this Jesus, whom I preach unto you, is Christ.
4 And some of them believed, and consorted with Paul and Silas; and of the devout Greeks a great multitude, and of the chief women not a few.
5 But the Jews which believed not, moved with envy, took unto them certain lewd fellows of the baser sort, and gathered a company, and set all the city on an uproar, and assaulted the house of Jason, and sought to bring them out to the people.
6 And when they found them not, they drew Jason and certain brethren unto the rulers of the city, crying, These that have turned the world upside down are come hither also;
7 Whom Jason hath received: and these all do contrary to the decrees of Caesar, saying that there is another king, one Jesus.
8 And they troubled the people and the rulers of the city, when they heard these things.
9 And when they had taken security of Jason, and of the other, they let them go.
10 And the brethren immediately sent away Paul and Silas by night unto Berea: who coming thither went into the synagogue of the Jews.
11 These were more noble than those in Thessalonica, in that they received the word with all readiness of mind, and searched the scriptures daily, whether those things were so.
12 Therefore many of them believed; also of honourable women which were Greeks, and of men, not a few.
13 But when the Jews of Thessalonica had knowledge that the word of God was preached of Paul at Berea, they came thither also, and stirred up the people.
14 And then immediately the brethren sent away Paul to go as it were to the sea: but Silas and Timotheus abode there still.

This passage is Luke's brief record of the coming of the gospel into two Macedonian cities. In both places the same pattern is traced: Christ is shared in the synagogue through the careful use of the Scriptures; large numbers of people turn to the Lord; opposition from unbelieving Jews initiates a general persecution; Paul, the center of the storm, is secretly sent away by the new converts. It is the story of triumph and trouble. The advance of the gospel, city by city, province by province, was no easy road. But Paul and Silas seem never to have entertained the idea of turning back. Theirs was a world mission, and so they moved forward in their costly ministry, knowing only that futher trials awaited them in the next city. Nothing could overshadow the high privilege of taking Christ to those who had never heard.

1. *The gospel always bears fruit* when faithfully presented. The response varies, but the gospel is "the power of God unto salvation to everyone that believeth; to the Jew first, and also to the Greek" (Rom. 1:16).

a. Paul's strategy was clearly to begin churches in strategic centers from which entire areas could be evangelized. The journey from Philippi to Thessalonica was about 100 miles. The two cities en route were passed through. That they, along with the whole region, were later reached by the Thessalonian believers we learn from 1 Thess. 1:8. Thessalonica was the capital city of Macedonia, a great commercial center and seaport on the Egnatian Way, next in importance in the Aegean only to Ephesus and Corinth.

b. Paul and Silas had outstanding success in Thessalonica. Unlike Philippi, this city had a Jewish element in its population. The synagogue provided an open door to begin their ministry. Some of the Jews cast in their lot with Paul and Silas, but a *great multitude* of the Greek God-fearers attached to the synagogue became Christians, and these included a number of the wives of the leading citizens. Many more women than men were ordinarily found among the Gentile worshippers at the synagogues.

Luke mentions that the synagogue ministry involved three Sabbaths. From what we learn in Paul's first letter to this church, we know that the congregation included Gentiles who had "turned to God from idols" (1 Thess. 1:9). It may well be that the full period of the ministry in the city extended well beyond the synagogue period, perhaps in Jason's house. We know that the Philippian church sent Paul gifts during this time, and also that he worked at his tent-making trade (Phil. 4:16; 1 Thess. 2:9). The first three chapters of Paul's first letter to the church provide a fascinating account of his in-depth ministry there, as well as of his deep feeling and concern for the believer.

c. The response to the gospel was negative as well as positive. Here again, Luke takes pains to record that the opposition sprang not from Gentiles but from the hostility of envious Jews. This time they resorted to completely unscrupulous methods. Judging from Paul's defense of his ministry in 1 Thessalonians 2, the Jews had mounted a vicious campaign of slander against him, Silas, and Timothy. When this failed to halt their work, the opposition decided on more violent measures.

Lounging about the city's marketplace were always a crowd of idlers, men without scruples, ready for any kind of excitement. The Jews used this rabble group to gather a crowd which they stirred up against Paul and Silas. The crowd mobbed Jason's house where apparently Paul and the others stayed. Either they wanted to expose them to mob violence or else to bring them before the popular assembly. (Thessalonica had a democratic style of government.) Probably Jason had hidden the apostles, so instead of them, Jason and others of the Christians were dragged before the magistrates (who are here called politarchs, a term only used in Macedonia, an interesting fact because it has confirmed the careful accuracy of Luke's record.)

Jason was charged with harboring Paul and Silas, *these that have turned the world upside down,* troublemakers, political agitators, revolutionaries. It was indirectly an immense tribute to the effectiveness of the Christian message in the world. Wherever the gospel went, it made a powerful difference; it could never be simply ignored as could other religious fads.

The bold and serious charge of treason could not be ignored by the politarchs. There was a slight plausibility to it. Paul *did* preach Jesus as Lord of all. We know that he taught at Thessalonica the doctrine of Christ's second coming in power and glory (cf. 2 Thess. 2:5). He seemed careful, however, to avoid using the term *king,* probably because it would be easily misunderstood in the Roman world. Among the Jews, he might have spoken of the kingdom of heaven. But the charge of treason against Caesar was knowingly trumped up.

d. In God's providence no real harm was done to the church. Jason and the others were required to provide guarantees against the recurrence of the trouble. This probably involved putting up a bond, a sum of money, with the magistrates, which would be forfeited if Paul returned. Perhaps this is what Paul means when he writes that he would have returned, "but Satan hindered us" (1 Thess. 2:18).

It was thus that Paul and Silas were at once sent by night to the smaller city of Berea, 60 miles to the south. Here the pattern was repeated: teaching in the synagogue; more success this time among Jews; many Gentile God-fearers converted to Christ, both of women of high social rank and of men. The persecution at Berea did not arise from the local Jews but was instigated by the fanatical Jews of Thessalonica, likely with the same tactics used there. The same kind of pursuit had taken place years earlier at Lystra (14:19). It is evident that Paul was the object of their hatred. He yielded to the solicitude of "the brethren" who loved him and feared for his life, and allowed them to escort him out of Berea and all the way to Athens. Silas and Timothy remained for a short time in Berea to establish the church.

2. *The Spirit honored the use of the Scriptures* in Thessalonica and Berea. At Thessalonica Paul *reasoned . . . out of the scriptures.* There was evidently opportunity for questions and answers, for discussion. This would likely suit the style of at least the Greek God-fearers in the congregation. Paul's method was to demonstrate first from the Old Testament that the prophecies concerning the Christ had foretold His sufferings and resurrection. A suffering, dying Messiah was a stumbling block to Jews. Having removed the barrier, Paul then proceeded to place the Scripture record alongside the person of Jesus, demonstrating that Jesus is Saviour and Lord.

The same method was even more effective with the Jews and God-fearers of Berea. Luke pays tribute to their nobility of character, in that they were eager searchers after truth, less affected than others by blinding prejudice. They allowed the Holy Spirit to guide them through their own careful investigation of Paul's message. They were not credulous, nor were they quickly persuaded. These are not the signs of nobility of mind. They examined the Scriptures over a period of days, thoughtfully and critically; and like all who do so with willing hearts, they were led into the truth of Christ. No doubt Paul delighted in this testing of his message. A preacher with such a congregation could not fail to be at his best.

The Bereans, whom Luke praises because they *searched the scriptures,* had given their honored name to many a church, school, or Bible class. Theirs was a solid foundation on which to build a church. May their tribe increase!

Encounter with the Philosophers

Acts 17:15-21

15 And they that conducted Paul brought him unto Athens: and receiving a commandment unto Silas and Timotheus for to come to him with all speed, they departed.
16 Now while Paul waited for them at Athens, his spirit was stirred in him, when he saw the city wholly given to idolatry.
17 Therefore disputed he in the synagogue with the Jews, and with

the devout persons, and in the market daily with them that met with him.
18 Then certain philosophers of the Epicureans, and of the Stoicks, encountered him. And some said, What will this babbler say? other some, He seemeth to be a setter forth of strange gods: because he preached unto them Jesus, and the resurrection.
19 And they took him, and brought him unto Areopagus, saying, May we know what this new doctrine, whereof thou speakest, is?
20 For thou bringest certain strange things to our ears: we would know therefore what these things mean.
21 (For all the Athenians and strangers which were there spent their time in nothing else, but either to tell, or to hear some new thing.)

There is a certain poignancy as well as heroic drama about the picture of Paul alone at Athens, the solitary Christian ambassador standing for Christ at the intellectual and artistic capital of the world, one lonely Christian witness at the headquarters of Greek mythology.

It is not possible to reconstruct the movements of Silas and Timothy with certainty. When Paul's kind escort from Berea left him alone at Athens, they carried a request back for the other two missionaries to join him quickly. In 1 Thess. 3:1, Paul writes of being "left at Athens alone" because Timothy had been sent back to Thessalonica in order to bring word of that church. If we harmonize this with Acts, then either Silas and Timothy rejoined Paul at Athens and were at once sent again to Macedonia, or else to be "left at Athens alone" *means to remain* alone at Athens. If the latter is true, then Paul countermanded his original request to his companions by way of the Berean brethren, and sent Timothy to Thessalonica and Silas elsewhere before they rejoined him. We know that he had gone on to Corinth before they caught up with him again.

But the lonely figure in the famous city of Pericles, Demonsthenes, Sophocles, and Euripedes (to name only a few), was God's man and adequate to the challenge. One man and God is an "overwhelming minority." Certain characteristics of the great apostle shine out in his encounter with the Athenians.

1. For one thing we sense *the intensity of Paul's passion*

for souls. His spiritual discernment and the clarity of his spiritual insights are evident.

Even though Athens, the cradle of democracy, was no longer of political importance in Paul's day, it still represented the highest culture of that ancient world. It was *the* university center of the empire; an aristocrat's education was incomplete without studies at Athens; it was crowded with real and would-be students from everywhere. It was the shrine of greatness in literature, oratory, sculpture, and philosophy. At Athens the immortals, like Socrates, Plato, Aristotle, Zeno, and Epicurus, had lived and taught.

Athens was the home of the most beautiful art in the world. Sculpture had reached near perfection. Even today, the mere ruins of the architectural splendor of the Parthenon and other buildings on the Acropolis quicken the pulse of the tourist. In the midst of all this, and not without appreciation for it, Paul walked.

But what most caught Paul's attention was the multiplicity of religious symbols. Athens was literally "full of idols," temples, and images to pagan gods. And with it all was a hollow emptiness, a vain show without meaning, a performance without even the sincerity of a misguided faith. It was this that made Paul's heart burn within him. He knew the reality of contact with the living God. He had grasped the joyous possibilities of God's grace in Jesus Christ. The futility, the heartache, the moral and spiritual slavery of the human spirit which he witnessed, moved his heart profoundly. He was "stirred," he was angry, exasperated.

Men were destined for freedom in Christ; the human heart was meant, in God's great plan, to soar in fellowship with the Creator. Everywhere in Athens there was evidence of the aspiration, the yearning, the creative quality of the human spirit. But alongside was also the evidence of the vanity and disillusionment of the quest. Luke comments (v. 21) that the Athenians were preoccupied with novelty. Culture had brought no lasting satisfactions. Paul saw past the outward facade into the inward emptiness. Athens in Paul's time is a picture of many of our great contemporary cities.

2. Further, we sense *the compulsion of Spirit which drove Paul to witness* in Athens. Athens was not, apparently, in his plans for a campaign; but while he waited, he could not be silent. He reasoned in the Jewish synagogue and with the God-fearing Greeks; but more significantly, he carried his message into the market, the *agora.* The agora was the heart of the city, the public square surrounded with public buildings, colonnades, and shops. Here was the marketplace and the center for civic affairs; here were the travelling teachers, the lecturers, the eager students, or the curious loungers. Here Socrates, 450 years earlier, had practiced his famous dialectic method. Did Paul use a similar style to preach Christ?

F. W. H. Myers, in his poem "St. Paul," has caught the spirit of the Christian man in the midst of the proud, decadent city.

Only like souls I see the folk thereunder;
Bound who should conquer, slaves who should be kings.
Hearing their one hope with an empty wonder,
Sadly contented with a show of things.

Then with a rush, the intolerable craving
Shivers through me, like a trumpet call—
Oh, to save these, to perish for their saving,
Die for their life, be offered for them all!

3. Further, we see Paul here as *the Christian man, in the certainty and simplicity of his faith, unabashed* by the trappings of culture.

a. Paul was unabashed by ridicule. One imagines that for him, a man of giant intellect, with a superb education, conscious of his mental grasp of truth, the jeering charge that he was an intellectual "seed picker" (the literal meaning of "babbler"), was harder to bear with dignity than was the beating at Philippi. "Seed picker" was slang for any clever, itinerant ignoramus who went about spouting off his bits of secondhand information, material which he had neither the originality nor the wit to think through for himself. It was a sharp and snobbish needling which must have stung Paul's sense of fairness.

b. The apostle was unashamed of his message. There is a line of interpretation which assumes that because Paul writes as follows about his coming to Corinth (right after Athens), "I . . . came not with excellency of speech or of wisdom . . . for I determined not to know any thing among you, save Jesus Christ, and him crucified" (1 Cor. 2:1-2), that he felt he had failed in his message at Athens. But at Athens he also *preached unto them Jesus, and the resurrection,* that is, the whole gospel.

It would be interesting to know what Paul said to the Stoics and the Epicureans. Doubtless he met them on their own level, and for such an encounter he was prepared, for he was familiar with Greek literature and thought.

These two philosophies, each with a history of more than 300 years, were the most influential systems of thought in Paul's day, the only two which had any semblance of vitality, Rather than being purely speculative systems, they aspired to promote creeds of practical morality, Each had religious overtones.

The Stoics were idealistic and dogmatic. They emphasized law and duty. Virtue ought to be practiced for its own sake. They believed in deity, a universal reason permeating everything, predestining everything, the spirit behind everything of which every man is a spark, and into which he is absorbed at last. They were really pantheists; nature was God or vice versa. The Stoics could inspire in some a certain staunchness of character, and yet the system was humanistic to the core.

The Epicureans were practical, pragmatic. Life's greatest good was the avoidance of pain, the achievement of happiness or pleasure. This meant more than sensual pleasure, as for example, freedom of the mind; but it tended to promote mere sensualism, the gratification of appetite. They were materialists, holding to a theory of atoms, and therefore there was no soul and no afterlife. They claimed deliverance from superstitions and fear of death, and viewed the appeasement of the gods with disdain. They believed in the existence of gods but that the gods did not matter to men.

Paul doubtless met the philosophers enthusiastically. His was a moral creed too, but more than a morality powerless like the law of Judaism to liberate in that it was "weak through the flesh." His was the good news that "the law of the Spirit of life in Christ Jesus hath made me free from the law of sin and death" (Rom. 8:2). The missionary even today meets the philosopher with "good news."

4. Paul left a *deep impression upon the culture and thought of Athens.* The request for him to address the prestigious court of Areopagus is proof of that. This council received its name from the word "Areopagus," meaning "hill of Ares or Mars," and so translated in v. 22. But the verse should refer to the council rather than to the location, for the council, or Court of Areopagus, went by the shortened name, "the Areopagus." Sometimes it met on Mars' hill, but it also convened at the agora. This venerable and aristocratic body superintended education and the moral, cultural, and religious life of the city. They evidently exercised the authority to permit or to deny the right of a teacher to lecture in Athens. Before this learned body Paul was asked to defend or explain his teachings. The request was courteous although there is the hint of a threat in the expression "strange gods." Centuries before, the court had condemned Socrates to death on the grounds that he had discredited the old gods and introduced new ones. But that was a different day.

Paul could not and did not care to avoid the issue of the essential intolerance in Christianity. If Jesus is Lord, then no one else can be. The Athenians were willing enough to entertain one more religious view for so far as it would fit comfortably into their present pattern of life. But the worship of God in Christ claims exclusive rights to a man's soul. The fact was then and is still the crucial point.

Confrontation with "the Unknown God"

Acts 17:22-34

22 Then Paul stood in the midst of Mars' hill, and said, Ye men of Athens, I perceive that in all things ye are too superstitious.
23 For as I passed by, and beheld your devotions, I found an altar with this inscription, TO THE UNKNOWN GOD. Whom therefore ye ignorantly worship, him declare I unto you.
24 God that made the world and all things therein, seeing that he is Lord of heaven and earth, dwelleth not in temples made with hands;
25 Neither is worshipped with men's hands, as though he needed any thing, seeing he giveth to all life, and breath, and all things;
26 And hath made of one blood all nations of men for to dwell on all the face of the earth, and hath determined the times before appointed, and the bounds of their habitation;
27 That they should seek the Lord, if haply they might feel after him, and find him, though he be not far from every one of us:
28 For in him we live, and move, and have our being; as certain also of your own poets have said, For we are also his offspring.
29 Forasmuch then as we are the offspring of God, we ought not to think that the Godhead is like unto gold, or silver, or stone, graven by art and man's device.
30 And the times of this ignorance God winked at; but now commandeth all men every where to repent:
31 Because he hath appointed a day, in the which he will judge the world in righteousness by that man whom he hath ordained; whereof he hath given assurance unto all men, in that he hath raised him from the dead.
32 And when they heard of the resurrection of the dead, some mocked: and others said, We will hear thee again of this matter.
33 So Paul departed from among them.
34 Howbeit certain men clave unto him, and believed: among the which was Dionysius the Areopagite, and a woman named Damaris, and others with them.

For the setting for Paul's address we accept the marginal reading of KJV: Paul stood in the midst of "the Court of the Areopagites," that is, he stood with this venerable and august body of men before him and around him. It is likely that the place was the agora, rather than Mars' hill. But the dignified atmosphere was far different from his previous "agora" experiences at Philippi and Thessolonica.

The address is a masterpiece in both form and content. It is aptly adapted to the occasion and the audience. It appeals to the reason but it is also aimed boldly at the conscience. It is both tactful and forthright. It argues but it also appeals. The approach was to pagans, and therefore the use of the Old Testament as proof or evidence is lacking. Instead there are allusions to the philosophers and quotations from the poets. And yet this is not a philosophical address or discussion. From beginning to end all its concepts are thoroughly biblical; it is the God of the Old Testament who is declared. At the close of the address the listeners are confronted with the Christ of the gospel.

1. *Paul declares the eternal God* in His relationships to the universe and to man.

a. Paul's introduction is brilliant. In a few well-chosen words he connects the contemporary life of his hearers to the great theme which is upon his heart. Swiftly, the audience's attention is gained and then riveted upon his theme: God, His nature, His will, His grace.

The reading "in every way you are very religious" (NIV) is preferred to "too superstitious," although both are possible translations. It is unlikely that Paul would begin with an uncomplimentary statement. "Beheld your devotions" (v. 23) means "beheld the objects of your worship."

Having found an altar inscribed "To the Unknown God," Paul takes it tactfully as acknowledgment or confession that in spite of the many gods they claimed to know, there was one whose name and attributes were not known. Just why the altar had been erected is not material to Paul's purpose. He puts the fact to his own use. With one deft stroke he deals with the charge concerning the importation of foreign deities (v. 18). This "Unknown God" he will now declare or set forth to them. No "babbler" is he. He has a word of certainty, firsthand knowledge of utmost importance.

b. God is introduced as Creator, personal and purposeful in His sovereign administration of the universe.

The Epicureans thought of matter as eternal and of the world as originating by chance. But if God is Creator, then the pagan idea of gods contained within temple walls and needing to be fashioned and served by men's hands, is clearly false. Indeed, the reverse is true: All men need Him and depend upon Him. He not only has created, but He sustains all things by His providential care. He is continually the Source of life and even breath.

God, then, is no mere abstraction. He is a personal Sovereign. He is transcendent, that is, apart from and independent of His creation, not confused with it, as the pantheistic Stoics taught. And yet He is immanent, providentially involved with His world, active and concerned with human history, overseeing both "the times" and "the bounds" of human existence. This challenged the Epicureans with their doctrine of chance, as well as the Stoics with their fatalistic creed. Paul also gently rebukes the Athenians' feeling of racial superiority. God sees all men in the same light since all came from a common origin.

c. But there is more. God is capable of personal relationships with men. It is not idols of gold, silver, stone, or wood, shaped by man's skill, which bear the image of God. The image of God is in men, who are His "offspring." Since this is true, God is close, accessible to men. Paul tactfully acknowledges (v. 27) the groping after God in the darkness of paganism. But it is God's will that men should actually find Him and know Him.

The quotation "for we are also his offspring" is from the Cilician poet Aratus, who was making reference to the Greek god Zeus. Paul accommodates the saying to his own use. "In him we live, and move, and have our being" is possibly a quotation from the Cretan poet Epimenides, but this is less certain.

2. *Paul declares the righteous God* who calls men to repentance.

a. God may be known and experienced, but the relationship is not fundamentally intellectual but moral. It is true that where there is no moral revelation of God such as in the law, there is no imputation of guilt, except insofar as man has denied and rebelled against the revelation in nature (cf. Rom. 2:11-16). This time of ignorance, as a child before the age of accountablilty, God has in mercy overlooked (this is a better translation than "winked at"). But a new day has dawned, and a new and better revelation has come in Jesus Christ.

b. Furthermore God has already set the day for the final tribunal of justice before which all shall be arraigned. The day has been set, the judgment is imminent. Therefore the pagans must repent of their idolatry and turn to the living God.

3. *Paul declares the gracious God* who has taken the initiative in meeting man's need.

a. God has guaranteed that the judgment will be "in righteousness" or absolute justice by appointing as final Judge a certain "man," who, being in all points like His fellowmen, sin excepted, will be both merciful and faithful (cf. John 5:27).

b. God has furnished assurance or confirming evidence of all this by raising the appointed "man" from the dead. By this Paul means that He was "declared to be the Son of God with power . . . by the resurrection from the dead" (Rom. 1:4). The Resurrection carries with it also the assurance of a new life now and personal resurrection in the hereafter. It is assurance also in the sense that it is a compelling invitation to exercise saving faith.

c. Paul did not name "that man." He was deliberately inviting further inquiry and in this he succeeded. The meeting adjourned and broke up. This address in Athens is sometimes cited as a failure, but when one considers the occasion and the audience, it was really a glorious success. True, some mocked at the doctrine of resurrection. To the idea of some kind of immortality of the soul the Greeks might have said yes; but to a bodily resurrection their philosophical bias was compelled to say no. On the other hand others wished to hear more at another time. It could have been only a polite dismissal, but more likely as J. S. Stewart has suggested, "Wistfully they hoped his message might be true." These pagans had for a moment caught sight of a light shining into the darkness and hopelessness of their existence. The good news, then as now, seemed "just too good to be true."

d. Some believed. Of these Luke named only two. One was a member of the erudite court itself. What a victory that was! Another was a woman of note who, being a woman, may not have been present for the address but may have contacted Paul on another occasion.

A climate of cultural and intellectual pride does not provide fertile soil for the gospel. Paul's rather brief efforts in Athens did not immediately produce a large harvest. Nevertheless he left behind him in that proud city a body of believers.

ACTS 18

Lights and Shadows at Corinth

Acts 18:1-17

1 After these things Paul departed from Athens and came to Corinth;
2 And found a certain Jew named Aquila, born in Pontus, lately come from Italy, with his wife Priscilla; (because that Claudius had commanded all Jews to depart from Rome:) and came unto them.
3 And because he was of the same craft, he abode with them, and wrought: for by their occupation they were tentmakers.
4 And he reasoned in the synagogue every sabbath, and persuaded the Jews and the Greeks.
5 And when Silas and Timotheus were come from Macedonia, Paul was pressed in the spirit, and testified to the Jews that Jesus was Christ.
6 And when they opposed themselves, and blasphemed, he shook his raiment, and said unto them, Your blood be upon your own heads; I am clean: from henceforth I will go unto the Gentiles.
7 And he departed thence, and entered into a certain man's house, named Justus, one that worshipped God, whose house joined hard to the synagogue.
8 And Crispus, the chief ruler of the synagogue, believed on the Lord with all his house; and many of the Corinthians hearing believed, and were baptized.

9 Then spake the Lord to Paul in the night by a vision, Be not afraid, but speak, and hold not thy peace:
10 For I am with thee, and no man shall set on thee to hurt thee: for I have much people in this city.
11 And he continued there a year and six months, teaching the word of God among them.
12 And when Gallio was the deputy of Achaia, the Jews made insurrection with one accord against Paul, and brought him to the judgment seat,
13 Saying, This fellow persuadeth men to worship God contrary to the law.
14 And when Paul was now about to open his mouth, Gallio said unto the Jews, If it were a matter of wrong or wicked lewdness, O ye Jews, reason would that I should bear with you:
15 But if it be a question of words and names, and of your law, look ye to it; for I will be no judge of such matters.
16 And he drave them from the judgment seat.
17 Then all the Greeks took Sosthenes, the chief ruler of the synagogue, and beat him before the judgment seat. And Gallio cared for none of those things.

This passage is concerned with Paul's ministry in the great city of Corinth, a ministry of at least 18 months, possibly somewhat longer. Because of the finding of an inscription at Delphi bearing to reference to the proconsulship of Gallio in a certain year of the emperor's reign, it is possible to date this period in Paul's life with considerable certainty. Gallio began at Corinth in the summer of either A.D. 51 or 52, likely the former. Paul had already been there for more than a year. It was from Corinth that he wrote his first and second letters to the Thessalonians.

The stay at Corinth was marked by great opportunities, great problems, great burdens, great successes, great consolations, great victories.

1. *There was happy fellowship in a sordid environment.* Corinth was only 50 miles to the west of Athens. The Gulf of Corinth, stretching westward to the Adriatic Sea, almost cuts Greece in two. The narrow neck of land, only five miles wide, which joined northern and southern Achaia, was the location of Corinth. Today a canal allows ships to pass between the eastern and western gulfs on either side of the isthmus; but in Paul's day, goods and even small ships were hauled across in order to avoid the rough voyage around the southern cape. Corinth stood on this land

bridge, a great cosmopolitan, commercial crossroads for traffic from all directions, flanked by a seaport on either side.

a. Corinth was the meetingplace of many cultures and languages. It had a considerable Jewish community. It was the capital of Achaia. It was the home of the famous Isthmian games. But its chief notoriety in Paul's day seems to have been its reputation throughout the world as a center of licentious immorality. All kinds of vice flourished, much of it allied with religion. Acrocorinth, the fortress hill which dominated the city, had a temple to Aphrodite and 1000 priestesses dedicated to prostitution. Corinth was identified with sexual vice to the degree that its name had passed into the language: to Corinthianize meant to corrupt morally; to "act the Corinthian" meant to practice fornication. It was in this city of Roman officialdom, Greek commerce, pagan religions,wealth, poverty, slavery, and moral pollution, that Paul planted a thriving Christian church.

To this church he wrote a little later: "Do not be deceived: neither the sexually immoral idolaters nor male prostitutes nor homosexual offenders nor thieves nor the greedy nor drunkards nor slanderers nor swindlers will inherit the kingdom of God. *And that is what some of you were.* But you were washed, you were sancitfied, you were justified in the name of the Lord Jesus Christ and by the Spirit of our God" (1 Cor. 6:9-11, NIV).

b. At the beginning of his stay Paul was blessed with the good fellowship and the congenial home of a couple recently come from Rome, Aquila and Priscilla. It was the beginning of a cherished friendship. Paul could describe them later as "my helpers in Christ Jesus: who have for my life laid down their own necks" (Rom. 16:3-4). Later they were associated with Paul at Ephesus. They had left Rome because of the decree of the Emperor Claudius in A.D. 49, banning Jews from Rome. This was a year before Paul's arrival at Corinth. We observe the providential strands of God's weaving.

Needing to support himself at Corinth, Paul had sought out in the city the tentmakers, since through this trade, learned in his youth, he often earned his bread, either by necessity or by his own choice (cf. 1 Thess. 2:9). And so he met Aquila and Priscilla, people of the same trade, and he arranged to live with them. Apparently the couple had become Christians at Rome, although Luke does not say so. We do not know the origin of the church at Rome, but we do know that it flourished at this time. Paul had much to dissuade him at Corinth. Without such a happy base of operations his work would have been greatly hindered.

2. There was also *renewed courage out of former victories.* Paul followed his usual practice of going first to the synagogue where he reasoned with the Jews and the Gentile God-fearers who attended (see the exposition on 17:1-4). But with the arrival of Silas and Timothy from Macedonia, his ministry took on a new dimension (v. 5).

Right after Timothy's report to Paul on his visit to Thessalonica, Paul wrote to the church: "But Timothy has just now come to us from you and has brought good news about your faith and love. He has told us that you always have pleasant memories of us and that you long to see us, just as we also long to see you. Therefore, brothers, in all our distress and persecution we were encouraged about you because of your faith. For now we really live since you are standing firm in the Lord" (1 Thess. 3:6-8, NIV).

The word from Macedonia revived Paul's flagging spirits. The ministry at the synagogue and in Corinth had not been going well. But now, Luke records, Paul became "completely absorbed in preaching the message" (Phillips); he "devoted himself exclusively to preaching" (NIV). (This is the preferred text to the KJV "pressed in the spirit"). He changed his method from "reasoning" (v. 4) to "testifying" (v. 5), meaning emphatic utterance or very solemn protestation. Evidently his ministry took on a new intensity and earnestness.

One is reminded of Samson, who refreshed himself

with honey out of the carcass of the lion he had slain. The news and memory of the victory for the gospel at Thessalonica against such great odds, brought fresh courage to Paul at Corinth.

3. There was *a great success after a temporary failure.* The ministry in the synagogue came to an abrupt close. The Jews set themselves up to do battle (literal meaning) against Paul and even blasphemed the name of Jesus. Paul withdrew with great emotion. In a symbolic act he shook out his garments as a testimony that he had done his best to help them. The act was similar to shaking the dust off one's feet on leaving an unhospitable city as Jesus had instructed His disciples to do (Luke 9:5). Paul declared his freedom from fault or guilt because of their rejection of Jesus. He could do no more. He would go to the Gentiles. It was the turning point at Corinth.

It was a bold and seemingly undiplomatic move for Paul to continue his preaching at the house of Justus, next door to the synagogue, but perhaps no other place was suitable. Certainly no one would have trouble finding him. Great success now attended Paul's efforts. Although comparatively few Jews were converted, no less a person than the ruler of the synagogue, Crispus, with his entire family, was converted. *Many of the Corinthians,* that is, the pagan residents of the city, believed and were baptized.

4. Finally, there was *a great victory through trust in God's promise.*

a. The words of the Lord to Paul in the night vision speak eloquently of the immense pressures under which he was laboring. Obviously he had been driven almost to the point of giving up his ministry at Corinth. To the Thessalonians he wrote about his "afflictions and distress" (1 Thess. 3:7) and requested their prayers for him "that we may be delivered from unreasonable and wicked men" and that "the word of the Lord may have free course" (cf. 2 Thess. 3:1-2). We know that the Corinthian church presented him with more problems than any other. There were moral failures, problems rising from an unruly enthusiasm, and from a tendency to factionalism and pride. On the other hand the Lord's admonition not to fear and not to cease preaching coupled with the promise that no one would hurt him, indicates that there were plots and threats from outside the church which caused Paul to fear for his life.

b. The special promise of God was not only that Paul would be protected, but even more encouraging was the word that God would establish His Church in that polluted environment. In the promise the Lord identifies himself with the Corinthian believers; they are His people, His flock, His responsibility. In a congregation where Paul had much trouble maintaining his own place of leadership, that must have been a comforting word.

But the heart of the promise was the word of the risen Lord, "I [myself] am with thee," a very gracious reaffirmation of a promise Paul already knew, "Lo, I am with you alway" (Matt. 28:20). So it is that the Lord reassures His servants in their often lonely task. Luke records that in response to the Lord's promise Paul continued a steady teaching ministry at Corinth over a period of a year and a half. Corinth, like Antioch, was to be a center for evangelism.

c. It is the incident of Paul's appearance before Gallio which is, however, the climactic event in the fulfillment of the Lord's promise. If the Jews had been able to persuade Gallio, the proconsul for all of Achaia, to render an unfavorable verdict against Paul and the Christians, the setback for the missionary enterprise would have been incalculable. As it turned out, Gallio's verdict constituted a precedent in Roman jurisprudence which meant an outstanding victory for the gospel enterprise in all Europe and Asia. Once again, Satan overstepped himself.

Gallio was a brother of the Roman philosopher Seneca, himself very influential at Rome. Gallio is known in secular history as a very intelligent, charming, and generous person. A tourist today at the excavated site of the agora in ancient Corinth can see the very spot where on a raised dais Gallio sat in judgment with Paul before him.

This time there was no mob violence, nor were the Jews so bold as to bring a charge of treason. With a man of Gallio's astuteness, that could have backfired. The charge was that Paul was propagating a religion which was not authorized by the Roman law. The Jewish religion *was* so authorized and could therefore be freely practiced. Paul's worship of God, the Jews charged, was so contrary to their own way of worship that it constituted an illegal religion. It was a sensitive and vital point of law in a superior court such as Gallio's.

Paul would have defended Christianity's legality as the true Jewish faith as he did before Felix (24:14-15) and Agrippa (26:6), but it was unnecessary. Gallio perceived that the charge was properly neither a matter of civil law ("of wrong") nor of criminal law ("wicked lewdness") and that therefore it was not legally within the domain of his court. It was, he noted, a religious struggle over doctrines ("words") and loyalties ("names"). Gallio may even have been informed as to the question of Jesus as the Jewish Messiah. It was, he declared, a question for their own courts, not his. The order was given to the lictors to clear the area around the judgment seat. The crowd was dispersed.

d. The rejoicing of Paul and his associates must have been chastened by the outburst of violence which followed the verdict. It is not clear who was responsible for the beating of Sosthenes, the chief ruler of the synagogue, which immediately marred the scene. The best manuscripts simply say "They . . . beat him." Lenski thought it was the lictors, because Sosthenes kept protesting the verdict. John Wesley thought it was the Jews themselves, probably because they suspected their own leader of secret sympathy for Paul's position. (It is true that Paul joined his salutation with that of "Sosthenes our brother" in his first letter to Corinth [1 Cor. 1:1], and this has resulted in speculation that this Christian Sosthenes is the same as in Acts 18. We do not know.) Probably the beating was the work of Greeks, a sample of the smouldering anti-Semitism of the times, triggered by the court issues. Gallio felt it was politic to turn a blind eye to this minor violence. This, however, should not be taken to mean that he was indifferent toward the issues before him as a judge.

So the opposition was stilled and the stage set for steady growth of the Church. Paul had won through in spite of great pressures. The Lord's promise had been verified.

Looking Forward to a Great New Challenge

Acts 18:18-23

18 And Paul after this tarried there yet a good while, and then took his leave of the brethren, and sailed thence into Syria, and with him Priscilla and Aquila; having shorn his head in Cenchrea: for he had a vow.
19 And he came to Ephesus, and left them there: but he himself entered into the synagogue, and reasoned with the Jews.
20 When they desired him to tarry longer time with them, he consented not;
21 But bade them farewell, saying, I must by all means keep this feast that cometh in Jerusalem: but I will return again unto you, if God will. And he sailed from Ephesus.
22 And when he had landed at Caesarea, and gone up, and saluted the church, he went down to Antioch.
23 And after he had spent some time there, he departed, and went over all the country of Galatia and Phrygia in order, strengthening all the disciples.

In these brief verses Luke passes over the period between the closing of Paul's ministry at Corinth and the beginning of a great ministry at Ephesus. About a year of time and many hundreds of miles of travel are condensed into a few words. We are reminded again that there is a significant part of Paul's ministry about which we have no knowledge.

1. The end of the second missionary journey comes at v. 22, and the beginning of the third journey at v. 23. Obviously Luke was not thinking of these journeys as divided in the formal sense that is usually employed. He seems rather, to be looking ahead to the coming ministry

at Ephesus. Events between Corinth and Ephesus are treated somewhat as an interlude.

We remember that Paul would have gone to Ephesus earlier but was not permitted to do so by the specific guidance of the Spirit (cf. 16:6). Now, after perhaps two years, the door to Ephesus, the greatest city of Asia Minor, was opening in the will and plan of God. But first Paul felt obliged to return to his original home base of Antioch in Syria, for the last time, as it turned out. Included would be a visit to Jerusalem. Contact with the "mother church" was important to Paul. We know how keenly he felt about cementing the ties between the Judean and the Gentile churches. The relief offering for the poor among the Judean churches would also be advanced by Paul's firsthand knowledge of conditions there.

2. At Cenchrea, the seaport to the east of Corinth, Paul caught a ship destined for Syria, perhaps a pilgrim ship on which many Jews had booked passage en route to Jerusalem. The clause regarding the feast at Jerusalem (v. 21) is not found in the most reliable manuscripts and is thus omitted in the later translations. However, it is no doubt factual. Priscilla and Aquila went with Paul as far as Ephesus, where the ship made a call. These good friends took this occasion to move their residence to Ephesus. One wonders if it was to prepare the ground for Paul's coming as well as to continue to provide him a home. As it turned out, they were able to render a great service to Apollos (v. 26).

Luke adds the detail that at Cenchrea someone (either Aquila or Paul: the grammar would permit either meaning) cut his hair because he had taken a vow. The Nazarite and other religious vows were usually expressions of special gratitude to God. The man making the vow let his hair grow for the duration of the vow and then shaved his head. The shaved hair would be presented and burnt at Jerusalem as an offering. Either Paul or Aquila had good reason for special thanksgiving. Luke's purpose in giving the detail was likely to illustrate once more the fact that Christian Jews were free to observe Jewish ceremonials, and often did (cf. 21:20-26).

3. Paul likely had only one sabbath at Ephesus where, as was his custom, he presented the gospel of Jesus the Messiah to the Jews. Doubtless they knew of him from Corinth. Their response was positive; they requested him to continue his scriptural expositions. At this point Paul could only promise to return in the will of God, something he must have eagerly anticipated.

His ship made port at Caesarea, and from there he went up to Jerusalem (the view of nearly all scholars even though Jerusalem is not named). After that he returned to Antioch, from which he and Silas had departed more than two years before. During the time in Antioch he had much to recount to the church which had furnished his first missionary support. Then he was gone again, travelling alone, in order to revisit all the Galatian and Phrygian churches, places known to both Barnabas and Silas on the two previous journeys.

The vital importance of this trip to the strengthening and confirming of the believers can be realized best by referring to the Galatian letter. An immense amount of strenuous and fruitful ministry is capsuled into one short sentence.

Having completed the visits to the Galatian churches, he moved directly westward through the high country toward Ephesus, this time unchecked by the Spirit. And so he came to Ephesus in God's good time (19:1).

Incomplete Christians

Acts 18:24—19:7

24 And a certain Jew named Apollos, born at Alexandria, an eloquent man, and mighty in the scriptures, came to Ephesus.
25 This man was instructed in the way of the Lord; and being fervent in the spirit, he spake and taught diligently the things of the Lord, knowing only the baptism of John.
26 And he began to speak boldly in the synagogue: whom when

Aquila and Priscilla had heard, they took him unto them, and expounded unto him the way of God more perfectly.
27 And when he was disposed to pass into Achaia, the brethren wrote, exhorting the disciples to receive him: who, when he was come, helped them much which had believed through grace:
28 For he mightily convinced the Jews, and that publickly, shewing by the scriptures that Jesus was Christ.

1 And it came to pass, that, while Apollos was at Corinth, Paul having passed through the upper coasts came to Ephesus: and finding certain disciples,
2 He said unto them, Have ye received the Holy Ghost since ye believed? And they said unto him, We have not so much as heard whether there be any Holy Ghost.
3 And he said unto them, Unto what then were ye baptized? And they said, Unto John's baptism.
4 Then said Paul, John verily baptized with the baptism of repentance, saying unto the people, that they should believe on him which should come after him, that is, on Christ Jesus.
5 When they heard this, they were baptized in the name of the Lord Jesus.
6 And when Paul had laid his hands upon them, the Holy Ghost came on them; and they spake with tongues, and prophesied.
7 And all the men were about twelve.

These are two entirely separate incidents which took place at Ephesus. They are nevertheless closely connected, because each points out the possibility of the existence of a subnormal or incomplete form of Christianity—a discipleship and a faith of an intellectual kind but devoid of the inward dynamic of the Holy Spirit. This is certainly implied in the first incident and clearly indicated in the second. Luke is concerned to set forth here, as he does throughout Acts, that the norm, not the exception, for Christians everywhere is that they should be filled with the Holy Spirit.

1. *Meeting the need of the preacher, Apollos.* Apollos was to play an important role in the Church, but apart from this passage and Paul's references to him in 1 Corinthians, New Testament information is lacking.

a. We know that he was endowed with excellent *abilities* and *qualities,* apparently both natural and acquired. He was a Jew from the North African city of Alexandria, a great metropolis said to have had 1 million Jews at this time. It was also a famous intellectual and university center. Philo, the Jewish philosopher who blended Judaism and Hellenistic thought and who taught the allegorical interpretation of the Old Testament, was still at Alexandria. Apollos may have come under Philo's influence. He was eloquent (the Greek word can also mean that he was learned, well educated). Besides this he was zealous, *fervent in . . . spirit.* He spoke *boldly in the synagogue* at Ephesus. This last furnished the occasion for Aquila and Priscilla, themselves synagogue attenders, to hear and meet him.

b. But with all his gifts and training, Apollos had a crippling *deficiency.* He knew only the baptism of John the Baptist, the forerunner of Jesus. He was instructed in the way of the Lord, that is, Jesus; but like John, his was a pre-Pentecost faith and experience. He taught Jesus as the Messiah and doubtless, like John, taught a baptism for repentance as a preparation for the coming kingdom. From what source Apollos' doctrine had come, and whether or not he knew of Jesus' death and resurrection, we are not told. He was *mighty in the scriptures.* He understood how they pointed to and were fulfilled in Jesus, so that he may even have preached them in relation to the Resurrection. But he had stopped with John's baptism of water unto repentance. He did not know Jesus' baptism with the Holy Spirit and fire. At Alexandria he had not been instructed by any who knew the outpouring of the Spirit upon the Church at Pentecost.

c. Equally as significant as Apollos' ability was his *receptivity* to additional light. Aquila and Priscilla were not highly educated, if at all. But they had been under Paul's ministry and Paul had lived in their home at Corinth. They recognized the need in Apollos' life and ministry. Tactfully they took him to their home and in private expounded the gospel more accurately. The implication is that Apollos, gifted and learned as he was, received their instruction with an open heart. One is reminded in this connection of the two ladies who prayed for the young Dwight L. Moody that he would be filled with the Spirit. What a vital ministry such laymen may have! Surely Aquila and Priscilla will share the rewards of the public ministry of Apollos.

d. At once Apollos, under the Spirit's anointing, began a greater *ministry.* One ancient manuscript adds the statement that he was invited by some visiting Corinthian Christians to go to Corinth. A letter of recommendation went with him to the believers in Achaia. He became a great blessing to the church there, and also had outstanding success amongst the Jews, preaching Jesus to them from the Scriptures.

In the church at Corinth the unfortunate factions ranked Apollos with Peter and Paul. Paul, in his letter, placed no blame for the division on Apollos. Grateful for his ministry, Paul wrote: "I have planted, Apollos watered; but God gave the increase" (1 Cor. 3:6). In 2 Cor. 16:12 Paul speaks of him as a "brother," evidently then laboring at Ephesus, and indicates that he had desired him to return again to Corinth but that Apollos had willed otherwise, possibly to avoid risk of further factionalism in that church.

ACTS 19

2. *Meeting the need of the Ephesian disciples.* Luke picks up the narrative left off at 18:23 and records Paul's arrival at Ephesus on the third missionary journey. But before he goes on with the usual account of the beginning of Paul's ministry at Ephesus, he interpolates this second related incident (19:1-7). It likely occured soon after Paul's arrival.

a. The incident illustrates a *defective Christian discipleship.* Paul acknowledges this certain group as believers (v. 2) and Luke calls them "disciples," a regular term used to describe Christians. The language seems to indicate, however, that their case was exceptional. In a great city like Ephesus they may well have been isolated from "the brethren" mentioned in 18:27. Apparently they were not in contact with Aquila and Priscilla who had been in Ephesus for several months at the least. There was as yet no organized church at Ephesus, but there were some believers attached to the synagogues. Further, Luke's statement that there were "about twelve" in the group suggests the meaning "only a small group"; which is to say, their ignorance was the exception among the Ephesian believers, not the rule.

While pleased to find disciples of Jesus, Paul must have recognized their defective faith at once. Paul's sense of priorities in the Christian life prompted his question. There were many questions which would have been pertinent but only one which was fundamental: "Have you received [or did you receive] the Holy Spirit?"

The grammatical construction of this question (in the original Greek) permits it to be translated either "since you believed" or "when you believed." Translators therefore tend to follow their theological bias. In any case the answer was no. More important than "since" or "when" is the true sense of their answer. It is extremely doubtful that they meant to say that they had never heard of the Holy Spirit. Any knowledge of John the Baptist's ministry, or of Jesus' ministry, or of the Old Testament, would have at least introduced them to *the fact* of the Holy Spirit. What they meant was that they had not heard of the Holy Spirit in the sense or in the context of Paul's question, that is, in the sense of "receiving" or being filled with the Spirit. So it is that the *New International Version* translates, "We have not even heard that the Holy Spirit has been given." In fact, John 7:39, which very literally says in the Greek, "The Holy Spirit was not yet," has the word "given" supplied in most versions and is a rather parallel case to this. These disciples had a truncated gospel, which had omitted the good news of the outpouring of the Spirit at Pentecost and His indwelling as the privilege of all believers. In various places historically this truth has likewise been obscured.

Their ignorance at this point was accounted for on the grounds that they, as in the case of Apollos, knew only the baptism of John the Baptist. They knew Jesus as the Messiah, as the Great Teacher, as the coming King, but they did not know Him as the indwelling Presence in the person of the other Comforter who abides forever. They knew of the promised Kingdom; they had not realized fully the present Kingdom which is "righteousness, and peace, and joy in the Holy Spirit." They had responded in repentance to Christ's call to holiness of life; they had not yet experienced the inward power of His Spirit which makes that holiness of heart and life possible. They knew the Jesus of history; they needed to experience "Christ in you, the hope of glory." We may infer that Paul explained the baptism of Jesus with the Holy Spirit.

b. This incident also illustrates the principle of *readiness or preparedness for the Spirit's coming.* The remedying of their defective understanding led to them being rebaptized, this time in the name of Jesus, confessing Him as their Saviour, signifying to all not only repentance but new life in Christ. Only then, Luke records, did Paul pray for them with the laying on of his hands (cf. 8:17), and then the Holy Spirit came upon them. This passage, along with the others, makes it clear that the Spirit's fullness is for those who are believers in the true meaning of the term.

c. Further, the incident illustrates *the Church's universality and oneness through the Spirit.* This is one of the three times in Acts where it is recorded that believers, upon being filled with the Spirit, spoke in unlearned languages. The other two occurrences are on the Day of Pentecost (c. 2) and at the house of Cornelius (c. 10). Here they "prophesied," that is, they preached (in a multiracial city), the plain sense of which is that they communicated in spoken languages. Ephesus was destined to be a great new center for the spread of Christianity among the pagans. Here Timothy would labor through the years as a general overseer, and here John the Beloved would minister at a later time. The pouring out of the Spirit upon this small group of believers in this pagan city was a kind of breakthrough, just as Pentecost was the inaugural breakthrough, and as the house of Cornelius' outpouring signalled the inclusion of Gentiles.

The miracle of languages signified that whether among Jews, or among Gentile proselytes, or among converted pagans far from Palestine, there was but one Church, universal in its mission and calling. "There is one body, and one Spirit, even as ye are called in one hope of your calling" (Eph. 4:4).

The Triumph of The Word

Acts 19:8-22

8 And he went into the synagogue, and spake boldly for the space of three months, disputing and persuading the things concerning the kingdom of God.
9 But when divers were hardened, and believed not, but spake evil of that way before the multitude, he departed from them, and separated the disciples, disputing daily in the school of one Tyrannus.
10 And this continued by the space of two years; so that all they which dwelt in Asia heard the word of the Lord Jesus, both Jews and Greeks.
11 And God wrought special miracles by the hands of Paul:
12 So that from his body were brought unto the sick handkerchiefs or aprons, and the diseases departed from them, and the evil spirits went out of them.
13 Then certain of the vagabond Jews, exorcists, took upon them to call over them which had evil spirits the name of the Lord Jesus, saying, We adjure you by Jesus whom Paul preacheth.
14 And there were seven sons of one Sceva, a Jew, and chief of the priests, which did so.
15 And the evil spirit answered and said, Jesus I know, and Paul I know; but who are ye?
16 And the man in whom the evil spirit was leaped on them, and overcame them, and prevailed against them, so that they fled out of that house naked and wounded.
17 And this was known to all the Jews and Greeks also dwelling at Ephesus; and fear fell on them all, and the name of the Lord Jesus was magnified.
18 And many that believed came, and confessed, and shewed their deeds.
19 Many of them also which used curious arts brought their books together, and burned them before all men: and they counted the price of them, and found it fifty thousand pieces of silver.
20 So mightily grew the word of God and prevailed.
21 After these things were ended, Paul purposed in the spirit, when

he had passed through Macedonia and Achaia, to go to Jerusalem, saying, After I have been there, I must also see Rome.
22 So he sent into Macedonia two of them that ministered unto him, Timotheus and Erastus; but he himself stayed in Asia for a season.

In Ephesus, as in no other place, Paul faced the demonic opposition of the spiritual underworld. Writing back to this church, he said, "For our struggle is not against flesh and blood, but against the rulers, against the authorities, against the powers of this dark world and against the spiritual forces of evil in the heavenly realms" (Eph. 6:12, NIV). All of 20:18-35 is a commentary on Paul's costly ministry at Ephesus. From there he wrote of standing "in jeopardy every hour," there he said "I die daily," and he spoke of having "fought with beasts at Ephesus" (1 Cor. 15:30-32). The latter is likely a figurative description of his vicious enemies. He later referred to "trouble" in Asia, being "pressed out of measure, above strength, insomuch that we despaired even of life" (2 Cor. 1:8). But in the next line he wrote of a great deliverance which came to him. Ephesus was the scene of tears and travail, but also of triumph.

We catch the great challenge of this city for Paul in his words to Corinth, "But I will tarry at Ephesus until Pentecost. For a great door and effectual is opened unto me, and there are many adversaries" (1 Cor. 16:8-9). Of Paul's sufferings at Ephesus Luke only hints.

Like Syrian Antioch and Corinth before it, Ephesus was chosen by Paul as the center of outreach. From here the whole Roman province of Asia was probably evangelized, including the seven churches of Revelation 2 and 3, as well as Colosse and Hierapolis. In Christian strategy this city was more significant than either Antioch or Corinth.

Ephesus was a meeting place of Greek and Roman civilization, pagan religion, occult superstition, emperor worship, commercial wealth, and great wickedness. The temple of Artemis was one of the seven wonders of the ancient world. The city was a cosmopolitan center at the crossroads of both sea and land travel, a free Roman city, the capital of the Asian province.

1. The Word triumphed *through Paul's sacrificial ministry* (8-10). The ministry in the synagogue was longer than usual, a period of three months. There must have been a considerable positive response. But in the end, as elsewhere, some hardened their hearts to the truth, became stubborn, and then began to malign and revile the gospel. When Paul could no longer carry on in the synagogue, he withdrew with his converts to form a congregation, a church. The meetinghouse was rather unusual. It was not the last time, however, that mission evangelism would be conducted in shared public facilities.

The school of Tyrannus would be a lecture hall in one of the several city gymnasia, public buildings set aside for recreational and cultural uses. One Greek text indicates that Paul had use of the facility between the hours of 11 a.m. and 4 p.m. daily. At those hours, in the heat of the day, everything else would be closed for a meal and the daily siesta. Paul doubtless used the earlier hours for labor at tent-making (cf. 20:33-35). At other times he engaged in a house-to-house ministry (20:20).

During a period of two years, this strenuous ministry, carried out with great personal hardship, reached out to all parts of Asia through numbers of visitors from the area as well as the evangelizing zeal of the converts. And to everything else that Paul did must be added his considerable correspondence including 1 Corinthians and another letter to Corinth now lost (1 Cor. 5:9).

2. The Word triumphed *by weak things confounding the mighty* (11-12). God ordained special or extraordinary miracles as countersigns to the false signs (magic) so prevalent at Ephesus. The handkerchiefs were literally the sweatbands which Paul wore on his head while laboring, to keep the sweat out of his eyes. The aprons were the cloths or towels he wore round his waist and on which he wiped his hands. God was pleased to use these symbols of

Paul's privation or limitation as instruments of His power. There is a lesson to that. Limitations turned into power signs! Sweat turned into miracles!

The cloths were mere tangible encouragements to faith. God wrought the miracles. It was the name of Jesus, not Paul, which was invoked in prayer.

3. The Word triumphed *against the false use of Jesus' name* (13-17). Ephesus in Paul's day was overrun by magicians and exorcists. Among them were a number of renegade Jews whose powers were especially sought after because of association with the awesome secrets of the Hebrews' God. Many of these invoked names like Abraham or Solomon. Many were mere imitators and charlatans. All sought to exploit superstition for gain. For the sons of Sceva to announce that their father was chief priest would suggest to the gullible that they possessed a special secret power.

The evil spirit, speaking through the possessed person, acknowledged the name of Jesus, the Name before which demons tremble and flee, and also acknowledged respectful acquaintance with Paul, the man of God. The satanic underworld forces are not ignorant of the forces of righteousness. But the wicked spirit seemed to be infuriated rather than intimidated by the attempt at exorcism by proxy or by the mere incantation of Jesus' name. The effort was powerless.

Only those who love and reverence the Name, those who live in obedience to Jesus' will, may invoke His name with power against evil or in blessing upon the needy. Secondhand, hearsay Christianity is impotent. A salutary and reverential awe fell upon all who heard of the incident. The name of Jesus was exalted.

4. The Word triumphed *over the grip of the old life upon the new converts* (18-20). So well was Ephesus known as a center of magic that books of magic in those days were commonly called "Ephesian letters." These manuscripts were often very costly; like rare works of art they were

likely family heirlooms. They were looked upon as containing the stored-up secret wisdom of centuries. They represented the means of livelihood for many.

Luke seems to indicate that the incident of the sons of Sceva spurred the consciences of and gave courage to many of the believers who had not fully separated themselves from their old habits and superstitions. These people might have rid themselves of their scrolls of magic spells by selling them. They would have brought a high price. Fifty thousand drachmas, considering their purchasing power at that time, would represent in our day a huge sum of money. A drachma then may have represented a day's wage for a laborer.

But good conscience would allow no compromise with evil. The scrolls were burned, their secrets made useless. Figuratively, these Ephesian believers burned their bridges behind them. They did not intend to go back. It was a clean break with all in the past that was evil. The truth is timeless: No one can hold to the new life in Christ with one hand and to his old life with the other. One or the other will claim his total allegiance.

5. The Word triumphed *through Paul's unquenchable spirit* (21-22). V. 20 is another of Luke's characteristic sentences indicating a summing-up and a new departure in the story. From this point on it is Rome which is in view in Luke's narrative. In the mind of Paul it was not Rome only but Spain and who knows what territories beyond (Rom. 15:24, 28). Rome would be a thrilling, long-awaited visit for the apostle; but there was a church there already, and his call was to pioneer, not to build on another's foundation. Always he dreamed far-reaching plans to carry the gospel to new regions. His was the spirit of David Livingstone: "I will go anywhere, provided it be forward!"

But first, two duties called. The churches in Macedonia and Achaia needed his personal touch before he departed, and a visit to Jerusalem was essential in order to deliver the famine relief offering which he was collecting from all the Gentile churches. Nothing would dissuade him from this latter decision. It was an offering of gratitude and love, and a cementing bond between the Judean and Gentile churches.

To prepare the way for Paul's coming, Timothy and Erastus (a helper of whom we have no other certain information) were dispatched to Macedonia. Very likely Timothy went on from there to Corinth (cf. 1 Cor. 4:17 and 16:10).

Christ Versus False Religion

Acts 19:23-41

23 And the same time there arose no small stir about that way.
24 For a certain man named Demetrius, a silversmith which made silver shrines for Diana, brought no small gain unto the craftsmen;
25 Whom he called together with the workmen of like occupation, and said, Sirs, ye know that by this craft we have our wealth.
26 Moreover ye see and hear, that not alone at Ephesus, but almost throughout all Asia, this Paul hath persuaded and turned away much people, saying that they be no gods, which are made with hands:
27 So that not only this our craft is in danger to be set at nought; but also that the temple of the great goddess Diana should be despised, and her magnificence should be destroyed, whom all Asia and the world worshippeth.
28 And when they heard these sayings, they were full of wrath, and cried out, saying, Great is Diana of the Ephesians.
29 And the whole city was filled with confusion: and having caught Gaius and Aristarchus, men of Macedonia, Paul's companions in travel, they rushed with one accord into the theatre.
30 And when Paul would have entered in unto the people, the disciples suffered him not.
31 And certain of the chief of Asia, which were his friends, sent unto him, desiring him that he would not adventure himself into the theatre.
32 Some therefore cried one thing, and some another: for the assembly was confused; and the more part knew not wherefore they were come together.
33 And they drew Alexander out of the multitude, the Jews putting him forward. And Alexander beckoned with the hand, and would have made his defence unto the people.
34 But when they knew that he was a Jew, all with one voice about the space of two hours cried out, Great is Diana of the Ephesians.
35 And when the townclerk had appeased the people, he said, Ye men of Ephesus, what man is there that knoweth not how that the city of the Ephesians is a worshipper of the great goddess Diana, and of the image which fell down from Jupiter?
36 Seeing then that these things cannot be spoken against, ye ought to be quiet, and to do nothing rashly.
37 For ye have brought hither these men, which are neither robbers of churches, nor yet blasphemers of your goddess.

38 Wherefore if Demetrius, and the craftsmen which are with him, have a matter against any man, the law is open, and there are deputies: let them implead one another.
39 But if ye enquire any thing concerning other matters, it shall be determined in a lawful assembly.
40 For we are in danger to be called in question for this day's uproar, there being no cause whereby we may give an account of this concourse.
41 And when he had thus spoken, he dismissed the assembly.

The tumultuous near riot at Ephesus is recounted by Luke in vivid, dramatic language. The precision of historical detail adds to Luke's luster as an historian as well as a storyteller. Several intriguing characters dominate the scenes. Paul, who hardly appears in the action, nevertheless is by far the most important human person involved. But the real confrontation is between the unseen antagonists, Christ and Diana, or Artemis of the Ephesians. The living Christ proclaimed by Paul and the disciples challenges and is challenged by the goddess backed by the wild acclaim of the multitude. The conflict is between the Way and not-the-way.

1. The worship of *the Ephesian Artemis,* here called Diana, had its center in Ephesus, and dominated all of the province of Asia. Her magnificent temple was one of the wonders of the ancient world. It contained no less than 100 immense columns, each 56 feet high. It was the depository of a vast amount of treasure and works of art. Great numbers of priests, priestesses, and other temple employees were involved. The great festivals in honor of the goddess brought to Ephesus hordes of devotees and pilgrims from Asia and beyond the province. Everywhere in the ancient world the goddess was known. The chief annual festival was called the Artemisia, and the month in which it occurred was known as Artemision. It may have been during the annual festival that this incident took place.

Although the Greeks connected the Ephesian goddess with Artemis and the Romans with Diana, she was in fact different. The devotees of this superstitious, immoral worship thought that her image had fallen from heaven. The idea may have originated from a meteorite. The image was an ugly carving showing at the top a many-breasted female form representing nature's fertility and nutritive powers, and at the bottom a square block adorned with various objects. It was a primitive nature deity. The chief attribute claimed was "greatness." It was the pagan concept of greatness as Jesus defined it, "They that are great exercise authority upon them" (Matt. 20:25). Conversely, the Son of Man came "to minister, and to give his life a ransom for many" (Matt. 20:28).

2. *Demetrius,* himself a silversmith, seems to have headed a guild of workmen in this and other crafts related to the making of shrines used in the worship of the goddess. These objects, some silver, some of cheaper materials, were likely small replicas of the goddess' image enclosed in a niche. They might be used as dedicated offerings at the temple, or as souvenirs, sacred ornaments in houses. Their sale provided a lucrative income to a great number of people.

At the meeting of the shrine-makers' guild, Demetrius gave a striking testimonial to the effectiveness of Paul's ministry, and to the power of the gospel in Ephesus and throughout Asia. Because of the Christian impact the shrine-making business was in peril. That, of course, was the real issue. The pocketbooks, the livelihood of these men had been affected. However, Demetrius either shrewdly saw that it would be in their interests to subordinate the real issue and clothe the matter in the cloak of religion, or else he unconsciously confused his economic motives with religious zeal. Unless Paul and the Christians were stopped, he said, the temple was threatened; indeed, even the goddess herself might be deposed from her place. It is worth noting that Demetrius was able to give an accurate statement of Paul's position about idols. He was not ignorant of the truth.

The union of religion, even great zeal in religion, with selfish or vested interest is a subtle thing and seldom is expressed so crassly as in this instance. It can appear in

Christianity as well as in paganism. Its real antidote is the deep, revealing heart-searching of the Holy Spirit. To try to use the Christian faith as the mere means to the acquisition of some self-seeking goal, no matter how legitimate the thing in itself may be, is to play Demetrius' game. God himself, not merely His favors, is the aspiration of true worship. God is not the mere means but the End of pure devotion. God's gifts are not footmen at our service. We ourselves are at the disposal of our Lord!

3. *The craftsmen, and then the mob* which they soon attracted, illustrate the superficiality and danger of mere religious sentiment and feeling divorced from careful concern for truth. It was easy to work up a storm of religious frenzy based on the shallowest of religious scruples. Some began to cry out, invoking the name of the goddess. Out in the street the pilgrims and citizens caught up the cry. Soon there was a mob, all chanting, "Great is Diana of the Ephesians." Luke adds, in undisguised disdain, that most of the people did not even know what was going on. That fact, however, did not prevent them from screaming along with the rest.

Religious emotion is not only beautiful but also essential when it is stirred by a deep response to truth and righteousness. It is a travesty when it is merely manipulated in isolation from the personal apprehension of God in truth and in obedience.

4. The relationship of *Paul* to his colleagues, to the disciples, and to certain of the chief rulers of the province, during the alarming uproar, speaks eloquently of his courage, the reciprocal love between himself and the church, and the high respect in which he was held by persons outside the body of believers.

It was Paul and he alone who was regarded as the source of the threat to the pagan worship. What a powerful impact one gifted, Spirit-filled man had made in so brief a time on that great city! Paul towers above the other personalities in the story. Even so, his assistants, Gaius and

Aristarchus, from Macedonia, were recognized, and because of their association with Paul were placed in a position of real danger.

The ruins of the great Ephesian amphitheater show that it could have seated more than 20,000 people. The mob naturally gravitated to this place of city-wide assembly. Paul's impulse was to be there at the side of his companions, but he was restrained by the disciples who could not tolerate the thought of harm to their beloved leader. Messages came to Paul also from certain chief men of Asia, literally, some of the Asiarchs, asking him to refrain from the risk of entering the theater.

These Asiarchs presided over the provincial council which managed provincial business. But their chief function seems to have been the supervision of the worship of the emperor, including the games, festivities, and expenditures involved. Since this was a matter of great importance to Rome, these officials had immense prestige, often coupled with great wealth. They retained the honorary title after their term of office was ended. Luke does not tell us anything about Paul's friendship with these officials. Evidently the apostle witnessed with telling effect to men of both high and low estate. Like Jesus, who had secret followers such as Nicodemus among the rulers, so Paul was respected by many who were not confessed believers.

5. Who was *Alexander,* and why did he attempt to speak? Luke says only that he was a Jew and was put forward by the Jews. He reached the stage and tried to quiet the mass assembly so that he could make a defense, obviously on behalf of the Jews. Undoubtedly the Jewish community had learned of Demetrius' protest and had become alarmed lest they be required to share the blame for the decline in the shrine-making business. The Jews, of course, were known as fanatical opponents of idolatry. This fact, plus the always-latent anti-Semitism, made the uproar appear very dangerous to them. Their strategy was to clear themselves of blame in this matter by diverting attention

to Paul and the Christians, while dissociating themselves entirely from Paul's message.

But Alexander had no opportunity to make his speech. As soon as he was recognized as a Jew, and therefore an unbeliever in the goddess, fresh fuel was poured on the fires of religious frenzy. For two hours the mob chanted and invoked the name of their goddess.

Twice in later years when Paul was writing to Timothy, then the pastor at Ephesus, he warned him concerning a certain Alexander. In 1 Tim. 1:20, Alexander is described as a blasphemer and an apostate who had put away a good conscience. In 2 Tim. 4:14, Alexander is called "the coppersmith" who "did me much evil." Timothy is to beware of him, "for he hath greatly withstood our words."

There is a reasonable probability that this is the same Alexander of Acts 19. If so, as a coppersmith and a renegade Jew, he was likely himself involved in the shrine-making. Perhaps that was why he was put forward to make the speech.

Alexander illustrates the impotence and futility of all compromising, fence-straddling, "Mr. Facing-both-ways" forms of religion.

6. *The townclerk* is the most interesting and admirable of the characters in this drama. Actually he was an official of considerable power and prestige, the secretary of the Ephesian assembly. As a free city Ephesus had a democratic assembly of all the voting citizens which met three times a month and which cared for domestic issues. The secretary convened, chaired, prepared the agenda of, and recorded the decisions of, these meetings. He was responsible to the Roman authority, the proconsul, for the orderly discharge of these duties. His speech, although favorable to Paul, was, like that of Demetrius, made in self-interest. The disorderly assembly had placed his position as secretary in jeopardy. He took the Christian cause momentarily under his patronage, not because he believed in it or cared for it, but because it was in his own interests and in the interest of the city to do so at that point. He was

a careful politician and a logical and effective speaker. Evidently he wisely waited until the crowd was weary of shouting. The interval also gave him time to acquaint himself with all the facts involved.

a. The secretary began with an appeal to the crowd's vanity, but it is full of scarcely hidden irony. Everyone, he said, knew the greatness of the goddess and likewise knew that Ephesus had the great honor of being her temple-keeper. There was no call for panic. A few strangers from out-of-province could not endanger the unquestioned majesty of Diana. They might shout themselves hoarse but none of the facts would be changed. There was also an implied sarcastic rebuke. If they believed so much in the goddess' greatness, why the panic and all the shouting? The argument is reminiscent of Gamaliel's in Acts 5. The religion which has behind it the force of truth and spiritual power will win out in the end.

b. The secretary scored a second point by reminding them of the innocence of their two hostages. He was evidently confident of his facts. Christians were not temple-robbers, a general term for sacrilegious people, nor were they blasphemers of Diana. It is noteworthy that the Christians had preached Jesus without a negative attack upon other faiths, and that they had impressed the authorities with their honest, wholesome living. All this could not be gainsaid.

c. In the third place the town clerk reminded the now subdued crowd that the regular courts were open to Demetrius and his guild if they had a legal grievance against anyone. They could sue the offenders before the proconsul if they had a case. On the other hand, if the citizens themselves wished to inquire further into this matter, they could do so at a special and lawfully convened meeting of the assembly. He reminded them finally that the present disorderly concourse was not legally constituted and therefore placed them all in peril. The one thing Rome would not tolerate was disorder.

With that the meeting was dismissed. The crisis was

past. Demetrius had been thoroughly thwarted. Paul and the Christians had been exonerated. Luke has added still another item to his list of evidence that the cause of Christ is not in opposition to law and order, is not treasonous, and has indeed enjoyed the favor of enlightened government officials.

Whether Paul was more comfortable under the smile of pagan officials or under their persecution is a matter to debate. At least he knew that worldly patronage of the church is a fickle thing at best, and is always a broken reed on which to lean. There are those who would connect the verdict and patronage of the town clerk with the final Bible verdict on the church at Ephesus: "I have somewhat against thee, because thou hast left thy first love" (Rev. 2:4).

The town clerk illustrates the nobility and justice of sound reason in matters of religion. Yet there is a sadness in the ending of the story. There is no decision for righteousness, no commitment to truth and to Christ. Without reason, faith is without foundations. But reason alone stops short of the fountain of cleansing and new life. After reason there must be decision, commitment, involvement, faith.

ACTS 20

Christian Constancy in Changing Circumstances

Acts 20:1-16

1 And after the uproar was ceased, Paul called unto him the disciples, and embraced them, and departed for to go into Macedonia.
2 And when he had gone over those parts, and had given them much exhortation, he came into Greece,
3 And there abode three months. And when the Jews laid wait for him, as he was about to sail into Syria, he purposed to return through Macedonia.
4 And there accompanied him into Asia Sopater of Berea; and of the Thessalonians, Aristarchus and Secundus; and Gaius of Derbe, and Timotheus; and of Asia, Tychicus and Trophimus.

5 These going before tarried for us at Troas.
6 And we sailed away from Philippi after the days of unleavened bread, and came unto them to Troas in five days; where we abode seven days.
7 And upon the first day of the week, when the disciples came together to break bread, Paul preached unto them, ready to depart on the morrow; and continued his speech until midnight.
8 And there were many lights in the upper chamber, where they were gathered together.
9 And there sat in a window a certain young man named Eutychus, being fallen into a deep sleep: and as Paul was long preaching, he sunk down with sleep, and fell down from the third loft, and was taken up dead.
10 And Paul went down, and fell on him, and embracing him said, Trouble not yourselves; for his life is in him.
11 When he therefore was come up again, and had broken bread, and eaten, and talked a long while, even till break of day, so he departed.
12 And they brought the young man alive, and were not a little comforted.
13 And we went before to ship, and sailed unto Assos, there intending to take in Paul: for so had he appointed, minding himself to go afoot.
14 And when he met with us at Assos, we took him in, and came to Mitylene.
15 And we sailed thence, and came the next day over against Chios; and the next day we arrived at Samos, and tarried at Trogyllium; and the next day we came to Miletus.
16 For Paul had determined to sail by Ephesus, because he would not spend the time in Asia: for he hasted, if it were possible for him, to be at Jerusalem the day of Pentecost.

1. *God's will is not thwarted by necessary changes in plans.* Christians plan as wisely as they can, then add, "God willing." Our best plans are subject to change.

Luke condenses about a year's ministry into the first three verses. As Paul later wrote to the Corinthians (2 Cor. 1:15-16), his original plan had been to go directly to Corinth. The altered plan took him through Macedonia (1 Cor. 16:5-6) by way of Troas. At Troas he expected to find Titus with word from Corinth (2 Cor. 2:12-13) and was disappointed. He pressed on to Macedonia under great personal pressure, but was filled with comfort when Titus arrived bearing good news (2 Cor. 7:5-7). There he also joined Timothy (cf. 19:22).

At this point (perhaps at Thessalonica) Paul wrote 2 Corinthians. Titus went on ahead to Corinth along with two other brethren (2 Cor. 8:6-8, 18, 22) likely carrying the letter. This letter contains much of Paul's spiritual autobiography. It details his struggles and feelings at this time.

Judging from Rom. 15:19, during this trip Paul likely reached the borders if not the province of Illyricum (or Dalmatia) at the extreme northwest of Macedonia. How his spirit burned to open up new territory for Christ! (Cf. Rom. 15:20 and 2 Cor. 10:16.)

Three months were spent in Greece (the popular name for Achaia) with most of the time likely spent at Corinth. There Paul wrote his letter to the Romans, that calm and systematic treatise on his mature faith. In it he expressed his intention to go to Jerusalem with the Gentile gifts, then to go on to Rome, and also Spain (Rom. 15:24-28).

Paul would have gone directly to Syria (Palestine) from Corinth, but the discovery of a Jewish plot to murder him at sea again altered the plans. Instead he returned to Macedonia. The Passover (the days of unleavened bread) was spent not at Jerusalem but at Philippi. To have the apostle there at the Easter season was a blessing which the Philippian church had not expected when they had last said good-bye to him. Paul now rescheduled his plans so as to spend Pentecost at Jerusalem (v. 16).

2. *Handling the Lord's money merits careful, extra effort.* Paul never intended that he himself would handle or convey the offering from the Gentile churches. Carefully selected representatives of the churches would do this and would accompany him to Jerusalem. Seven of them are named here. There were eight if we include Luke. That Luke rejoined the group at Philippi is indicated by his use of "we" instead of "they," beginning at vv. 5-6. Perhaps Sopater went only as far as Asia with Paul. Part of the group, perhaps the two Asians, joined Paul at Troas.

A great deal of effort and time was expended to insure that no criticism could be sustained regarding the handling of these funds, as well as to enhance the act of presentation at Jerusalem. The effort was justified. The example should be emulated.

3. *Worship on the Lord's Day is a priority.* Paul seems not to have given much time to Troas on previous visits. This time he stayed seven days, concluding with the first day of the week, the Christian Lord's Day. Evidently the disciples gathered on Sunday evening. To "break bread" could refer to a fellowship meal, the *Agape,* or to the sacrament of the Lord's Supper, or to both. There is no reason to think that both were not involved.

Paul's message was long, "until midnight," and, after the interruption, his discourse continued again until "break of day." He had so much to say to them, they were so eager to hear, and this was their last opportunity! It is impossible not to compare this occasion with Jesus' discourse to the disciples at the Last Supper. The disciples at Troas, on the Lord's Day, worshipped in the assurance of the risen Lord and in the power of His Spirit.

4. *There is divine strength to face life's emergencies.* The night meeting may well have been the only time that some of the disciples, perhaps slaves, could attend. Eutychus, a young man who may have worked hard at manual labor, struggled valiantly to keep awake, as indicated by the Greek verbs. But to no avail. The many oil-burning torches may have aggravated his overwhelming drowsiness. Unconscious at last, he fell from his place on the windowsill three stories to the ground below. Luke describes it vividly as an eyewitness. Luke, the physician, says they picked him up dead. On the face of it, it was a disastrous end to Paul's visit.

In the restoration of Eutychus, Paul's apostolic office was again demonstrated, and the sovereign administration of the gift of healing was illustrated. Prompted by the Spirit, Paul ministered in much the manner of Elijah (1 Kings 17) and Elisha (2 Kings 4) under similar circumstances. The case of Jesus' raising of Jairus' daughter (Mark 5) has several parallels.

The sleepiness, the infirmity of Eutychus is so human! The sovereign compassion and power of the Spirit through

Paul is so divine! And yet, not every sleepy "Eutychus" is saved from death by a miracle. Sometimes God's strength is made perfect through infirmity. God is sovereign.

5. *God gives patience to cope with human limitations.* Luke's listing of the six ports on the Asian coast where their ship cast anchor reads like a personal trip-diary, which it doubtless is. The problem was that the sailing vessel depended entirely on the wind. Sir William Ramsay says that the wind from the north (they were travelling south) rises in the early morning and becomes calm at sundown. Without the wind and the daylight, the ship anchored overnight.

Why Paul gave orders (the expression in v. 13 is strong) to the party to go ahead by sea while he went the 20 miles to Assos by land, is unknown, Perhaps he was so tired he needed to be by himself. Perhaps the wind was up, the ship waiting, and he was not yet ready. Even our Lord in His humanity needed at times to be alone (cf. Matt. 14:22-23).

Does 2 Timothy 4:13 mean that Paul left Troas so hurriedly that he forgot a cloak and some parchments? Or was it done intentionally because of limited baggage space? At any rate these familiar limitations required the grace of patience.

Portrait of a Man of God

Acts 20:17-38

17 And from Miletus he sent to Ephesus, and called the elders of the church.
18 And when they were come to him, he said unto them, Ye know, from the first day that I came into Asia, after what manner I have been with you at all seasons,
19 Serving the Lord with all humility of mind, and with many tears, and temptations, which befell me by the lying in wait of the Jews:
20 And how I kept back nothing that was profitable unto you, but have shewed you, and have taught you publickly, and from house to house,
21 Testifying both to the Jews, and also to the Greeks, repentance toward God, and faith toward our Lord Jesus Christ.
22 And now, behold, I go bound in the spirit unto Jerusalem, not knowing the things that shall befall me there:

23 Save that the Holy Ghost witnesseth in every city, saying that bonds and afflictions abide me.
24 But none of these things move me, neither count I my life dear unto myself, so that I might finish my course with joy, and the ministry, which I have received of the Lord Jesus, to testify the gospel of the grace of God.
25 And now, behold, I know that ye all, among whom I have gone preaching the kingdom of God, shall see my face no more.
26 Wherefore I take you to record this day, that I am pure from the blood of all men.
27 For I have not shunned to declare unto you all the counsel of God.
28 Take heed therefore unto yourselves, and to all the flock, over the which the Holy Ghost hath made you overseers, to feed the church of God, which he hath purchased with his own blood.
29 For I know this, that after my departing shall grievous wolves enter in among you, not sparing the flock.
30 Also of your own selves shall men arise, speaking perverse things, to draw away disciples after them.
31 Therefore watch, and remember, that by the space of three years I ceased not to warn every one night and day with tears.
32 And now, brethren, I commend you to God, and to the word of his grace, which is able to build you up, and to give you an inheritance among all them which are sanctified.
33 I have coveted no man's silver, or gold, or apparel.
34 Yea, ye yourselves know, that these hands have ministered unto my necessities, and to them that were with me.
35 I have shewed you all things, how that so labouring ye ought to support the weak, and to remember the words of the Lord Jesus, how he said, It is more blessed to give than to receive.
36 And when he had thus spoken, he kneeled down, and prayed with them all.
37 And they all wept sore, and fell on Paul's neck, and kissed him,
38 Sorrowing most of all for the words which he spake, that they should see his face no more. And they accompanied him unto the ship.

While the ship lay in harbor at Miletus, Paul requested the elders or overseers of the church at Ephesus to come the 30 miles so that he might say farewell to them. Luke has preserved a careful account of the message of Paul to this Christian audience. By way of both example and precept it provides a portrait of those who are leaders or pastors in the Church.

1. *Paul's example as a pastor* (vv. 18-21). This should be compared with 1 Thess. 2:1-11. Paul was unafraid of scrutiny of his record.

a. "At all seasons," that is, with constancy and perseverance he had labored.

b. Service was the keynote; serving Christ by serving people.

c. Lowliness and tenderness of heart describe his attitude. "Tears" suggests how deeply he shared the people's needs.

d. Trials and dangers were proof of the personal costliness of his ministry.

e. Both public meetings and house-to-house visitation characterized his teaching and preaching methods.

f. Courage to speak the truth to all parties with solemn words ("testifying") regarding the fundamentals of repentance and faith indicate the content of his message. These two terms really summarize the ethical requirements and the glorious privileges of the gospel.

2. *Paul's consecration to his calling* (vv. 22-25)

a. He was bound by his devotion to duty. "Bound in the spirit" may refer either to Paul's spirit or the Holy Spirit. Indeed, in their interaction, it was both. He was sure that it was right and necessary in the interests of the gospel to go to Jerusalem. An inward constraint sent him on even though the Spirit was forewarning and thus forearming him concerning the things he would have to endure. No doubt those who conveyed these messages urged him not to go, but he could not be moved from his sense of duty.

b. He considered himself to be expendable for the sake of Christ. This was not recklessness. It was not that he did not care about life or care about himself, but rather that he cared more about his commission, his ministry, the gospel, and the approval of his Lord. All of this testimony was made more solemn by his belief at this time that he would not see the Ephesians again.

3. *Paul's charge to the church elders* (vv. 26-32).

a. "All the counsel of God" had been laid upon them. By implication, they were to pass it on. This means that God's whole plan of salvation, the entire scope of Christian truth, is to be inculcated. Only then may pastors leave the responsibility for decision with their hearers. Paul did not shrink back, for personal reasons, from declaring unpopular truths. Neither may they. But it is the changeless counsel of God, not men's own ideas, which is to be declared.

b. In their spiritual concern for others, they were to remember that their first concern must be for their own souls. Pastors cannot teach unless they are first taught. They cannot bring others to God if they are not themselves abiding in Him.

c. Paul used three descriptions of these pastors. They were elders or presbyters. They were overseers or bishops. They were shepherds or pastors. In the Primitive Church these terms might all refer to the same function. The commission was from the Holy Spirit; they were accountable to God. The pastor cares for, feeds, protects, loves his people as a good shepherd oversees his flock.

The seriousness of pastoral care is seen in the fact that the flock is the Church of God, those whom God has called out and acquired for His own possession, and at very great cost! The cost is "his own blood," or, as it may be rendered, the blood of His own One, that is, Jesus, the Son of God. Paul was aware that every man with whom he dealt was a person "for whom Christ died" (cf. 1 Cor. 8:11).

d. The shepherds were to protect the flock against false teachings from two sources. From outside the congregation "wolves" would come, intent on destruction, tearing the flock. From inside the church itself would come self-seeking, self-appointed leaders, hungry for a personal following, creating divisions and schism. We know that the doctrines of the Judaizers, and later, of the Gnostics, challenged this church. Even so, the Revelator was able to commend its orthodoxy (cf. Rev. 2:2-4).

The fact of false doctrine calls for constant watchfulness in the spirit of love, with "tears," according to the example of Paul himself (v. 31).

e. The only sufficiency for the shepherd of souls is God and "the word of his grace." The gracious word is of God's free gift of salvation. It is receiving what God freely gives that builds up believers; this includes their future "inheritance," reserved for all who are set apart as God's possession. But the present inheritance of believers is the sanctifying and indwelling fullness of the Holy Spirit.

4. *Paul's example concerning money and things* (vv. 33-35). If this were not a critical matter, it would not have been included at the close of the address. Material things are contrasted with the spiritual riches of the preceding verse.

a. Paul was conscious of a heart cleansed of covetousness or greed (cf. Rom. 7:7-8).

b. However, he had gone far beyond this, refusing even to exercise his right to support, working with his own hands, so as to undercut any suspicion regarding his motives.

c. Even beyond personal independence, he had shared his small means with others in need, especially "the weak" or the sick who could not support themselves.

d. All of this was in keeping with the words and the spirit of Jesus.

This beatitude which Paul cites from Jesus, is not found in the Gospels, but it is characteristically beautiful. Those who give in the Lord's name are twice blessed. They already know the happiness of humbly receiving their own supply from the Lord's bounty: this is blessedness. But greater still is the joy of being a channel of God's bounty to others, and discovering that in so doing one's own supply is being continually refurnished.

5. *Paul's affectionate farewell* (vv. 36-38). The tender and sorrowful parting paid eloquent tribute to Paul's ministry and to the place he held in the hearts of these believers. Luke remembered the scene vividly: the kneeling company; the fervent, tender prayer against the background of

quiet sobbing; the farewell kiss, as one by one they embraced their mentor and father in the gospel. The ship was read to sail, and Paul was given a sorrowful escort to the water's edge. Finally they were able to tear themselves away (as 21:1 suggests), and the destiny of the great Ephesian church was in the hands of its elders and of God.

The Defense of the Gospel at Jerusalem, Caesarea, and Rome

Acts 21:1—28:31

ACTS 21

The Will of the Lord Be Done

Acts 21:1-16

1 And it came to pass, that after we were gotten from them, and had
launched, we came with a straight course unto Coos, and the day fol-
lowing unto Rhodes, and from thence unto Patara:
2 And finding a ship sailing over unto Phenicia, we went aboard, and
set forth.
3 Now when we had discovered Cyprus, we left it on the left hand,
and sailed into Syria, and landed at Tyre: for there the ship was to un-
lade her burden.
4 And finding disciples, we tarried there seven days: who said to Paul
through the Spirit, that he should not go up to Jerusalem.
5 And when we had accomplished those days, we departed and went
our way; and they all brought us on our way, with wives and children,
till we were out of the city: and we kneeled down on the shore, and
prayed.
6 And when we had taken our leave one of another, we took ship;
and they returned home again.
7 And when we had finished our course from Tyre, we came to
Ptolemais, and saluted the brethren, and abode with them one day.
8 And the next day we that were of Paul's company departed, and
came unto Caesarea: and we entered into the house of Philip the evan-
gelist, which was one of the seven; and abode with him.
9 And the same man had four daughters, virgins, which did prophesy.
10 And as we tarried there many days, there came down from Judaea
a certain prophet, named Agabus.
11 And when he was come unto us, he took Paul's girdle, and bound
his own hands and feet, and said, Thus saith the Holy Ghost, So shall
the Jews at Jerusalem bind the man that owneth this girdle, and shall
deliver him into the hands of the Gentiles.
12 And when we heard these things, both we, and they of that place,
besought him not to go up to Jerusalem.

13 Then Paul answered, What mean ye to weep and to break mine heart? for I am ready not to be bound only, but also to die at Jerusalem for the name of the Lord Jesus.
14 And when he would not be persuaded, we ceased, saying, The will of the Lord be done.
15 And after those days we took up our carriages, and went up to Jerusalem.
16 There went with us also certain of the disciples of Caesarea, and brought with them one Mnason of Cyprus, an old disciple, with whom we should lodge.

From this point on in Luke's story it is Paul the prisoner, rather than Paul the missionary, who is in view. The prospect of captivity dominates the trip to Jerusalem.

1. Luke paints *a lovely picture of Christian fellowship* en route to Jerusalem. With favoring winds their vessel from Miletus quickly reached Patara, keeping near the coastline, passing inside the islands of Cos and Rhodes, with stops at their ports. At Patara they changed ships and took to the open sea in a larger commercial vessel, moving across the Mediterranean to the Palestinian port of Tyre, sailing southeast and only sighting Cyprus on their port side. The voyage took about a week.

a. There were still nearly three weeks until Pentecost. A whole week was spent in Tyre with the disciples. Jesus himself had preached in this Gentile region. By the time the week was over, Paul and his party said farewell to those who had become dear friends in the gospel. The kneeling company at the seashore, comprised of entire families, remained a vivid and precious memory.

Doubtless by the same ship, which had unloaded and loaded again, they made the short trip to Ptolemais, just to the south. Only one day was spent there, but "the brethren" were contacted.

b. The next day "Paul's company" departed for Caesarea, 40 miles further south, but whether on foot or by sea Luke does not say. Their host at Caesarea was none other than "Philip the evangelist," whose ministry, some 20 years earlier, is recorded in Acts 8. What memories must have been evoked and discussed during the days that Paul lodged in Philip's house! Saul's persecution of the Jerusalem believers had led directly to Philip's preaching at Samaria. How Philip must have revelled in Paul's missionary exploits! Paul's resolution may have been strengthened by the recounting of Stephen's martyrdom.

c. The title "evangelist" seems to have meant something such as "missionary" means to us. Evangelists ranked high in the Early Church (cf. Eph. 4:11). All four of Philip's unmarried daughters were prophetesses, that is, they ministered the Word of God, a significant comment on the place of women in the Church, at least in some areas of it. Church tradition says that these women later lived many years in Asia Minor and were renowned as a source of information on the early Judean church. Luke likely drew on this information for his own narrative, especially during the two years of Paul's imprisonment in Caesarea. In those same years, this family doubtless ministered often to Paul.

The expression in v. 15 means that the party packed their baggage for the trip to Jerusalem. Leaving Caesarea, thoughtful and careful arrangements were made for Paul to stay at the house of a disciple named Mnason, a Cypriot, one whose roots in the Church likely went right back to Pentecost. Verse 16 can be translated, "They brought us to Mnason," perhaps at Jerusalem, although others prefer to think Paul lodged at this home en route to Jerusalem.

2. Luke also portrays *the strenuous testing of Paul's Christian resolution.* The disciples at Tyre warned Paul not to go to Jerusalem. Again at Caesarea, Agabus, no doubt the same Jerusalem prophet mentioned in Acts 11:28, prophesied by the Holy Spirit that at Jerusalem the Jews would bind Paul and "deliver him into the hands of the Gentiles." In fulfillment, Paul was actually bound by the Roman authorities, but at the instigation of the Jews. The dramatic manner of Agubus' message made it even more solemn. One is reminded of other acted-out prophecies by Isaiah (Isaiah 20) and Ezekiel (Ezekiel 4). Agabus did not, however, request Paul not to go to Jerusalem.

a. These were not the first solemn warnings Paul had received. At Ephesus he had stated that "the Holy Ghost witnesseth in every city, saying that bonds and afflictions abide me" (20:23).

It is evident that Paul regarded these Spirit-directed warnings as God's gracious way of preparing and forarming him for the trials ahead. He remained unmoved in his purpose to fulfill his mission at Jerusalem. The Christian brethren on the other hand, including at last the members of his own travelling group (v. 12), began to intreat him even with tears not to go.

We can understand the loving concern and overpowering human sentiment which swayed the brethren to beg Paul to avoid the course he had set. We need not judge them harshly. This is a human situation which is often repeated. It is not their decision but Paul's. The could not know the deep convictions of Paul's heart. Yet Paul reveals by his gentle rebuke how they had allowed their sympathy and sentiment to become a stumbling block to him: "Why do you crush my heart?" The words indicate tremendous pressure on his will, the temptation to weaken in his resolution. Sometimes one's most serious temptation to take an easier, lesser way comes from well-meaning friends.

b. Why was Paul so sure that he ought to go to Jerusalem, even to the point of suffering death if necessary? Without question he was motiviated by his passion to fulfill the call of Christ upon his life. He saw in the presentation of the Gentile offering for the Jewish Christians a means of healing misunderstandings and making the two sections of the Church one in Christ. It was to him the tangible expression of his desperate desire to win for Christ his brethren after the flesh, the Jews (cf. Rom. 9:1-5). This mission was, for him, God's will, a conviction of long standing, and he could not swerve from it. To their credit, his friends acquiesced, whether or not they really understood Paul's determination, saying, "The will of the Lord be done."

There are remarkable parallels, perhaps consciously drawn, between this story and the account of Jesus going up to Jerusalem to His death. Then also there were warnings, entreaties by friends, and at last, the agony in the Garden, climaxed by the prayer "Nevertheless, not as I will, but as thou wilt." Like his Lord, Paul set his face to go to Jerusalem.

Every man called of God will somewhere face his own Jerusalem road struggle. In that lonely hour God will give him strength to go on.

A Matter of Expediency

Acts 21:17-26

> 17 And when we were come to Jerusalem, the brethren received us gladly.
> 18 And the day following Paul went in with us unto James; and all the elders were present.
> 19 And when he had saluted them, he declared particularly what things God had wrought among the Gentiles by his ministry.
> 20 And when they heard it, they glorified the Lord, and said unto him, Thou seëst, brother, how many thousands of Jews there are which believe; and they are all zealous of the law:
> 21 And they are informed of thee, that thou teachest all the Jews which are among the Gentiles to forsake Moses, saying that they ought not to circumcise their children, neither to walk after the customs.
> 22 What is it therefore? the multitude must needs come together: for they will hear that thou art come.
> 23 Do therefore this that we say to thee: We have four men which have a vow on them;
> 24 Them take, and purify thyself with them, and be at charges with them, that they may shave their heads: and all may know that those things, whereof they were informed concerning thee, are nothing; but that thou thyself also walkest orderly, and keepest the law.
> 25 As touching the Gentiles which believe, we have written and concluded that they observe no such thing, save only that they keep themselves from things offered to idols, and from blood, and from strangled, and from fornication.
> 26 Then Paul took the men, and the next day purifying himself with them entered into the temple, to signify the accomplishment of the days of purification, until that an offering should be offered for every one of them.

At Jerusalem, Paul and his party of delegates from the Gentile churches were received with glad hospitality. James, the Lord's brother, still presided over the Jewish church supported by the elders or overseers, who by this time had likely grown to a considerable number. At a meeting with this group the delegates no doubt presented the offerings from the Gentile churches. Then Paul recited God's work among the Gentiles. That the Gentiles were being saved by faith in Christ without works of the law, presented no problem to this group. Indeed, for this "they glorified the Lord."

Nevertheless, they confronted a problem concerning Paul's presence in Jerusalem which involved the believers and the populace as a whole.

1. *The position of most Jewish believers,* "all zealous of the law," and numbering a great multitude, posed a barrier to reconciliation with the Gentile church. To these believers, Paul's reception of Gentile converts into the church without circumcision could at least be tolerated. (To unbelieving Jews Paul was, of course, a renegade, because he saw Jews and Gentiles as equals in God's sight.) It was rumored, however, that Paul also taught Christian *Jews* to abandon the Mosaic rituals and even to disregard circumcision. This they could not tolerate.

These "law-keeping" Christian Jews were likely the overwhelming majority in the Jerusalem church, although there were also others more mature in faith and with broader vision.

2. *The position of James and the elders* was one of mediation. They did not accept the rumor regarding Paul's position, but they feared that the influence of the Judaizers would undo Paul's mission to Jerusalem and turn it into a defeat. They proposed a plan to prove to all and sundry that the rumor was false.

There were four believers who had taken a Nazarite vow; for what reason is unimportant. Evidently they had also incurred some ceremonial defilement from which they had to be purified after "seven days" (v. 27). At the fulfillment of a Nazarite vow a man shaved his head and burned the hair at the door of the Temple. Then he offered two lambs and a ram, along with meal and drink offerings. Frequently poor worshippers could not afford these offerings, and then some wealthy person provided the money for them as an act of piety. The elders proposed that Paul pay the charges for the four men involved, as well as participate with them in the Temple ritual of purification. This would prove to all that Paul himself reverenced the law.

The elders made it clear that they still concurred fully with the decision of the Jerusalem conference regarding the relation between Gentile Christians and the law (see exposition on c. 15).

3. *The position of Paul* in this matter has been the occasion of conflicting interpretations. His consent to the plan of the elders is an illustration of his own teaching on the subject of expediency in ethical concerns where matters of moral principle are not at stake (cf. 1 Corinthians 8 and 9). In the light of this it was not *wrong* for Paul to do as he did. Whether it was *wise* has often been debated. There is little evidence that the action produced the desired effect; it did lead to his arrest and nearly to his death.

Paul did, at times, make use of his ancestral Jewish law customs in his personal devotional life (cf. Acts 18:18). These things were for him matters of indifference without any vital connection with salvation. He would have contended even with his life that justification was by faith without the works of the law. He insisted that Gentiles should be entirely free of the Mosaic ceremonial law. Circumcision was to him nothing in itself (1 Cor. 7:19). Jewish Christians might keep the ceremonial law if they chose, but they would do it as Jewish custom, not as a Christian obligation.

On this occasion Paul was doubtless motivated by his great passion to win his countrymen to Christ and to cement the Church. He would become "as under the law" so that he might win those under the law (cf. 1 Cor. 9: 19-22).

Keeping on Course in the Storm

Acts 21:27-40a

27 And when the seven days were almost ended, the Jews which were of Asia, when they saw him in the temple, stirred up all the people, and laid hands on him,
28 Crying out, Men of Israel, help: This is the man, that teacheth all men every where against the people, and the law, and this place: and further brought Greeks also into the temple, and hath polluted this holy place.
29 (For they had seen before with him in the city Trophimus an Ephesian, whom they supposed that Paul had brought into the temple.)
30 And all the city was moved, and the people ran together: and they took Paul, and drew him out of the temple: and forthwith the doors were shut.
31 And as they went about to kill him, tidings came unto the chief captain of the band, that all Jerusalem was in an uproar.
32 Who immediately took soldiers and centurions, and ran down unto them: and when they saw the chief captain and the soldiers, they left beating of Paul.
33 Then the chief captain came near, and took him, and commanded him to be bound with two chains; and demanded who he was, and what he had done.
34 And some cried one thing, some another, among the multitude: and when he could not know the certainty for the tumult, he commanded him to be carried into the castle.
35 And when he came upon the stairs, so it was, that he was borne of the soldiers for the violence of the people.
36 For the multitude of the people followed after, crying, Away with him.
37 And as Paul was to be led into the castle, he said unto the chief captain, May I speak unto thee? Who said, Canst thou speak Greek?
38 Art not thou that Egyptian, which before these days madest an uproar, and leddest out into the wilderness four thousand men that were murderers?
39 But Paul said, I am a man which am a Jew of Tarsus, a city in Cilicia, a citizen of no mean city: and, I beseech thee, suffer me to speak unto the people.
40*a* And when he had given him licence, Paul stood on the stairs, and beckoned with the hand unto the people.

The seven-day period concerning the vow was nearly over when the storm of which Paul had been warned broke over his head. Luke gives the vivid detailed description of an eyewitness. After his conversion Paul had never been welcome in Jerusalem. This is the final rejection of the man and his gospel.

1. *Fanatical zeal for religion devoid of love* is the impression one gains from the mob action of the Jews.

Present at the Feast of Pentecost were Asian Jews who

knew Paul by sight and hated him. Trophimus, one of Paul's party and a Gentile, was also known to them. They easily induced in their minds the conclusion that because they had seen Paul with Trophimus, Paul had taken the Gentile into the inner Temple area beyond the Court of the Gentiles, an area forbidden to Gentiles on pain of death. This act would ceremonially defile or pollute the Temple, the meaning of the last charge which they brought against Paul. Such a charge was very serious. Furthermore, nothing they could have said would have been more inflammatory of the volatile religious passions of the people.

The false word was quickly spread. A great, excited, angry crowd gathered at the Temple. Paul was dragged from the inner Temple area, manhandled, and beaten. The gates which guarded the inner court were closed. It was an ugly scene. The mob was intent upon murder.

2. In contrast, Paul was enabled to demonstrate *a clear sense of direction and purpose in the midst of the storm.* Paul's presence of mind and unrelenting earnestness of spirit stand out in the incident. Even in the roughest seas the Spirit enables a fully dedicated man to keep his buffeted ship pointed in the right direction.

a. Paul would have been killed momentarily but for the timely intervention of the Roman authority. The tower of Antonia, the Roman garrison for the city, was adjacent to and overlooked the Temple courts. Two flights of stairs led down from the fortress to the outer Temple area. When its complement was full, the garrison contained a cohort, 1,000 troops, comprised of both infantry and cavalry. The military tribune, Claudius Lysias, was alerted to the riot and immediately rushed to the scene with a contingent of troops. On his orders Paul was seized and chained by each arm to two soldiers. With the prisoner secured, the tribune demanded to know who he was and what he had done. In the confusion he could make no sense of the accusation and so ordered Paul taken up to the tower barracks. So dense and violent was the crowd, Luke recalls, that the soldiers hoisted Paul over their heads when they reached the tower stairs. All the while the mob was yelling, "Kill him." It was the same cry that echoed in the Jerusalem streets at the trial of Jesus.

b. Luke was not unmindful of the debt Paul owed, on this and other occasions, to the Roman passion for law and order. The tribune appears as an intelligent, reasonable soldier. In spite of his beating, Paul had the courage and determination to address the mob. As they mounted the stairs, he courteously addressed the tribune. Evidently the officer had conjectured that Paul was a revolutionary who had incurred the revenge of the Jews. He had assumed that he was a certain Egyptian Jew who, three years earlier, had lured a large following of Jewish fanatics as far as the Mount of Olives on the promise that the city walls would fall down and the Romans would be driven out. The procurator, Felix, had repulsed the uprising with a slaughter. Such fanatics were common. A conspiracy of terrorists known as the assassins, or Sicarii, because they carried hidden daggers, carried on an organized campaign of political murder against those who cooperated with Rome.

Paul's cultured use of the Greek tongue, along with his remarkable demeanor, convinced the tribune that he was at least no terrorist. Paul's response to the tribune's question suggests the surge of a sudden, almost incredible dignity on the part of the torn and battered prisoner. There, in all the fierce hubbub, he was, as always, no mere victim of circumstances, but "the prisoner of the Lord." Strangely impressed, the officer granted him permission to speak to the crowd.

No man ever had a stranger pulpit or congregation. Standing on the stairs above the people, chained on either side to a soldier, and separated from the staring crowd by a company of soldiers, Paul gestured with a chained hand to the upturned faces, and the crowd fell silent.

Paul's Defense to the Jewish People

Acts 21:40b—22:21

40*b* And when there was made a great silence, he spake unto them
in the Hebrew tongue, saying,
1 Men, brethren, and fathers, hear ye my defence which I make now
unto you.
2 (And when they heard that he spake in the Hebrew tongue to them,
they kept the more silence: and he saith.)
3 I am verily a man which am a Jew, born in Tarsus, a city in Cilicia,
yet brought up in this city at the feet of Gamaliel, and taught according to the perfect manner of the law of the fathers, and was zealous
toward God, as ye all are this day.
4 And I persecuted this way unto the death, binding and delivering
into prisons both men and women.
5 As also the high priest doth bear me witness, and all the estate of
the elders: from whom also I received letters unto the brethren, and
went to Damascus, to bring them which were there bound unto Jerusalem, for to be punished.
6 And it came to pass, that as I made my journey, and was come nigh
unto Damascus about noon, suddenly there shone from heaven a
great light round about me.
7 And I fell unto the ground, and heard a voice saying unto me, Saul,
Saul, why persecutest thou me?
8 And I answered, Who art thou, Lord? And he said unto me, I am
Jesus of Nazareth, whom thou persecutest.
9 And they that were with me saw indeed the light, and were afraid;
but they heard not the voice of him that spake to me.
10 And I said, What shall I do, Lord? And the Lord said unto me,
Arise, and go into Damascus; and there it shall be told thee of all things
which are appointed for thee to do.
11 And when I could not see for the glory of that light, being led by
the hand of them that were with me, I came into Damascus.
12 And one Ananias, a devout man according to the law, having a
good report of all the Jews which dwelt there,
13 Came unto me, and stood, and said unto me, Brother Saul, receive thy sight. And the same hour I looked up upon him.
14 And he said, The God of our fathers hath chosen thee, that thou
shouldest know his will, and see that Just One, and shouldest hear the
voice of his mouth.
15 For thou shalt be his witness unto all men of what thou hast seen
and heard.
16 And now why tarriest thou? arise, and be baptised, and wash away
thy sins, calling on the name of the Lord.
17 And it came to pass, that, when I was come again to Jerusalem,
even while I prayed in the temple, I was in a trance;
18 And saw him saying unto me, Make haste, and get thee quickly
out of Jerusalem: for they will not receive thy testimony concerning me.
19 And I said, Lord, they know that I imprisoned and beat in every
synagogue them that believed on thee:
20 And when the blood of thy martyr Stephen was shed, I also was
standing by, and consenting unto his death, and kept the raiment of
them that slew him.
21 And he said unto me, depart: for I will send thee far hence unto
the Gentiles.

The charge against Paul was that he as a Jew, taught a message which was "against the people, and the law, and this place [the temple]" (21:28). The crux of the matter was his teaching that Gentiles could have an equal place with Jews in God's kingdom.

In summary, the defense of Paul was straightforward and plain: He was and remained a patriotic Jew; but God had intervened in his life so unmistakably that his former life had been completely changed. His life and his teaching were now in obedience to the divine command. His message had come by divine revelation. It was God's doing, not his own. This is the classic apology for Christianity.

ACTS 22

1. *Paul* presented himself as *a thoroughgoing patriotic Jew* (vv. 1-5). The language is strikingly tactful and conciliatory. Paul's use of "the Hebrew tongue" (here it means the commonly spoken Aramaic) so surprised and pleased the crowd that they listened intently. Likewise, Paul's form of address was most courteous: "Men, brethren, and fathers." He was doing his utmost to win them over.

Paul made it clear that he fully understood the Jewish faith. Born outside of Palestine in a Hellenistic culture, he was nevertheless "brought up" in Jerusalem and was taught the law with studious exactness by no less a rabbi than the great Gamaliel, one of the most famous teachers of the time. He had lived an exemplary life as a strict Pharisee.

His education had been backed up with deeds. He had been "zealous toward God." Paul tactfully and pointedly adds "as ye all are this day." To the Romans he had already written about his countrymen: "They have a zeal of God, but not according to knowledge" (Rom. 10:2). In our time there are many in the cults whose misdirected zeal for God hinders Christ's work. Paul's mistaken zeal had flung him into furious persecution of the Church. He had written, "Beyond measure I persecuted the Church of God, and wasted it . . . being more exceedingly zealous of the traditions of my fathers" (Gal. 1:13-14).

There were still those in Jerusalem who had known the young, fiery Saul of Tarsus, commissioned to go to Damascus and bring back the disciples of Jesus in chains. There was no question about what Paul had once been; no question of his qualifications as a Jew.

2. *Paul* proceeded to present himself as *a divinely transformed person* (vv. 6-16). The conversion of Paul has been discussed in detail in the exposition of c. 9. Here were need only note the main emphases related to his defense.

It was Paul's personal encounter with Jesus of Nazareth which had transformed his life. The same Jesus who was crucified in that very city of Jerusalem was therefore alive in the unseen glory, and was caring for and directing His people. Paul had seen Him and conversed with Him. Such a revelation was utterly convincing. The evidence, if admitted, was irrefutable. No greater authority could be asked. Paul was saying, in effect, "If you ask of me why I do as I do and teach as I teach, I simply reply, 'Because I have been apprehended for this very purpose by the highest of all authorities. I am what I am by the will and grace of God.'"

Tactfully, Paul spoke of Ananias, God's human messenger to him, as "a devout man according to the law, having a good report of all the Jews." It was Ananias who had referred to Jesus as "that Just One," a Jewish term for the Messiah, the Christ. It was such a one as Ananias who had confirmed him in his new faith. Paul was saying implicitly that in the truest interest of the law, the defenders of the law had nothing to fear from him or from the Christian faith.

Paul's new life had begun with the repentance sign of baptism, with a new allegiance to his living Lord.

3. *Paul* finally presented himself as *a man serving under divine orders* (vv. 17:21). The reference to his worshipping

in the Temple, *after* his conversion, was another conciliatory answer to the charges against him. So also was his seeming argument with the Lord over the directive to depart from Jerusalem.

Two things are implied in his response to the Lord. First, he is revealing his reluctance to leave the beloved city of Jerusalem, coupled with his intense desire to witness to his own people, the Jews. Second, he is making a twofold argument as to why he should stay. His rejection by the Jews is understandable: They know what a persecutor of Christians he had been, and so now they naturally see him as an untrustworthy renegade. He is excusing their attitude. However, this very fact regarding his past makes his witness to Christ's transforming power that much more convincing. He is the logical one, as he sees it, to testify to the gospel in Jerusalem.

Notwithstanding such feelings on his part, the Lord's command was clear: "Depart: for I will send thee far hence unto the Gentiles." The mission to the Gentiles, the thing which was particularly offensive to his audience, was not his own doing, but God's.

The reference to Stephen's death is especially poignant. It is the painful acknowledgment of a terrible crime, but one deliberately made so as to make the point as sharp as possible. What piercing memories of God's boundless grace must have flooded his heart as he spoke! He refers, with a great sense of debt, to Stephen as the Lord's witness (the Greek word is *martyr,* but the word at that time had not taken on the meaning which it now has in English). Paul's debt to Stephen was profound and in several dimensions.

Tested, but Not Beyond Your Strength

Acts 22:22-30

22 And they gave him audience unto this word, and then lifted up their voices, and said, Away with such a fellow from the earth: for it is not fit that he should live.
23 And as they cried out, and cast off their clothes, and threw dust into the air,

24 The chief captain commanded him to be brought into the castle, and bade that he should be examined by scourging; that he might know wherefore they cried so against him.
25 And as they bound him with thongs, Paul said unto the centurion that stood by, Is it lawful for you to scourge a man that is a Roman, and uncondemned?
26 When the centurion heard that, he went and told the chief captain, saying, Take heed what thou doest: for this man is a Roman.
27 Then the chief captain came, and said unto him, Tell me, art thou a Roman? He said, Yea.
28 And the chief captain answered, With a great sum obtained I this freedom. And Paul said, But I was free born.
29 Then straightway they departed from him which should have examined him: and the chief captain also was afraid, after he knew that he was a Roman, and because he had bound him.
30 On the morrow, because he would have known the certainty wherefore he was accused of the Jews, he loosed him from his bands, and commanded the chief priests and all their council to appear, and brought Paul down, and set him before them.

Some few years before this day in his life Paul had written: "God is faithful, and he will not let you be tempted beyond your strength, but with the temptation will also provide the way of escape, that you may be able to endure it" (1 Cor. 10:13, RSV). He was now to experience once again the truth of these words.

1. *The final rejection* of Paul and his gospel by Jerusalem had taken place. At the mention of his call to the Gentiles, the enraged screams of the crowd brought his defence to an end. The mob would have killed him except that he was protected by soldiers. The tossing of outer garments and the throwing of dust was the oriental way of expressing their abhorrence and total rejection of Paul's person. Perhaps it also suggested their desire to stone him. In his rejection Paul had become one with Jesus and His witness, Stephen.

2. *The ethics of suffering* are pointed up in the incident which followed.

a. Completely frustrated by the situation and by his inability to understand the reasons for the hatred against Paul, the military tribune made a peremptory decision to extract the truth from the prisoner through the torture of the lash. Roman scourging was much more terrible than the beatings Paul had already experienced. The lash consisted of several leather thongs tied to a handle, but with pieces of metal or bone imbedded in the thong tips. Soldiers on either side of the victim struck alternate blows. Scourged prisoners were usually permanently maimed; frequently they died. In his weakened condition following the mob beating, Paul would hardly have survived.

b. The means of Paul's deliverance was in this case not a divine intervention but the announcement of his Roman citizenship. As he was being tied up for the scourging (this could have meant suspension from the ground, or being stretched over a low pillar with hands and feet fastened to rings in the floor), he spoke to the centurion in charge. The centurion at once halted proceedings and excitedly reported to the tribune. His warning to take heed was well taken, for Roman law severely safeguarded the rights of citizens in matters of arrest. Scourging of citizens had been outlawed. Had his order been carried out, the tribune might have jeopardized his high rank and even his life. To make matters worse, Paul was uncondemned; indeed, he had not even been properly questioned. Paul's protest had actually saved the tribune from a destructive blunder.

The tribune seemed unable at first to comprehend that this poor, bedraggled object of Jewish scorn, now calmly claiming citizenship, was really a Roman. "A great price I had to pay to become a citizen," he exclaimed. The implication was: How could a person like this prisoner have achieved so difficult a thing? Paul replied with dignity, "I was born a citizen!" Citizenship was sold at Rome as a means of raising funds. Claudius Lysias had bought this freedom. Paul had been born of Jewish parents who were already citizens of Tarsus. We know from the history of that city that Jews had been granted citizenship on more than one occasion.

c. Paul's deliverance from further mistreatment was instantaneous. The soldiers and the centurion who were involved with the scourging vanished. Paul was unbound.

Greatly disturbed by his near-fatal mistake, the tribune was forced to a new course of action. Since he was now obliged to give a proper account of his prisoner, he determined to obtain charges against him by bringing him before the Jewish Council. Using his authority as the procurator's representative, the next day he summoned the council and brought Paul before it.

d. Paul has sometimes been faulted for appealing to his legal rights as a Roman, rather than suffering silently. In fact, this appeal did sever him completely from the Jerusalem community. But they had already rejected him. Needless suffering, even for righteousness' sake, is not a Christian virtue. It is wrong to court martyrdom or to recklessly throw one's life away. Paul's work was not done. Human life and strength are vehicles for God's work in the world, but they are also intrinsically precious in God's sight.

ACTS 23

Christ's Presence in the Dark, Lonely Night

Acts 23:1-11

1 And Paul, earnestly beholding the council, said, Men and brethren, I have lived in all good conscience before God until this day.
2 And the high priest Ananias commanded them that stood by him to smite him on the mouth.
3 Then said Paul unto him, God shall smite thee, thou whited wall: for sittest thou to judge me after the law, and commandest me to be smitten contrary to the law?
4 And they that stood by said, Revilest thou God's high priest?
5 Then said Paul, I wist not, brethren, that he was the high priest: for it is written, Thou shalt not speak evil of the ruler of thy people.
6 But when Paul perceived that the one part were Sadducees, and the other Pharisees, he cried out in the council, Men and brethren, I am a Pharisee, the son of a Pharisee: of the hope and resurrection of the dead I am called in question.
7 And when he had so said, there arose a dissension between the Pharisees and the Sadducees: and the multitude was divided.
8 For the Sadducees say that there is no resurrection, neither angel, nor spirit: but the Pharisees confess both.
9 And there arose a great cry: and the scribes that were of the Pharisees' part arose, and strove, saying, We find no evil in this man: but if a spirit or an angel hath spoken to him, let us not fight against God.
10 And when there arose a great dissension, the chief captain, fearing

lest Paul should have been pulled in pieces of them, commanded the soldiers to go down, and to take him by force from among them, and to bring him into the castle.
11 And the night following the Lord stood by him, and said, Be of good cheer, Paul: for as thou hast testified of me in Jerusalem, so must thou bear witness also at Rome.

Jesus himself had appeared to Paul in his hours of deepest gloom and discouragement on at least two previous occasions: once before at Jerusalem on his early visit (Acts 22:18-21), and again at Corinth (Acts 18:9-10). Paul had special need for the Lord's reassurance on this particular night (v. 11). A survey of the events of the previous day, not to say those of the day before that, will suggest the reasons. The apostle's intended defense before the Sanhedrin had turned out badly, judged in the light of the immediate results.

Each of Paul's four statements before the Jewish Council presents difficulties in interpretation and understanding.

1. *The profession of a good conscience* before God until that very hour raises at once the serious question of Paul's meaning regarding his pre-Christian life. In another setting he described himself as the chief of sinners (1 Tim. 1:15).

The meaning of *conscience* is important here. When we consciously pronounce judgment upon the moral quality of our actions, we call that function of personality *conscience.* Conscience innately tells us that there is a distinction between right and wrong, and that we ought to do the right. A healthy conscience also produces in us a sense of approbation when we do right, or a sense of disapproval when we do wrong. But conscience is dependent upon our moral judgment or discernment or training with respect to what *is* right and what *is* wrong. Thus it was that Paul could say that even in persecuting the Church, he had acted ignorantly in unbelief (cf. 1 Tim. 1:13), but not in violation of his conscience as it was informed at that time. When his moral judgment had been purged and corrected he saw, with remorse, that what he had done was utterly wrong. But sinning, in any proper sense, lies in the intention. It is a *known* transgression.

It must be noted, however, that Paul here refers to his outer life and not to the inward quality of his spirit, when he claims to have lived in good conscience (cf. Rom. 7:7 ff. for the problem of inward failure). The Greek words for "I have lived" suggest that Paul means, "in my outward actions." He therefore refused to be classed as a criminal in this arraignment before the Sanhedrin. Without waiting to be asked to speak, and with little attempt at conciliation, he at once protested his innocence of wrongdoing.

2, *Paul's indignant and severe retort* after the high priest had commanded him to be struck on the mouth, has occasioned criticism. Should he have submitted meekly and silently? Certainly we see that he was a man of "like passions" to our own. Admittedly, his reaction fell below the level of our Lord's in the same circumstances (cf. John 18:19-23). On the other hand, Paul had every reason to be properly indignant. He was correct in pointing out the violation of the code regarding the treatment of those on trial. Complacency toward evil and evil men is not a sign of piety.

What Paul said about Ananias was prophetic. The man was notoriously cruel and avaricious, and practiced even violence and robbery in his pursuit of wealth and power. He was deposed in A.D. 58 and assassinated by Jewish zealots in the uprising of A.D. 66. He was indeed a "whitewashed wall" tottering toward ruin.

3. *Paul's statement that he did not know he was addressing the high priest* has produced still greater questions. How, it is asked, could one so well versed in Sanhedrin procedures fail to recognize the high priest?

Possibly, Paul heard the voice but did not see the speaker. More likely, he meant to say (and the language may be taken in this sense) that his quick and indignant retort had come before he had time to reflect on the fact that he was obligated to respect the high priest's office even if he could not respect the man. The statement was a confession of error. It also indicated his conscientious respect for the law.

4. *Paul's declaring himself a Pharisee,* and his deliberate dividing of the council on the issue of the Resurrection, has by some been considered a ploy unworthy of the apostle. In v. 8 Luke explains that theological basis of the quarrel between the Sadducees and the Pharisees. Actually the quarrel included political motives. The Sadducees, the high priestly party, collaborated with the Romans and thus retained their power. In the council, they were held in check by the Pharisaic party.

In the view of the Sadducees, Paul had to be disposed of, just as they had done with Jesus, because they held him responsible for the disturbance and unrest in the city. On the other hand Paul's reputation concerning his Gentile mission had created new animosity toward him and the Church on the part of the Pharisees. Paul saw it was expedient for several reasons to avoid at all cost the apparently inevitable sentence of condemnation by the Sanhedrin. The subsequent story of his trial shows that his reasoning was wise. His strategy was successful. The meeting broke up without a verdict being given.

a. Before the people Paul had presented himself as a Jew. Here he declares himself a Pharisee. He could claim that his allegiance to Jesus Christ fulfilled in the highest sense all that was truly meant by his life as a Jew and as a Pharisee. It should be recalled that "Pharisee" was not at that time a synonym for "hypocrite" as it now tends to be.

The "hope" to which Paul referred was the Messianic hope of Israel. It concerned the restoration of all things and was bound up, so far as Paul was concerned, with Christ's second coming and the resurrection of the dead.

b. We need not believe that Luke has recorded all that Paul spoke in his defense. Indeed, in v. 9 there may be a reference to his testimony to his conversion and call. In the division within the council, the Pharisees, largely for partisan reasons, stood and declared Paul innocent of the charges. In the confusion which followed, all remaining dignity within the court was cast to the winds. Once again Paul was rescued by the intervention of the Roman tribune.

c. The personal word of Jesus during the night gave assurance to Paul at three vital points. There was encouragement in the midst of the seeming failure. In the words, "as thou hast testified of me," there was balm to his spirit, no doubt wounded and chagrined by his encounter with the council. There was also the promise of a future witness at Rome. "Just when I need Him, Jesus is near!"

God Has a Thousand Ways

Acts 23:12-35

12 And when it was day, certain of the Jews banded together, and bound themselves under a curse, saying that they would neither eat nor drink till they had killed Paul.
13 And they were more than forty which had made this conspiracy.
14 And they came to the chief priests and elders, and said, We have bound ourselves under a great curse, that we will eat nothing until we have slain Paul.
15 Now therefore ye with the council signify to the chief captain that he bring him down unto you to morrow, as though ye would enquire something more perfectly concerning him: and we, or ever he come near, are ready to kill him.
16 And when Paul's sister's son heard of their lying in wait, he went and entered into the castle, and told Paul.
17 Then Paul called one of the centurions unto him, and said, Bring this young man unto the chief captain: for he hath a certain thing to tell him.
18 So he took him, and brought him to the chief captain, and said, Paul the prisoner called me unto him, and prayed me to bring this young man unto thee, who hath something to say unto thee.
19 Then the chief captain took him by the hand, and went with him aside privately, and asked him, What is that thou hast to tell me?
20 And he said, The Jews have agreed to desire thee that thou wouldest bring down Paul to morrow into the council, as though they would enquire somewhat of him more perfectly.
21 But do not thou yield unto them: for there lie in wait for him of them more than forty men, which have bound themselves with an oath, that they will neither eat nor drink till they have killed him: and now are they ready, looking for a promise from thee.
22 So the chief captain then let the young man depart, and charged him, See thou tell no man that thou hast shewed these things to me.
23 And he called unto him two centurions, saying, Make ready two hundred soldiers to go to Caesarea, and horsemen threescore and ten, and spearmen two hundred, at the third hour of the night;

24 And provide them beasts, that they may set Paul on, and bring him safe unto Felix the governor.
25 And he wrote a letter after this manner:
26 Claudius Lysias unto the most excellent governor Felix sendeth greeting.
27 This man was taken of the Jews, and should have been killed of them: then came I with an army, and rescued him, having understood that he was a Roman.
28 And when I would have known the cause wherefore they accused him, I brought him forth into their council:
29 Whom I perceived to be accused of questions of their law, but to have nothing laid to his charge worthy of death or of bonds.
30 And when it was told me how that the Jews laid wait for the man, I sent straightway to thee, and gave commandment to his accusers also to say before thee what they had against him. Farewell.
31 Then the soldiers, as it was commanded them, took Paul, and brought him by night to Antipatris.
32 On the morrow they left the horsemen to go with him, and returned to the castle:
33 Who, when they came to Caesarea, and delivered the epistle to the governor, presented Paul also before him.
34 And when the governor had read the letter, he asked of what province he was. And when he understood that he was of Cilicia;
35 I will hear thee, said he, when thine accusers are also come. And he commanded him to be kept in Herod's judgment hall.

The reassuring message of the Lord had transformed Paul's dark night of disappointment and distress into the calm light of assurance and peace. He had the Lord's explicit word, "So must thou bear witness also at Rome." How, and when, he did not yet know, but of the fact he was sure.

1. *"No weapon that is formed against thee shall prosper;* and every tongue that shall rise against thee in judgment thou shalt condemn. This is the heritage of the servants of the Lord" (Isa. 54:17). Perhaps these familiar words of Isaiah were in Paul's mind.

The plot against Paul's life shows the depth of fanatical hatred as well as the reckless daring of the Jewish zealots. Had they attacked Paul as planned, some of them would certainly have been killed by the soldiers. However, the curse under which they placed themselves was likely removed by the ingenuity of those who were practised in the subtleties of the law.

Luke's story of the part which Paul's nephew played in saving him from the plot is told with the touch of detail of an eyewitness account. That may be because Luke was present with Paul in the Antonia fortress. At any rate Paul, although in custody, was now being treated with the deference due a Roman citizen. One privilege was to have visitors.

The bare reference to Paul's family is tantalizing. Did his sister live in Jerusalem, or was his nephew a student there as he himself had been years before? Had a reconciliation with his family taken place? Did they possibly supply him with financial help at this time? We can only conjecture.

The young nephew may have come upon word of the plot through some association he had as a student at the Temple. Concern and admiration for his uncle caused him to risk a good deal to give the warning. Thus he became another link in a chain of divine providences. We can imagine the warm and fruitful relationship which continued between Paul and his nephew.

2. "And the sons of strangers shall build up thy walls, *and their kings shall minister unto thee*" (Isa. 60:10). Perhaps Paul also remembered these words of Isaiah as he rode to Caesarea, escorted and protected by a detachment of Caesar's imperial army.

If the military escort seems to us excessively large as a guard for one prisoner, it does provide a commentary on the political unrest and common violence of those times. The tribune was taking no chances of Paul's being ambushed. This also explains the suddenness of departure by nine o'clock the same night. Once Paul was safe at Antipatris, about halfway to Caesarea, and in more open country, the foot soldiers were ordered back to Jerusalem, and the escort for the remaining journey became the 70 cavalry troops.

The letter of the tribune, Claudius Lysias, to Felix, the Roman procurator of Judea, is noteworthy for its fairness, and for its statement of Paul's innocence of any crime worthy of imprisonment. An interesting sidelight is its arrangement of the details of Paul's arrest in a manner favorable to the tribune, and its obvious omission of reference to the near scourging.

Felix was a former slave who had been liberated and elevated to high office through special influence at Caesar's court. Tacitus, the Roman historian, held him in very low esteem as a man. He had become notorious for his unscrupulous dealings, his excessive cruelty, and his addiction to violence.

Learning that Paul was a citizen of Cilicia, a Roman province, Felix deemed it proper for him, as procurator of Judea, to adjudicate in the case. Accordingly Paul was held prisoner in the praetorium, the procurator's headquarters, which was the palace built by Herod the Great. Doubtless the believers in Caesarea were now able to minister to Paul, and to commit to God in prayer the portentous events just ahead.

ACTS 24

Paul's Defense Before Felix

Acts 24:1-21

1 And after five days Ananias the high priest descended with the elders, and with a certain orator named Tertullus, who informed the governor against Paul.
2 And when he was called forth, Tertullus began to accuse him, saying, Seeing that by thee we enjoy great quietness, and that very worthy deeds are done unto this nation by thy providence,
3 We accept it always, and in all places, most noble Felix, with all thankfulness.
4 Notwithstanding, that I be not further tedious unto thee, I pray thee that thou wouldest hear us of thy clemency a few words.
5 For we have found this man a pestilent fellow, and a mover of sedition among all the Jews throughout the world, and a ringleader of the sect of the Nazarenes:
6 Who also hath gone about to profane the temple: whom we took, and would have judged according to our law.
7 But the chief captain Lysias came upon us, and with great violence took him away out of our hands,
8 Commanding his accusers to come unto thee: by examining of whom thyself mayest take knowledge of all these things, whereof we accuse him.

9 And the Jews also assented, saying that these things were so.
10 Then Paul, after that the governor had beckoned unto him to speak, answered, Forasmuch as I know that thou hast been of many years a judge unto this nation, I do the more cheerfully answer for myself:
11 Because that thou mayest understand, that there are yet but twelve days since I went up to Jerusalem for to worship.
12 And they neither found me in the temple disputing with any man, neither raising up the people, neither in the synagogues, nor in the city:
13 Neither can they prove the things whereof they now accuse me.
14 But this I confess unto thee, that after the way which they call heresy, so worship I the God of my fathers, believing all things which are written in the law and in the prophets:
15 And have hope toward God, which they themselves also allow, that there shall be a resurrection of the dead, both of the just and unjust.
16 And herein do I exercise myself, to have always a conscience void of offence toward God, and toward men.
17 Now after many years I came to bring alms to my nation, and offerings.
18 Whereupon certain Jews from Asia found me purified in the temple, neither with multitude, nor with tumult.
19 Who ought to have been here before thee, and object, if they had ought against me.
20 Or else let these same here say, if they have found any evil doing in me, while I stood before the council,
21 Except it be for this one voice, that I cried standing among them, Touching the resurrection of the dead I am called in question by you this day.

The high priest Ananias, supported by the Jewish elders, had lost no time and had gone to considerable pains in pursuit and prosecution of Paul. That in itself indicates the strategic importance of the case. Doubtless Paul and the Caesarean believers had been in earnest prayer. As yet Christianity, as a form of the Jewish faith, continued to enjoy the protection of the law, because the Jewish religion was recognized under Roman law. Far more important to Paul than his own safety was the status of the Christian faith in Judea and eventually in the whole empire. The high priest was attempting not only to finish Paul but also to create enmity between Christ and Caesar.

1. *The case for the prosecution* (vv. 2-9). Tertullus was a professional pleader, a hired lawyer. His speech demonstrates his skill with words. The case against Paul was so weak as to be practically nonexistent; by lies and innuendo Tertullus attempted to influence Felix, the judge.

a. The flattery with which Tertullus began was customary in the circumstances. It was true that Felix had suppressed certain outlaws and terrorists in Judea, but any good he had done was greatly overbalanced by his cruel and mercenary regime. The ascriptions of nobility, providence, and clemency, and the servile expression of gratitude toward Felix would have turned the stomach of the average Palestinian Jew had he heard.

b. The charges were three: the first was political, the second merely religious, and the third a question of Jewish Temple law. All were false in their import.

c. The first charge was that Paul was a subversive person, an anarchist, a disturber of the peace of the land, a "mover of sedition." The word "pest" sums it up. Such a charge could indeed be serious if believed. Rome did not tolerate those who might provoke insurrection. Felix would have to give attention.

It was an evil charge against the apostle who everywhere preached peace with God, reconciliation of man with man through Christ our Peace, and respect for and obedience to civil law and authority. But it was a charge to be more and more repeated against the Church. The gospel can make no truce with sin and entrenched evil. It was in that sense that Jesus came "not to send peace, but a sword" (Matt. 10:34).

d. The second charge, that Paul was "a ringleader of the sect of the Nazarenes," is difficult to interpret. This is the only place where believers are referred to as Nazarenes, meaning obviously, followers of Jesus of Nazareth, himself called a Nazarene. Perhaps it was intended as an epithet to conjure up the picture of a troublesome Messianic movement; perhaps by this they intended to disown "the Nazarenes" as a legitimate Jewish sect; perhaps they supposed that to Felix it connoted the memory of the crucifixion of Jesus under Pontius Pilate. As a merely religious charge it could hardly carry much force in a Roman court. Thus, one supposes that it was intentional innuendo. There was, in fact, an unconscious tribute to Paul as the recognized effective leader of the followers of Jesus.

e. The third charge had been reduced from the original one of profaning the Temple to *attempting* to profane the Temple (cf. 21:28). Since the Romans upheld the Jewish right to punish Temple violaters with death, this charge could have led, if substantiated, to serious consequences. Tertullus made an implicit appeal to have Paul returned to Jewish jurisdiction. The statement against Lysias, the tribune, was a lie. The "great violence" was on the part of the Jews who were about to tear Paul limb from limb in the Temple court. The tribune had prevented a lynching.

To these accusations all the elders present gave assent and thus perjured themselves.

2. *The prisoner's defense* (vv. 10-21). The trial was conducted according to Roman custom, with which Paul was evidently familiar. The procurator nodded to Paul, giving him permission to defend himself against his accusers. It is noteworthy that Paul, in a straightforward statement of facts completely demolished the charges, and at the same time witnessed to his faith. He began without flattery but with an acknowledgement of Felix' experience in Jewish affairs.

a. The charge of sedition or trouble-making Paul flatly denied, and challenged his accusers to produce any evidence to substantiate it (vv. 11-13). He had gone up to Jerusalem to worship, and since this had been only 12 days ago, his movements and the facts could easily be verified. Various theories have been advanced in order to count the 12 days. Perhaps the best way is to assume that Paul did not join the four men with the vow (cf. 21:23-27) until the seven days of their purification had nearly expired. In this way all the events after 21:17 can be included in a 12-day span.

b. Paul took up the second charge (vv. 14-16) by declaring proudly that he worshipped the God of his fathers according to the Way (it should be capitalized) which Tertullus had described as a sect (the Greek word *hairesis,* here translated "heresy," is everywhere else in Acts translated "sect" in the KJV). If the term implied the holding of certain peculiar tenets while denying others (cf. Acts 5:17), Paul was implicitly protesting it when he affirmed that he believed "all things which are written in the law and the prophets." His was a whole faith, founded on the whole Scriptures.

Going further, Paul also identified himself with the "hope towards God" shared by his people, the Jews, that is, the resurrection of the dead. For Paul, that hope was embodied in Christ, the risen Saviour. But this reference was a turning of the tables on his accusers, who were of the Sadducean party and denied the resurrection. Who is it after all, Paul was saying, who has denied the faith?

It seems to follow that one who looked forward to the resurrection, and by the same token to the judgment, should take great pains to preserve an unsullied conscience (v. 16). So, here in this court, Paul was speaking as one who must give account to God. Those who deny the resurrection may not be so well motivated.

c. In Paul's reply to the third charge (vv. 17-21) we have, curiously, the only reference in Acts to the "alms," the collection which Paul took from the Gentile churches for the Judean poor. But we know from the Epistles that it was mainly this which impelled him to return to Jerusalem.

Paul's denial of the charge of profaning the Temple was supported by the fact that none of those who had found him in the Temple had appeared as witnesses against him. All the so-called evidence was merely hearsay. If they were honest, Paul declared, the Jews would admit that the only real evidence they could muster was in reference to his declaration of belief in the resurrection while standing before the Sanhedrin. And that, of course, could hardly be a crime, since the Pharisees in the Sanhedrin itself believed the same!

Paul thus ended his defense on an ironic note, as if he

had said, "And that, your honor, is all the case they have—in fact, it is no case at all!"

Today Is the Day of Salvation

Acts 24:22-27

22 And when Felix heard these things, having more perfect knowledge of that way, he deferred them, and said, When Lysias the chief captain shall come down, I will know the uttermost of your matter.
23 And he commanded a centurion to keep Paul, and to let him have liberty, and that he should forbid none of his acquaintance to minister or come unto him.
24 And after certain days, when Felix came with his wife Drusilla, which was a Jewess, he sent for Paul, and heard him concerning the faith in Christ.
25 And as he reasoned of righteousness, temperance, and judgment to come, Felix trembled, and answered, Go thy way for this time; when I have a convenient season, I will call for thee.
26 He hoped also that money should have been given him of Paul, that he might loose him: wherefore he sent for him the oftener, and communed with him.
27 But after two years Porcius Festus came into Felix' room: and Felix, willing to shew the Jews a pleasure, left Paul bound.

No man ever had a more favorable opportunity to hear and respond to the gospel than did Felix. Due possibly to contacts he had made with Christians during his Judean residence, Felix had, for a Roman, a rather accurate knowledge of the Christian faith. He saw the emptiness of the case against Paul and ought to have freed him. The deferral of his decision until Lysias could testify in person seems to have been no more than a way out for the moment. It is unlikely that Lysias ever testified in the case.

Although unconvicted, Paul's case was only adjourned. He remained in custody, albeit a custody in which his friends had free access to him. Doubtless he enjoyed the ministry of Luke, Philip the evangelist, and many others among the Christians of Caesarea.

As on several other occasions described in Acts, Luke vividly pictures the way in which the positions of prisoner and judge became reversed under the pungent preaching of the gospel.

1. *The faithful word.* One textual tradition says that it was at the request of Drusilla, the wife of Felix, that a

private audiance was arranged where Paul witnessed of "the faith in Christ." What a special hour of grace and high privilege that was for the procurator and his wife!

Drusilla was the daughter of Herod Agrippa I, the Herod of c. 12 (see comments there on the family). Her brother was Herod Agrippa II, and her sister was Bernice (cc. 25 and 26). As a young girl she had been given in marriage by her brother to the king of Emesa (Emesa was a small Syrian state), but Felix had persuaded her to abandon her husband and to marry him. At this time she was still under 20 years of age.

In his declaration of the Christian faith Paul "reasoned of righteousness, temperance, and judgment to come."

a. "Righteousness," because of the setting here, has usually been thought of only in ethical terms, the just requirements of a righteous God. But it is unlikely that Paul could warm to this theme without declaring "the righteousness of God which is by faith of Jesus Christ" (Rom. 3:22). Doubtless Paul preached on the remission of sins and justification by "grace through the redemption that is in Christ Jesus" (cf. Rom. 3:20-26).

b. "Temperance" means self-control, self-mastery, a deliverance from the blight of lust, greed, covetousness, violence, and vacillation which had ravaged the character of Felix.

c. "Judgment to come" is the truth that all men, the great as well as the small, must give an account to God of the deeds done in the body.

2. *The fearful conscience.* Felix, deeply convicted of his sins, was shaken to the core. Confronted, not with a strange itinerant preacher, not with a sect, not with an argument about religion, but with the living God, he became terrified. Paul had not accused him of his adulterous life nor of his past crimes. There had been no need. The Holy Spirit had aroused his conscience and arraigned him before the tribunal of God's truth and holiness.

3. *The fateful decision.* How lofty and awful is the power of choice! Felix' decision was polite but fatal. The postponement of the issues until another time, "a convenient season," was only a way to still his conscience, stifle the Word, and break off the gracious contact. Although on future occasions he sent for Paul and conversed with him, so that many additional opportunities were permitted him, he seems to have been motivated by his lust for gold rather than by any hunger for truth. Convicted of his guilt, and at one time terrified of judgment, he yet clung to his sins. The statement that he "left Paul bound" is chilling in its import. Compromiser to the last, he could decide neither entirely for nor against Paul or his opponents. Yet his indecision was, in fact, his fateful decision.

On what grounds Felix assumed that Paul had funds with which to pay a bribe we do not know. Perhaps it was the reference to "alms" (v. 17). Perhaps at this time Paul was in command of funds from some source. At any rate Paul steadfastly refused the suggestion.

Felix was finally recalled by Caesar because of the great bloodshed with which he dealt with the strife between Jews and Gentiles at Caesarea. He hoped that leaving Paul in custody would partially placate the Jews. In this he failed, for the Jews bitterly accused him to Nero when he returned to Rome.

ACTS 25

Government and the Christian

Acts 25:1-12

1 Now when Festus was come into the province, after three days he ascended from Caesarea to Jerusalem.
2 Then the high priest and the chief of the Jews informed him against Paul, and besought him,
3 And desired favour against him, that he would send for him to Jerusalem, laying wait in the way to kill him.

4 But Festus answered, that Paul should be kept at Caesarea, and that he himself would depart shortly thither.
5 Let them therefore, said he, which among you are able, go down with me, and accuse this man, if there be any wickedness in him.
6 And when he had tarried among them more than ten days, he went down unto Caesarea; and the next day sitting on the judgment seat commanded Paul to be brought.
7 And when he was come, the Jews which came down from Jerusalem stood round about, and laid many and grievous complaints against Paul, which they could not prove.
8 While he answered for himself, Neither against the law of the Jews, neither against the temple, nor yet against Caesar, have I offended any thing at all.
9 But Festus, willing to do the Jews a pleasure, answered Paul, and said, Wilt thou go up to Jerusalem, and there be judged of these things before me?
10 Then said Paul, I stand at Caesar's judgment seat, where I ought to be judged: to the Jews have I done no wrong, as thou very well knowest.
11 For if I be an offender, or have committed any thing worthy of death, I refuse not to die: but if there be none of these things whereof these accuse me, no man may deliver me unto them. I appeal unto Caesar.
12 Then Festus, when he had conferred with the council, answered, Hast thou appealed unto Caesar? unto Caesar shalt thou go.

Little is known concerning Festus, the procurator appointed to succeed Felix. He served some three years and died in the office. The extreme disorders of his realm which he inherited were never adequately controlled. On the whole, Luke pictures him as generally honorable in his ideal of justice, but not immune to the pressures toward compromise. In that he was not unlike great numbers of his modern political counterparts.

1. *Civil government and human failure.* Festus' first act was to pay his respects to Jerusalem, the real capital of Judea. The ruling Jews assumed that in reviving the case against Paul, they could take advantage of a new procurator, perhaps even intimidate him. Although Ananias had been deposed in the meantime, and a new high priest appointed, the hatred against Paul still burned. The plot to ambush and kill him on the way to Jerusalem was also revived.

At first, and providentially, Festus was firm in denying the request to move the case to Jerusalem. He would be prompt with the trial, however. Those in authority among the Jews (the meaning in v. 5) should go to Caesarea to make their charges against the prisoner before his formal judgment seat. The immediate attention of Festus in the case indicates that he saw it to be very important for Roman-Jewish relations.

Paul's accusers apparently appeared in force. What they lacked in proof or legality they tried to make up in vehemence, insult, and slander (cf. 25:24). Paul's defense, which Luke only suggests, shows that the charges were substantially the same ones, three in number, which were completely refuted in the trial before Felix. They were no more successful on this occasion.

Festus, however, was impressed by the fury of the prosecution, and sought for a compromise which would conciliate the Jews without a complete miscarriage of justice. He ought to have set Paul free. Instead, he proposed what the Jews had first asked, moving the trial to Jerusalem. Whether he meant to transfer Paul to Jewish jurisdiction is not quite clear. Probably not, since the trial would still be before the procurator (cf. v. 9).

2. *The duties of human authorites.* Confronted with this disastrous proposal, Paul boldly reminded the procurator of what he well knew. He had a right to a verdict without delay. Simple justice demanded acquittal. He had done no wrong. A Roman provincial tribunal, such as that of Festus, ought not to postpone, or defer, or compromise in dispensing justice.

Paul's philosophy and doctrine of civil government he had already written in his letter to the church at Rome, especially with respect to the duties of subjects (cf. Rom. 13:1-4). He had a lofty view of government and civil authority. But here in this noble statement to Festus, he declared the duties of governments toward their subjects.

To use the structure to escape a just condemnation, even death itself, is wrong for a Christian, Paul declared. On the other hand, a Christian does not blindly invite or tolerate injustice. There was no hope of justice at Jerusalem. To consent to go there would be to close the jaws of a well-set trap. Although he must have done it with a wrench of pain, since he was making a final repudiation of his hope of justice under the Mosaic system, Paul chose the only alternative left to him, and appealed to Caesar. *Caesarem appello!* With these words any Roman citizen might appeal to what was then the supreme civil authority in the world.

Ironically, the Caesar was Nero. At the time, however, in the early years of his reign, there was no warning of the cruelties to come. Paul's appeal was for justice under the law.

Festus was likely relieved to get the case off his hands. After a brief conference with his legal advisors, he formally granted the appeal. The wolves who lusted for Paul's blood could only look on in frustration and rage. For Paul, the words "unter Caesar shalt thou go," were merely the echo of the earlier words of his Lord, "Thou must bear witness also at Rome." He was still "the prisoner of the Lord."

Taking the Long View of Life

Acts 25:13-27

13 And after certain days king Agrippa and Bernice came unto Caesarea to salute Festus.
14 And when they had been there many days, Festus declared Paul's cause unto the king, saying, There is a certain man left in bonds by Felix:
15 About whom, when I was at Jerusalem, the chief priests and the elders of the Jews informed me, desiring to have judgment against him.
16 To whom I answered, It is not the manner of the Romans to deliver any man to die, before that he which is accused have the accusers face to face, and have licence to answer for himself concerning the crime laid against him.
17 Therefore, when they were come hither, without any delay on the morrow I sat on the judgment seat, and commanded the man to be brought forth.
18 Against whom when the accusers stood up, they brought none accusation of such things as I supposed:
19 But had certain questions against him of their own superstition, and of one Jesus, which was dead, whom Paul affirmed to be alive.
20 And because I doubted of such manner of questions, I asked him whether he would go to Jerusalem, and there be judged of these matters.
21 But when Paul had appealed to be reserved unto the hearing of Augustus, I commanded him to be kept till I might send him to Caesar.

22 Then Agrippa said unto Festus, I would also hear the man myself. To morrow, said he, thou shalt hear him.
23 And on the morrow, when Agrippa was come, and Bernice, with great pomp, and was entered into the place of hearing, with the chief captains, and principal men of the city, at Festus' commandment Paul was brought forth.
24 And Festus said, King Agrippa, and all men which are here present with us, ye see this man, about whom all the multitude of the Jews have dealt with me, both at Jerusalem, and also here, crying that he ought not to live any longer.
25 But when I found that he had committed nothing worthy of death, and that he himself hath appealed to Augustus, I have determined to send him.
26 Of whom I have no certain thing to write unto my lord. Wherefore I have brought him forth before you, and specially before thee, O king Agrippa, that, after examination had, I might have somewhat to write.
27 For it seemeth to me unreasonable to send a prisoner, and not withal to signify the crimes laid against him.

The great importance which Luke attached to Paul's appearances before the Roman officials, followed by repeated declarations of his innocence, is indicated by the fact that three chapters (24—26) are given to these accounts.

In the present passage there is purposeful contrast between the worldly pomp and temporal glory of the court with its obscure and contemptuous treatment of great truths, and the humble circumstances of God's man as he represents the everlasting life-and-death salvation issues.

1. *God's man in action: true greatness.* King Agrippa and his sister Bernice had come from Agrippa's capital at Caesarea Philippi on a formal visit to welcome to office the new procurator, Festus. Herod Agrippa II, at this time about 30 years of age, was the last of the Herods. Although he had Jewish blood, he had been reared at the court of Claudius Caesar, in Rome. He might have succeeded his father, Herod Agrippa I (cf. c. 12), as king of Judea, except that at his father's death he was only 17 years of age. Instead, Judea had reverted to the rule of procurators, and Agrippa had later, over a period of time, received from Claudius areas to the northeast including some cities and villages around the Sea of Galilee, as his kingdom. Moreover, he was also the secular head of the Jewish religious system, with the right to appoint the high priests, and he

maintained a palace at Jerusalem. He was said to be something of an authority on Jewish religious affairs. He was evidently pleased at the chance to gain personal knowledge of Paul.

Bernice was a year younger than her brother. She had been married to her uncle, Herod of Chalcis, had married again after his death, had deserted her husband, and was living, for the second time, with her brother. Their relationship became an odious scandal, even at Rome. In later years she was the mistress of the emperor Titus. Her influence on her brother was evil.

Festus rehearsed Paul's case to Agrippa, along with considerable flattery of himself in the handling of it, and with proud words about his adherence to the principles of Roman law. (It should be noted that "Augustus" in v. 21 is not used as a proper name but as a title for Caesar, at that time Nero). Agrippa was eager to hear more. With all his Roman culture and tastes, he retained keen Jewish sympathies and insights. And so, the next day an informal hearing took place in the palace auditorium, to which all the elite from the military establishment, the city, and the court were invited.

It was a glittering scene, replete with ceremony, beautiful robes, and bright uniforms, and at the center, the king, his sister, and their host, the procurator. Finally, Paul was led in, dressed simply in his tunic and robe, a prisoner, but the center of attention. Festus presented him to the assemblage as the man whom "the multitude of the Jews" were pursuing to the death, "crying, that he ought not live any longer." Festus' rationale for the hearing, which was really nonlegal, was that Agrippa might assist him in formulating a proper bill of charges against Paul to send to Caesar. Luke is careful to record Festus' statement that Paul had "committed nothing worthy of death."

What emotions, what thoughts, must have filled Paul's heart! He had faced many a crowd, both unbelieving and hostile, but none like this! Neither the Sanhedrin, nor Gallio's court, nor Mars' hill, nor the mob in the Temple courtyard were truly comparable. Doubtless he exulted in the opportunity to witness for his Lord.

Luke's description is a brilliant study in true greatness. Festus described Nero as "my lord" (v. 26) and referred to Paul offhandedly as "the man" (v. 17). And yet, the names recorded in Luke's narrative would have passed from history with no more than a ghostly, fleeting nod except for the fact that on this occasion they were linked for an hour with the name of a little, despised Jew, a prisoner in bonds for the sake of Jesus Christ. That man in bonds, bearing in his body the scars of his Christian service, bestrides the centuries and towers above his contemporaries as the skyscrapers dwarf the huts beneath them. The writer to the Hebrews, describing the faith-heroes who were often destitute and tormented, adds parenthetically, "of whom the world was not worthy" (Heb. 11:37).

2. *God's act in Christ: true hope.* Even in his spiritual blindness Festus had instinctively gotten to the heart of the matter and had put his finger upon the one towering issue in the whole case. That was when he had noted that the accusations seemed to focus on the matter "of one Jesus, which was dead, whom Paul affirmed to be alive" (v. 19). That was the core of the controversy.

The fact of the Resurrection had changed everything in Paul's personal life and in his relationship to his ancestral faith. It was the living Christ who had compelled him to say that neither circumcision nor uncircumcision mattered any longer, but only the power of new life in Christ (cf. Gal. 6:15). It was for a living Lord that Paul had suffered the loss of all things, and counted them as mere refuse (cf. Phil. 3:7-11). He had written to the Corinthians that the Resurrection was the very heart of the gospel, and that Christian faith would be utterly without meaning if Jesus were, after all, still dead (cf. 1 Cor. 15:12-19). His Jewish opponents would have been little concerned about the followers of one more false Messiah, long since dead and buried. They could tolerate the mere intellectual belief in resurrection as held by the Pharisees. But Paul was different; for him it was a dynamic fact, a transforming reality.

Festus was right in his analysis of the case. To his pagan Roman mind the whole thing could be firmly dismissed as superstition. How far the world is from the truth! In that one casual and cynical remark of the Roman procurator was imbedded all the hopes of all men for all time, Festus included.

ACTS 26

Paul's Defense Before the World

Acts 26:1-23

1 Then Agrippa said unto Paul, Thou art permitted to speak for thyself. Then Paul stretched forth the hand, and answered for himself:
2 I think myself happy, king Agrippa, because I shall answer for myself this day before thee touching all the things whereof I am accused of the Jews:
3 Especially because I know thee to be expert in all customs and questions which are among the Jews: wherefore I beseech thee to hear me patiently.
4 My manner of life from my youth, which was at the first among mine own nation at Jerusalem, know all the Jews;
5 Which knew me from the beginning, if they would testify, that after the most straitest sect of our religion I lived a Pharisee.
6 And now I stand and am judged for the hope of the promise made of God unto our fathers:
7 Unto which promise our twelve trives, instantly serving God day and night, hope to come. For which hope's sake, king Agrippa, I am accused of the Jews.
8 Why should it be thought a thing incredible with you, that God should raise the dead?
9 I verily thought with myself, that I ought to do many things contrary to the name of Jesus of Nazareth.
10 Which thing I also did in Jerusalem: and many of the saints did I shut up in prison, having received authority from the chief priests; and when they were put to death, I gave my voice against them.
11 And I punished them oft in every synagogue, and compelled them to blaspheme; and being exceedingly mad against them, I persecuted them even unto strange cities.
12 Whereupon as I went to Damascus with authority and commission from the chief priests,
13 At midday, O king, I saw in the way a light from heaven, above the

brightness of the sun, shining round about me and them which journeyed with me.
14 And when we were all fallen to the earth, I heard a voice speaking unto me, and saying in the Hebrew tongue, Saul, Saul, why persecutest thou me? it is hard for thee to kick against the pricks.
15 And I said, Who art thou, Lord? And he said, I am Jesus whom thou persecutest.
16 But rise, and stand upon thy feet: for I have appeared unto thee for this purpose, to make thee a minister and a witness both of these things which thou hast seen, and of those things in the which I will appear unto thee;
17 Delivering thee from the people, and from the Gentiles, unto whom now I send thee,
18 To open their eyes, and to turn them from darkness to light, and from the power of Satan unto God, that they may receive forgiveness of sins, and inheritance among them which are sanctified by faith that is in me.
19 Whereupon, O king Agrippa, I was not disobedient unto the heavenly vision:
20 But shewed first unto them of Damascus, and at Jerusalem, and throughout all the coasts of Judaea, and then to the Gentiles, that they should repent and turn to God, and do works meet for repentance.
21 For these causes the Jews caught me in the temple, and went about to kill me.
22 Having therefore obtained help of God, I continue unto this day, witnessing both to small and great, saying none other things than those which the prophets and Moses did say should come:
23 That Christ should suffer, and that he should be the first that should rise from the dead, and should shew light unto the people, and to the Gentiles.

This passage includes the third account in Acts of Paul's conversion, a fact which suggests the prime apologetic importance of that event. For the blending of accounts see the exposition of c. 9. Paul had previously rehearsed the story in his defense before the Jews (c. 22). The basic arguments used on that occasion are repeated on this. But this speech is more carefully worded, and the style is more literary. Even though it was addressed to a Jewish king and has much Jewish content that even Festus was unable to cope with, there are indications that Paul also had in mind a Gentile or world audience.

Festus had placed the examination in charge of Agrippa, and so, with all eyes upon him, the king formally invited Paul to speak on his own behalf. Paul's gesture may have been a courteous salutation or just a characteristic movement of the hand. The opening compliment was not flattery. It was indeed a happy thing to defend his way of life before a judge who was expertly versed in Jewish customs and law, as Agrippa was known to be, something that could not be said to the same degree of the procurators. He did not promise to be brief, but rather begged for a patient hearing of his intended careful presentation.

1. *God's own man,* apprehended, commissioned, and obedient—in these terms Paul outlined and defended his remarkable and often stormy career.

a. He is, he declares, *a man whose life has been turned around and transformed* by a direct encounter with the resurrected Jesus. To give this an intelligible setting, he first establishes the fact that in his former life he had been educated and had also lived in Jewish orthodoxy, according to the strictest rules of the Pharisees. Indeed, it was because of his proclamation of Israel's ancient hope, the hope which infused the worship of Israel's 12 tribes, that he had been charged by the Jews. The charges are not specifically mentioned here since the hearing was not technically a trial. Israel's hope, the resurrection of the dead, and specifically, the resurrection of Jesus, were closely intertwined in Paul's thinking. The paradox was that although the Pharisees believed in the resurrection in a creedal way, they opposed and persecuted Paul for his specific declaration of Jesus' resurrection.

As a Pharisee Paul had himself denounced the claims of the Christians as incredible and had been the leader of a violent persecution of believers. He does not spare himself in his vivid description. The language of v. 11 should be understood to mean that he did his best to make believers blaspheme. He does not mean that he succeeded (cf. other versions). Then came the encounter with Christ which turned his life in the opposite direction (see the discussion of c. 9).

b. Paul also declares that he is *a man entrusted with a glorious work,* a divine commission. The words used to express this (vv. 16-18) constitute a summary of Paul's directives from the Lord on the Damascus road, from the lips of Ananias, and later in his vision at Jerusalem. Especially, he was to go to the Gentiles, who were to be "no more strangers and foreigners, but fellowcitizens with the saints, and of the household of God" (Eph. 2:19).

c. Paul presents himself as a *man with one Master,* fully obedient to His will. His explanation for his way of life was simple: He was a man under orders, under a divine compulsion. Both his life-style and his message were God's doing, not his own. And it was for *this* that he had been arrested and accused. If Agrippa wished to formulate the charges for Caesar, he had his answer.

d. Finally, Paul confesses himself to be *a man kept under the care and providence of God* (v. 22). "To this day," he declared, "I have had the help that comes from God, and so I stand here, testifying" (RSV). It is the same concept of victory in Christ which is expressed in Eph. 6:13-14. Having overcome by the help of God on every battlefield, the Christain warrior still stands erect. He was much aware that only by God's intervention and continual providence had he been delivered from the plots against him and sustained in his purpose.

2. *The essential elements of the gospel* which Paul preached are contained in his defense.

a. The fact of the resurrection of Jesus runs like a connecting thread throughout the discourse. It is Paul speaking, and speaking about his own experience and life; and yet one cannot escape the impression that it is Christ, alive, exalted, powerful to save, who is at center stage. At vv. 6,15, and 23, the Resurrection is in view. In the dramatic rhetorical question of v. 8, the whole issue comes suddenly into focus. Paul has in mind not so much Agrippa as his pagan audience with their pagan presuppositions which make resurrection incredible. In one swift sentence he shatters the objections; there is nothing incredible about resurrection if you are dealing with *God,* the *living* God. Rather it is *no* resurrection which is incredible! The cross and the death of Christ are implicitly in view as deriving their meaning from the Resurrection.

b. The work of salvation is depicted in the words of Paul's commission, largely in the language of the Old Testament. The gospel will bring spiritual illumination ("open their eyes"), and it will be manifested in transforming, life-changing power.

The totality of the radical change in conversion is pictured by two sets of contrasting spheres. "Darkness" is contrasted with "light": There is hope for the hopeless, purpose for the aimless, guidance for the lost, understanding for the confused, love and peace for the outcast. The "power of Satan" is contrasted with the realm of God: There is deliverance from moral failure, moral bondage and despair, into a dynamic, sustaining, value-building fellowship with God himself.

The twofold benefits of salvation are summarized as "forgiveness of sins" and "inheritance among them which are sanctified by faith" in Christ. Those who "take their place with all those who are made holy by their faith in me" (Christ), as J. B. Phillips puts it, already possess in their hearts, by the indwelling of the Spirit, the down payment on what will one day be their full inheritance, by the will of God, and through their adoption as sons.

c. The human side of the gospel Paul presents as threefold: (1) repentance, that is, sorrow for and forsaking of sin; (2) turning to God, involving faith and obedience; and (3) "Works meet for repentance," meaning the entire ethical life of discipleship (v. 20). God takes the initiative in salvation, and without the Spirit's ministry men are hopeless, so that salvation is all of grace. Nevertheless, men have the perilous power of choice to exercise. Paul was quick to reject any saving merit in human works, but at the same time was ready to insist that good works are the necessary consequence of saving faith and a holy, obedient life.

d. The foundation of the Christian faith is not in

men's searching or philosophizing but in the certain revelation which God has given in the Scriptures. Paul's witnessing includes "none other things that those which the prophets and Moses did say should come" (v. 22). It is likely that we do not have the full account of Paul's speech. No doubt he expounded passage after passage from the Old Testament Scriptures, showing that Christ should suffer as an offering for sin, that His resurrection from the dead was foretold in prophecy, and that the offer of salvation to the Gentiles throughout the whole world was in God's plan from the beginning.

The only true subject for preaching is the gospel, and the only sure foundation for the gospel is the inspired Scriptures.

Coming to Grips with the Gospel

Acts 26:24-32

24 And as he thus spake for himself, Festus said with a loud voice, Paul, thou art beside thyself; much learning doth make thee mad.
25 But he said, I am not mad, most noble Festus; but speak forth the words of truth and soberness.
26 For the king knoweth of these things, before whom also I speak freely: for I am persuaded that none of these things are hidden from him; for this thing was not done in a corner.
27 King Agrippa, believest thou the prophets? I know that thou believest.
28 Then Agrippa said unto Paul, Almost thou persuadest me to be a Christian.
29 And Paul said, I would to God, that not only thou, but also all that hear me this day, were both almost, and altogether such as I am, except these bonds.
30 And when he had thus spoken, the king rose up, and the governor, and Bernice, and they that sat with them:
31 And when they were gone aside, they talked between themselves, saying, This man doeth nothing worthy of death or of bonds.
32 Then said Agrippa unto Festus, This man might have been set at liberty, if he had not appealed unto Caesar.

Paul did not finish his discourse. As he was demonstrating the fulfillment of the Scriptures through the sufferings, death, and resurrection of Jesus, and through his saving mission to the whole world, there was a sudden interruption. It will help to understand the scene which followed if we remember that at this point all was charged with emotion. The discussion had become much more than academic. As always, an unseen Presence was at work.

Brief exchanges with Festus and Agrippa ended the hearing and precipitated the judgment that Paul was innocent.

1. Festus is typical of *the person* who understands little of the gospel but *who does not wish to understand more.* The serious discussion of supernatural events and meanings frustrated and scandalized his practical Roman mind. And yet Paul was obviously learned, transparently sincere, and completely committed. New, never-before-dreamed-of ideas, a bold new concept of life's possibilities, stirred within the heart of Festus. Suddenly the tension made him forget that not he but Agrippa was acting as judge. Out of keeping with the procedures, in a quite undignified way, man to man, he shouted: "Paul, you're raving, all your studying has driven you mad!" It was a defensive action. It arrested the strange pull of the gospel on his heart.

Jesus too had been accused of madness (Mark 3:21). In the ancient world madness (insanity) was often popularly equated with frenzied utterance, thought to be inspired.

2. Paul's response was really *an appeal to reason.* His reply to the outburst was respectful and courteous. Both his manner and his words denied the charge. The expression "speak forth" hinted at divine authority behind his words, if not inspiration. His message, however, was not ecstatic ravings but sober truth.

In a moment it was the prisoner, not the judge, who seemed to be in charge of the inquiry. Sensing his advantage, Paul swung to the offensive, trying to summon the king as a witness to the truth of his words. The events of which he spoke, including, no doubt, the sufferings of Jesus, were common knowledge. If he would, Agrippa could corroborate Paul's testimony concerning the prophets. Putting the witness of the prophets side by side with the well-known events regarding Jesus of Nazareth, there could be only one reasonable response: faith. Boldly Paul challenged the king: "Do you believe the prophets?" Then, while Agrippa hesitated, searching for words, Paul replied for him, "I know that you believe!" Every Jew revered the prophets.

3. Agrippa is typical of *the person who understands the gospel but who refuses to receive it.* The young king's alert mind had leaped ahead of Paul's question. He saw the conclusion to which a reasonable answer must lead. To answer yes would seem to place him on Paul's side before the great pagan assemblage. The next challenge was all too obvious. But to answer no would be to deny his Jewish heritage. He decided on evasive action.

Although the long discussion among scholars as to the real import of Agrippa's response will likely never be fully resolved, there is general agreement that the "almost thou persuadest me" of the King James Version is not a feasible translation. Literally, the Greek means, "In a little you are persuading me to make [or act or do] a Christian." The import of the words "in a little" is difficult to determine. Did Agrippa say, "You are trying to move too fast"? Was he implying, "Do you think you can persuade me in such a brief time?" This seems to be the import.

Whether Agrippa meant to say that Paul's appeal was to make him a believer, or only to gain his cooperation in playing the role of a Christian in order to convince Festus, is likewise uncertain. If the latter, then he was saying, "Rapidly, you are persuading me to act the Christian!" Without having heard the inflection of the voice, we cannot know if the words were a serious rebuff or an attempted jest. It is certain that he was evading the question and rejecting the appeal. The diversionary tactic saved him from facing the real issue.

4. The second response of Paul was *the gracious appeal of Christian love.* Whether or not Agrippa had replied with sarcasm, Paul clearly responded with courtesy and compassion. "Whether with little or with much persuasion" (or, as a possible translation, "Both quickly and to the

fullest extent") came the apostles closing words, "My prayer is that not only you, but all who hear me this day, should become as I am," and then, with a fine touch of winsome grace, "except, of course, for my bonds." It was the loving prayer that his hearers might share his faith, his hope, and his peace; that, in a word, they might know his Lord.

5. *The appeal for personal decision was the crossroads moment.* Agrippa would listen no longer. Academic inquiry into Paul's faith was tolerable, even intriguing. But Paul was getting uncomfortable close to issues that could shake life to its foundations. The meeting broke up. The guests filed out formally according to rank and protocol. The status quo had been preserved.

They were agreed on one thing. Paul was innocent of any wrongdoing. Nevertheless, the inept handling of the case by Festus had forced Paul's appeal to Caesar, and by accepting the appeal Festus had tied his own hands. Agrippa put the matter politely: Paul *might have been set free.* Without doubt, Festus reported nothing of an incriminating nature in his letter to Caesar. The commonly accepted tradition says that when Paul's case finally gained attention at Rome, he was promptly released.

ACTS 27

Storm, Darkness—and God

Acts 27:1-26

1 And when it was determined that we should sail into Italy, they delivered Paul and certain other prisoners unto one named Julius a centurion of Augustus' band.
2 And entering into a ship of Adramyttium, we launched, meaning to sail by the coasts of Asia; one Aristarchus, a Macedonian of Thessalonica, being with us.
3 And the next day we touched at Sidon. And Julius courteously entreated Paul, and gave him liberty to go unto his friends to refresh himself.
4 And whon we had launched from thence, we sailed under Cyprus, because the winds were contrary.

5 And when we had sailed over the sea of Cilicia and Pamphylia, we
came to Myra, a city of Lycia.
6 And there the centurion found a ship of Alexandria sailing into
Italy; and he put us therein.
7 And when we had sailed slowly many days, and scarce were come
over against Cnidus, the wind not suffering us, we sailed under Crete,
over against Salmone;
8 And, hardly passing it, came unto a place which is called The fair
havens; nigh whereunto was the city of Lasea.
9 Now when much time was spent, and when sailing was now dan-
gerous, because the fast was now already past, Paul admonished
them,
10 And said unto them, Sirs, I perceive that this voyage will be with
hurt and much damage, not only of the lading and ship, but also of our
lives.
11 Nevertheless the centurion believed the master and the owner of
the ship, more than those things which were spoken by Paul.
12 And because the haven was not commodious to winter in, the
more part advised to depart thence also, if by any means they might
attain to Phenice, and there to winter; which is an haven of Crete, and
lieth toward the south west and north west.
13 And when the south wind blew softly, supposing that they had ob-
tained their purpose, loosing thence, they sailed close by Crete.
14 But not long after there arose against it a tempestuous wind, called
Euroclydon.
15 And when the ship was caught, and could not bear up into the
wind, we let her drive.
16 And running under a certain island which is called Clauda, we had
much work to come by the boat:
17 Which when they had taken up, they used helps, undergirding the
ship; and, fearing lest they should fall into the quicksands, strake sail,
and so were driven.
18 And we being exceedingly tossed with a tempest, the next day they
lightened the ship;
19 And the third day we cast out with our own hands the tackling of
the ship.
20 And when neither sun nor stars in many days appeared, and no
small tempest lay on us, all hope that we should be saved was then tak-
en away.
21 But after long abstinence Paul stood forth in the midst of them, and
said, Sirs, ye should have hearkened unto me, and not have loosed
from Crete, and to have gained this harm and loss.
22 And now I exhort you to be of good cheer: for there shall be no loss
of any man's life among you, but of the ship.
23 For there stood by me this night the angel of God, whose I am, and
whom I serve,
24 Saying, Fear not, Paul; thou must be brought before Caesar: and,
lo, God hath given thee all them that sail with thee.
25 Wherefore, sirs, be of good cheer: for I believe God, that it shall
be even as it was told me.
26 Howbeit we must be cast upon a certain island.

The graphic detail in Luke's account of the voyage to Rome reveals how indelibly stamped on his mind were all the incidents of the terrible ordeal. Here again he begins his use of "we." Of special interest is the fact that every geographical and chronological detail of the story has long since been painstakingly scrutinized and found to be entirely accurate. The chapter becomes, therefore, one of the important evidences of the trustworthiness of the book.

Paul, the prisoner and the man of God, dominates the story. The character of men is best revealed at times of great emergency or crisis. Paul stands forth as the man of practical good sense, great courage, human feelings, but supremely as the man of faith.

Moreover, the space given to this story justifies the feeling that Luke had a conscious regard for the rich symbolism of the sea. In the Scriptures, the sea often symbolizes the mystery of much in life, the domain of evil, and especially, separation from fellowship or from the good. One characteristic of the new heaven and the new earth is "no more sea" (Rev. 21:1).

1. *Storm and darkness: the loss of human hopes.*

a. The voyage began, presumably from Caesarea, on a ship working out of a northwest port in Asia Minor. The centurion charged with the prisoners bound for Rome was likely one of a select corps of couriers, from a proud, special cohort. Paul's companions were Luke and Aristarchus, the latter having been mentioned earlier (19:29 and 20:4), and later, at Rome he was still with Paul (cf. 4:10). Paul evidently enjoyed the centurion's respect (cf. v. 3).

They did not sail directly westward, but to the north, passing to the east of Cyprus, on to the Asian coast, and from there working slowly westward because of the prevailing westerly winds. At Myra, a chief port, they transferred to a large Alexandrian grain ship, one of a large, government-controlled fleet supplying Egyptian grain to Rome.

The northwest winds made it hard sailing to Cnidus at the extreme southwest of Asia Minor. It took "many days" to travel some 130 miles. There the winds cancelled out any alternative but to turn south. Doing this, they made better time, passing around the eastern end of the island of Crete, and in the lee of the land, they reached the Cretan harbor of Fair Havens. There they waited for a favoring wind.

b. Paul's advice that they should winter in Fair Havens was apparently given a fair hearing. After all, he was a seasoned traveller. But 40 miles further west at Phenice (or Phoenix) was a much superior semicircular harbor. The ship's operators allowed their desire for commodious facilities to overcome their better judgment. The centurion, who had the final word, was persuaded by the majority. It was a fateful decision.

"The fast" referred to would be the Jewish Day of Atonement, which fell annually between late September and early October. After mid-September sailing was dangerous, and ceased altogether on the open sea between early November and early February. If the ship left Fair Havens at mid-October (the likely time), the three months on Malta would be November, December, and January (cf. 28:11). Sailing would begin again in February.

How often legitimate human desire overrules good judgment and sometimes, the previously known guidance of God! The "south wind blew softly," and they supposed "that they had obtained their purpose." But it was only presumption. Luke is careful to say "they," not "we." Hugging the shore, they moved slowly westward, but not for long. The wind suddenly shifted to the northeast. In a little the ship was helplessly caught in a furious, typhoon-like tempest, known to the experienced sailors as Euroclydon (or better, Euraquila).

c. Driven off course before the wind, they had a brief partial respite in the lee of the island of Clauda. They were able to get the swamped lifeboat on board. They passed cables or ropes under the keel and winched them tightly around the ship to hold its great planks, much as barrel hoops hold the staves in place. They lowered to the deck all the unnecessary rigging and set their storm sails. Soon they were again at the mercy of the wind on the open sea. Fearing that they would be driven on the sandbanks off the African coast, they held the ship's right side to the wind and thus drifted slowly toward Malta, 500 miles to the west. By the third day, tossing like a cork and taking water, they had thrown overboard part of the cargo and, to further lighten the ship, had mustered the help of all to throw over the ship's main spar (or so it would seem). When life is at stake, we discover much we can get along without! And so, for 14 days, they endured the storm.

d. Many a Christian man or woman who has passed through some "dark night of the soul" on his own personal voyage can empathize with the ship's passengers. No sun by day, nor stars by night. No bearings, no sense of direction. No interest in food or any of life's ordinary pleasures. No hope from human resources. Helplessness, a trapped feeling, growing fears, and finally the inpulse to total despair. Through it all, the mystery of a hidden providence, a circumstance without sense. Jonah's case was unlike Paul's. Paul had done nothing wrong.

2. *The promise and the character of God: the way through.*

a. When we come to the end of ourselves, we are sometimes beginning in a new way to lay hold on God. When human hope was gone, "there stood by . . . the angel of God." Paul too had been afraid; else why had the angel said, "Fear not, Paul"? We may assume that the three brethren prayed a good deal, but in deeply depressing circumstances even the exercise of prayer becomes very difficult. Shaken though he was, Paul had not surrendered two great principles: first, his own integrity ("whose I am, and whom I serve"); and second, his confidence in the character of God, against all odds ("for I believe God"). His faith was not grounded (no pun intended) on any ray of light in the circumstances, or any human rationale, or any special insight. There was none. Faith rested solely on his conviction of God's unchanging character. God had promised, and God cannot lie. To this alone he clung, and it was enough.

b. Through all of this, Paul was made the means of saving the entire company. Those who pass through deep waters become qualified as no others can to bring hope to their fellow travellers in the hour of trouble.

Shipwreck, and God's Promise Fulfilled

Acts 27:27-44

27 But when the fourteenth night was come, as we were driven up and down in Adria, about midnight the shipmen deemed that they drew near to some country;
28 And sounded, and found it twenty fathoms: and when they had gone a little further, they sounded again, and found it fifteen fathoms.
29 Then fearing lest we should have fallen upon rocks, they cast four anchors out of the stern, and wished for the day.
30 And as the shipmen were about to flee out of the ship, when they had let down the boat into the sea, under colour as though they would have cast anchors out of the foreship,
31 Paul said to the centurion and to the soldiers, Except these abide in the ship, ye cannot be saved.
32 Then the soldiers cut off the ropes of the boat, and let her fall off.
33 And while the day was coming on, Paul besought them all to take meat, saying, This day is the fourteenth day that ye have tarried and continued fasting, having taken nothing.
34 Wherefore I pray you to take some meat: for this is for your health: for there shall not an hair fall from the head of any of you.
35 And when he had thus spoken, he took bread, and gave thanks to God in presence of them all: and when he had broken it, he began to eat.
36 Then were they all of good cheer, and they also took some meat.
37 And we were in all in the ship two hundred threescore and sixteen souls.
38 And when they had eaten enough, they lightened the ship, and cast out the wheat into the sea.
39 And when it was day, they knew not the land: but they discovered a certain creek with a shore, into the which they were minded, if it were possible, to thrust in the ship.
40 And when they had taken up the anchors, they committed themselves unto the sea, and loosed the rudder bands, and hoised up the mainsail to the wind, and made toward shore.
41 And falling into a place where two seas met, they ran the ship aground; and the forepart stuck fast, and remained unmoveable, but the hinder part was broken with the violence of the waves.
42 And the soldiers' counsel was to kill the prisoners, lest any of them should swim out, and escape.
43 But the centurion, willing to save Paul, kept them from their purpose; and commanded that they which could swim should cast themselves first into the sea, and get to land:
44 And the rest, some on boards, and some on broken pieces of the ship. And so it came to pass, that they escaped all safe to land.

The details of the shipwreck narrative have been carefully and critically sifted by more than one investigator. The best known of these is James Smith, a seaman and a scholar, whose book *The Voyage and Shipwreck of St. Paul* was published in London in 1880. Smith's detailed study was able to fully confirm the accuracy of the story. It is generally acknowledged that the place of the shipwreck was at a bay at the northwest corner of the island of Malta, a place now known as St. Paul's Bay.

God's promise and Paul's prediction were fulfilled to the letter. One of the remarkable lessons is discovered in the conjunction of divine providence and human cooperation, especially courage and common sense, in accomplishing God's promise of deliverance.

Paul, God's man of faith, still dominates the story. At three critical points Paul's advice, example, and character saved the situation.

1. *The test of unity.* By the fourteenth night after leaving Fair Havens, the ordeal was nearing its end. "Drifting across the sea of Adria" (RSV), meaning, the central Mediterranean, the sailors apparently heard the crash of great breakers off the island's point. Taking soundings, they found they were in shallow water, and, to keep from drifting onto rocks in the darkness, they cast out four anchors. The anchors were from the stern rather than the usual bow anchors, in order to keep the ship pointed toward land.

The sailors' morale was at such low ebb that they plotted to abandon ship and reach land by using the lifeboat. On the pretext of placing more anchors from the front of the ship, they lowered the boat. Paul's alertness and experience revealed the plot in time to warn the centurion. Without the sailors it would have been impossible to beach the ship in the morning. If all shared the peril together, all could be saved. Otherwise, the enterprise was lost.

The action of the soldiers was extreme because the

needed lifeboat was lost. On the other hand it gave the sailors no alternative but to stay aboard.

2. *The test of confidence.* The weakened, bedraggled, and discouraged condition of both passengers and crew gave little promise of effective action at the dawn's critical challenge. Paul's advice to take food, and most of all, his personal example before their eyes, served as the catalyst to restore hope and a measure of confidence for the morrow's undertaking.

With the ship still shuddering and tossing under the pounding of the seas, in the flickering glare of whatever few lights they still possessed, Paul, holding a portion of food in his hands, offered solemn thanksgiving to God, broke the bread, shared it, and ate. Never was thanksgiving more heartfelt nor offered in stranger circumstances! The spell of depression was broken. "Then were they all of good cheer . . ." They immediately went to work to lighten the ship in preparation for beaching. Luke here records the number of those aboard, 276, perhaps because they had numbered in dividing the food. What strength there is in the prayer of thanks, and the courageous example of one good man!

3. *The test of character.* In the morning the beach could be seen. The anchors were cast off, the steering oars were untied, the foresail (rather than "mainsail") was hoisted, and they made for the beach. But the ordeal was still not ended. Before they could reach the beach, the ship's bow stuck fast on a muddy reef built up by the crosscurrents. The stern of the ship, pounded by the violent surf, began to break up under the strain.

At that point, with land so near, death for Paul and the prisoners was only narrowly averted. In a situation where it would be "every man for himself," the prisoners might escape. The soldiers, whose own lives would become a forfeit for their escaped charges, would have used their swords to dispatch the prisoners on the spot, except for the orders of Julius, the centurion. Again it was the person and character of Paul, coupled with the centurion's gratitude and sense of honor, which saved the day.

"And so . . . they escaped all safe to land." Not without immense struggle, not without loss, even through shipwreck; nevertheless, they reached the land. Swimming, clinging to planks and parts of the ship, in complete disorder, certainly with no dignity whatever, yet, they reached shore.

Through many dangers, toils, and snares
I have already come.
'Tis grace hath brought me safe thus far,
And grace will lead me home.

ACTS 28

Rome at Last

Acts 28:1-15

1 And when they were escaped, then they knew that the island was called Melita.
2 And the barbarous people shewed us no little kindness: for they kindled a fire, and received us every one, because of the present rain, and because of the cold.
3 And when Paul had gathered a bundle of sticks, and laid them on the fire, there came a viper out of the heat, and fastened on his hand.
4 And when the barbarians saw the venomous beast hang on his hand, they said among themselves, No doubt this man is a murderer, whom, though he hath escaped the sea, yet vengeance suffereth not to live.
5 And he shook off the beast into the fire, and felt no harm.
6 Howbeit they looked when he should have swollen, or fallen down dead suddenly: but after they had looked a great while, and saw no harm come to him, they changed their minds, and said that he was a god.
7 In the same quarters were possessions of the chief man of the island, whose name was Publius; who received us, and lodged us three days courteously.
8 And it came to pass, that the father of Publius lay sick of a fever and of a bloody flux: to whom Paul entered in, and prayed, and laid his hands on him, and healed him.
9 So when this was done, others also, which had diseases in the island, came, and were healed:
10 Who also honoured us with many honours; and when we departed, they laded us with such things as were necessary.

11 And after three months we departed in a ship of Alexandria, which had wintered in the isle, whose sign was Castor and Pollux.
12 And landing at Syracuse, we tarried there three days.
13 And from thence we fetched a compass, and came to Rhegium: and after one day the south wind blew, and we came the next day to Puteoli:
14 Where we found brethren, and were desired to tarry with them seven days: and so we went toward Rome.
15 And thence, when the brethren heard of us, they came to meet us as far as Appii forum, and The three taverns: whom when Paul saw, he thanked God, and took courage.

Following blow after blow of trouble as already described, the story of the remainder of the journey has the contrasting atmosphere of recurring waves of encouragement. The long, dark night of trial is over, the sun is shining, and there is a note of triumph in the narrative.

1. *Encouragement through kindness and hospitality.* The Phoenicians had settled the island of the shipwreck, and had called it Melita, meaning "refuge." It is the modern Malta. The term "barbarian" simply meant non-Greek-speaking. Certainly these native people acted in a very civilized fashion. How welcome must have been the fire, the warmth, the provisions!

One further instance of divine providence is provided in the incident of the snake fastening of Paul's hand. (The picture of Paul industriously gathering wood for the fire is in itself instructive and intriguing.) The story infers that the snake was poisonous, that Paul was bitten but, in spite of the venom, suffered no ill effects. In the light of what he had already suffered, such a deliverance seems almost routine.

The superstitious beliefs of the islanders are illustrated by their reaction. They had a fatalistic view of justice as a kind of retributive nemesis, perhaps even personified, from which there was no escape. They were also quite ready to accept any man who could so easily survive a vemonous snake as one of the gods come to earth. With what joy Paul and his two brethren must have later witnessed of divine forgiveness for sinners through the Son of God incarnate among men! The snake incident did serve to open the door for a hearing.

2. *Encouragement through an open door for ministry.* "Chief man" or "first man" of the island is now known, because of inscriptions discovered, to have been an official title, and is another instance of Luke's accuracy. Publius had an estate nearby, and Paul, along with Luke and possibly others, became his guest for three days. When one remembers that Paul was a prisoner, the implications are remarkable. This is one in a long list of courtesies shown to Paul by Roman officials and carefully recorded by Luke.

The healing of Publius' father, ill with fever and dysentery, resulted. How bountifully the governor's kindness was repaid! It would seem that following this opening, Paul exercized the gift of healing through prayer while Luke exercized the same gift through medicine, such as he had. Doubtless, all was done in the name of Jesus. Christ was exalted, and the gospel brought its healing to hearts as well as bodies.

The gratitude of the islanders, who loaded their benefactors with gifts and provisions for their journey, was an eloquent testimonial to a gracious ministry.

3. *Encouragement through the welcome of the Roman brethren.* When sailing was again possible, likely in February, passage was arranged on another Alexandrian vessel bearing the figurehead of Castor and Pollux, the twin sons of Jupiter in ancient mythology, and the patron gods of sailors. Syracuse, the great port of Sicily, was the first stop. Rhegium, on the toe of Italy, was reached by tacking into the wind, but a day later a south wind took the ship the 180 miles to Puteoli, in the bay of Naples, in less than two days. There, probably while the centurion was on business, Paul and his companions found Christian brethren, and were allowed to accept their hospitality for an entire week (cf. the same privilege at Sidon in 27:3).

Puteoli, an important southern port, was the destination of many grain ships from Alexandria. The party therefore proceeded on foot, and en route reached the Appian Way, the great Roman north-south road. Word of Paul's coming had somehow reached the Christians at Rome. Evidently two welcoming groups eagerly came forward to meet him. The first he greeted at the Appii Forum, some 40 miles south of Rome, and a little later he was again welcomed at the Three Taverns, 10 miles closer to the city.

Paul had, for a long time, longed to visit the believers at Rome. To see their faces fulfilled a hope which had seemed to ever elude his grasp. Some three years earlier he had written and sent his Roman letter. His prayer had been answered. He "thanked God and took courage." It was an hour of fulfillment, of immense comfort, and of strengthening for whatever lay ahead.

A Story Without an Ending

Acts 28:16-31

16 And when we came to Rome, the centurion delivered the prisoners to the captain of the guard: but Paul was suffered to dwell by himself with a soldier that kept him.

17 And it came to pass, that after three days Paul called the chief of the Jews together: and when they were come together, he said unto them, Men and brethren, though I have committed nothing against the people, or customs of our fathers, yet was I delivered prisoner from Jerusalem into the hands of the Romans.

18 Who, when they had examined me, would have let me go, because there was no cause of death in me.

19 But when the Jews spake against it, I was constrained to appeal unto Caesar; not that I had ought to accuse my nation of.

20 For this cause therefore have I called for you, to see you, and to speak with you: because that for the hope of Israel I am bound with this chain.

21 And they said unto him, We neither received letters out of Judaea concerning thee, neither any of the brethren that came shewed or spake any harm of thee.

22 But we desire to hear of thee what thou thinkest: for as concerning this sect, we know that every where it is spoken against.

23 And when they had appointed him a day, there came many to him into his lodging; to whom he expounded and testified the kingdom of God, persuading them concerning Jesus, both out of the law of Moses, and out of the prophets, from morning till evening.

24 And some believed the things which were spoken, and some believed not.

25 And when they agreed not among themselves, they departed, after that Paul had spoken one word, Well spake the Holy Ghost by Esaias the prophet unto our fathers,

26 Saying, Go unto this people, and say, Hearing ye shall hear, and shall not understand; and seeing ye shall see, and not perceive:
27 For the heart of this people is waxed gross, and their ears are dull of hearing, and their eyes have they closed; lest they should see with their eyes, and hear with their ears, and understand with their heart, and should be converted, and I should heal them.
28 Be it known therefore unto you, that the salvation of God is sent unto the Gentiles, and that they will hear it.
29 And when he had said these words, the Jews departed, and had great reasoning among themselves.
30 And Paul dwelt two whole years in his own hired house, and received all that came in unto him,
31 Preaching the kingdom of God, and teaching those things which concern the Lord Jesus Christ, with all confidence, no man forbidding him.

On reaching Rome, the centurion at once turned his prisoners over to a superior officer, but Paul was given the special privilege of living by himself along with a soldier who guarded him. The close contact with a number of guards over the two years of detention opened up the way to witness to some of Caesar's choicest military personnel. Doubtless, many a soldier left Paul's quarters a new man in Christ. Paul's own estimate of this ministry is given in Phil. 1:12-14.

1. *An unquenched compassion* (vv. 17-23). Paul's burning desire to give the gospel to his kinsmen after the flesh remained unquenched. They had hounded his steps and used every means in their power to destroy him; and yet, at Rome his first thought was to give them opportunity to know his Lord.

a. There were numerous Jewish synagogues in Rome. Evidently there had been little communication between the Christian community and the Jews. If Paul could win the Jewish leaders to Christ here in the world's capital, the results for the gospel would be incalculable.

Paul seems to have had unlimited privileges with respect to visitors, although he was unable to move about himself. The Jewish leaders responded to his invitation. Eagerly, he explained the circumstances of his being in Rome. Frankly, he spoke of his condemnation by Jerusalem officials. Carefully, he disarmed their fears by disclaiming any intention of bringing countercharges against the Jews before Caesar. His purpose, he warmly declared, was only to share with them "the hope of Israel," the one consuming passion of his life.

b. The profession of the Roman Jews that they had received neither official nor private information regarding Paul is somewhat puzzling. Apparently the Sanhedrin had dropped the matter, and the Jews of Rome, for their part, deemed it wise to remain aloof from Paul's case before Caesar. All that they knew of Paul's faith, they said warily, was that "everywhere it is spoken against."

Nonetheless, on an appointed day, the leaders of Rome's Jewry came in numbers to hear Paul out. All day long he expounding the Scriptures, testified of his faith, and persuaded them concerning Jesus. It was a notable and strategic gathering. We need not think Paul did all the talking. There were questions, exchanges, and debates among themselves and with the apostle. We know from previous instances what Paul's message was. The Scriptures outlined God's ways with men, His plan of salvation, which included the whole world. The prophecies were fulfilled in Jesus of Nazareth, in His death, resurrection, and coming in power. Prisoner Paul was, but the Word of God was not bound! (Cf. 2 Tim. 2:9.)

2. *An undefeated purpose* (vv. 24-29). Only Paul, with his unparalleled grasp of the issues, could have so witnessed at Rome. Some believed and doubtless bore much fruit for the gospel. Some closed their eyes and hardened their hearts.

Paul had cited many Old Testament passages, but he closed with a warning from Isa. 6:9-10. It was, he said, not his word, nor Isaiah's word, but the word of the Holy Spirit. Their fathers long ago had refused to heed the prophet. Paul was pleading, "Don't make the same mistake which they made!" Light rejected produces blindness. None are so deaf or so blind as those who *will* not hear or see. Hearing, they do not comprehend; and seeing, they perceive no meaning.

Long and bitterly Paul had wrestled with the problem, even the mystery, of Israel's rejection of Jesus. In Romans 9—11 he had grappled with it. Whatever Israel's failure, God's purposes remained undefeated. In it all God had opened the door, Paul saw, for the reception of the Gentiles. The Gentiles had, and would, receive the gospel. In that he rejoiced. And, in the end, Israel too, would be saved.

(V. 29 is based on an inferior Greek text and is therefore omitted in later translations.)

3. *An unending conquest* (vv. 30-31). For two years Paul lived in the great pagan city, the crossroads of the world, the melting pot for people of all nations. Although always under guard, living at his own expense near, probably, to the military camp, he nevertheless carried on a constant ministry of preaching and teaching.

a. These were productive years on behalf of the Church. The letters to Philemon, to the Colossians, to the Ephesians, and to the Philippians were written. Their contents tell us that he looked forward to release, that he rejoiced in his preaching ministry, and that he carried a deep concern for the welfare of all the churches.

These letters also inform us of a number of his companions. Luke and Aristarchus, companions on the voyage, were there. Mention is made also of Mark, later to serve him again; of Demas, who later deserted him; and of Jesus called Justus. Timothy rejoined him (Phil. 2:19-23). Epaphras came from Colossae with news which became the occasion for writing Colossians, and is called a fellow prisoner (Philem. 23; Col. 1:3-8). Onesimus, the runaway slave, was rescued by Paul at Rome and returned to Philemon, his master, as a Christian brother. Tychicus returned with Onesimus and carried the Colossian and Ephesian letters (Col. 4:7-8; Eph. 6:21-22). Epaphroditus brought to Paul a gift from the Philippian church and returned with a letter to them (Phil. 2:25-30; 4:18).

b. The tradition that Paul was released and, after

several years of travel and ministry, was rearrested and suffered martyrdom at Rome, has already been noted. The tradition fits well with the evidence of the later Pauline Epistles.

c. Luke ends his story on a note of optimism and triumph. His saga of the Church, which began some 30 years before at Jerusalem, ends fittingly at Rome. The gospel has triumphantly penetrated the great cities of the world and reached to its capital. There, under the very eye of imperial Rome, it is being preached unhindered, "no man forbidding."

Luke's task is ended, but the story is just beginning. Jesus' ministry through His Church will go on and on. It is an open-ended, unfinished story. The pattern has been established, and a pioneer trail blazed, for unending conquest.

Bibliography

BARCLAY, WILLIAM. *The Acts of the Apostles,* in *The Daily Study Bible.* Edinburgh: The Saint Andrew Press, 1953.

———, *et al. The Bible and History.* London: Lutterworth Press, 1968.

———. *The Mind of St. Paul.* New York: Harper and Row, 1958.

BLAIKLOCK, E. M. *The Acts of the Apostles,* in *The Tyndale New Testament Commentaries.* Grand Rapids, Mich.: Wm. B. Eerdmans Publishing Co., 1959.

BRUCE, F. F. "Commentary on the Book of the Acts." *The New International Commentary on the New Testament.* Grand Rapids, Mich.: Wm. B. Eerdmans Publishing Co., 1954.

CARTER, CHARLES W., and EARLE, RALPH. *The Acts of the Apostles.* Grand Rapids, Mich.: Zondervan Publishing House, 1959.

EARLE, RALPH. "The Acts of the Apostles." *Beacon Bible Commentary.* Kansas City: Beacon Hill Press of Kansas City, 1965.

FILSON, FLOYD V. *A New Testament History.* Philadelphia: The Westminster Press, 1964.

GERSTNER, JOHN H. "Acts." *The Biblical Expositor.* Philadelphia: A. J. Holman Co., 1960.

GOODWIN, FRANK J. *A Harmony and Commentary on the Life of St. Paul.* Grand Rapids, Mich.: Baker Book House, 1951.

GUTHRIE, DONALD. *New Testament Introduction.* London: The Tyndale Press, 1965.

LADD, GEORGE ELDON. "The Acts of the Apostles." *The Wycliffe Bible Commentary.* Chicago: Moody Press, 1962.

———. *A Theology of the New Testament.* Grand Rapids, Mich.: William B. Eerdmans Publishing Co., 1974.

———. *The Young Church.* New York and Nashville: Abingdon Press, 1964.

LEHMAN, CHESTER K. *Biblical Theology*, vol. 2. Scottdale. Pa.: Herald Press, 1974.

LENSKI, R. C. H. *The Interpretation of the Acts of the Apostles.* Minneapolis: Augsburg Publishing House, 1934.

MACGREGOR, G. H. C. "The Acts of the Apostles" (exegesis), *The Interpreter's Bible*, Vol. IX. New York: Abingdon-Cokesbury Press, 1954.

MARSHALL, I. HOWARD. *Luke: Historian and Theologian.* Grand Rapids, Mich.: Zondervan Publishing House, 1971.

MORGAN, G. CAMPBELL. *The Acts of the Apostles.* Westwood, N.J.: Fleming H. Revell Co., 1924.

PACKER, J. I. *"Acts of the Apostles." The Cambridge Bible Commentary.* Cambridge: The University Press, 1966.

RACKHAM, RICHARD BELWARD. *The Acts of the Apostles.* London: Methuen and Company, Ltd., 1901.

RAMSAY, WILLIAM M. *The Christ of the Earliest Christians.* Richmond, Va.: John Knox Press, 1959.

RAMSAY, SIR WILLIAM MITCHEL. *Pictures of the Apostolic Church.* Grand Rapids, Mich.: Baker Book House, 1959 (reprint).

———. *St. Paul the Traveller and the Roman Citizen.* London: Hodder and Stoughton, 1920.